Presented to _____

From _____

In honor of _____

Date _____

"I thank God for every remembrance of you."

PHILIPPIANS 1:3

My Big Book *of*
Catholic

BIBLE STORIES

Compiled by Heidi Hess Saxton

A Division of Thomas Nelson Publishers

NASHVILLE   DALLAS   MEXICO CITY   RIO DE JANEIRO   BEIJING

Nihil Obstat
Most Reverend David R. Choby, S.T.B., J.C.L.
Bishop, Diocese of Nashville
September 3, 2009

Imprimatur
Most Reverend David R. Choby, S.T.B., J.C.L.
Bishop, Diocese of Nashville
September 3, 2009

Published in Nashville, Tennessee, by Tommy Nelson. Tommy Nelson is a registered trademark of Thomas Nelson, Inc.

Page design by Mandi Cofer.

Thomas Nelson, Inc., titles may be purchased in bulk for educational, business, fund-raising, or sales promotional use. For information please e-mail SpecialMarkets@ThomasNelson.com.

Library of Congress Cataloging-in-Publication Data

My big book of Catholic Bible stories / compiled by Heidi Hess Saxton.
    p. cm.
  ISBN 978-1-4003-1538-3 (hardcover)
  1. Families—Religious life. 2. Spiritual life—Catholic Church. 3.
Religious education—Activity programs. 4. Christian education—Home
training. 5. Bible stories, English. I. Saxton, Heidi Hess.
  BX2351.M9 2009
  220.9'505—dc22
                2009032128

Mfgr: R R Donnelley
Shenzhen, China
November/2009 – PPO #96661

+LDM

My dear Children

God loved the world so much that He sent us His only Son to
save us from sin. And Jesus brought us the Good News that
God loves each one of us with a most tender love. We are
precious to Him. He has carved us in the palm of His hand.
And we are created for greater things: to love and to be loved.

It is so important for us to know the Word of God. Because if
we know it, we will love it; and if we love it, we will keep it
and live it. Let us ask Mary, the Mother of Jesus and our
Mother, for the grace to imitate her. She kept the Word of
God and pondered it in her heart. And to be able to do that,
we must pray. Prayer gives a clean heart, and a clean heart
can see God and know His will for us.

Jesus tells us, "Love one another as I have loved you."
And how do we do that? Love begins in the family. I begin
by loving my father and my mother, my brothers and sisters;
my friends in the neighbourhood and at school and all those
I meet in my town or city. Love to be true must hurt, must
cost us something. When we love like that, ready to make a
sacrifice, we will find peace and joy.

Look around and see if there is anyone around you who is sick,
poor, lonely, or feeling unloved or unwanted. We don't have
to do big things. What counts is that we do small things with
great love - giving a smile, a kind word, a helping hand,
bringing a glass of water, sharing a sweet. Remember that we
do it to Jesus because He said, "Whatever you do to the least,
you do it to Me." So let us pray much that we may be the
sunshine of God's love to all we meet.

Let us pray.

God bless you
Mc Teresa mc

Contents

God Wants Us to Grow . . . Together!

WE ARE PART OF GOD'S FAMILY

God gives us family to provide guidance, fellowship, and love for the good times and the bad.

All this is true with God's family too. Each of us is brought into the family through the sacraments of baptism and confirmation and called to have a personal and intimate relationship with God our heavenly Father, through Jesus his Son and in the Holy Spirit. We, the Church, are the Bride of Christ, members of his Body. And so, we approach God not just as individuals, but as a family.

OUR BROTHERS AND SISTERS IN FAITH

Part of our Church family is already in heaven. The Church Triumphant is made up of our brothers and sisters in faith who are in heaven, and whose lives and writings have been preserved for us, in the "Deposit of Faith." This includes the Scriptures as well as other, less authoritative, spiritual writings and stories. Some of these stories have been included in this book to help you get to know some of the spiritual giants of the faith!

Why is it important to read about other men and women of the faith, or to read sources such as the *Catechism of the Catholic Church* as we study the Scriptures? In the same way we can learn from our families, the lives of saints can also teach us about God. That is why Jesus left a group of his followers to pass the gospel message on to others.

ABOUT THIS BOOK

St. Jerome said, "The New Testament is hidden in the Old; the Old Testament is fulfilled in the New." We read Scripture and interpret it with this in mind, and the readings we hear at Mass each week are arranged along these lines as well. If you go to Mass each day and listen attentively, you will become familiar with most of the Bible in the course of three years.

Because most of us don't make it to church every day, cultivating the habit of regular spiritual reading is important. A family that wishes to grow strong in the faith must study the Scriptures and then seek ways to apply what they have read in daily life. Reading this book as a family can help you do just that!

HELPFUL RESOURCES

As you read through the stories in the book, take note of the additional resources for your family:

The deuterocanonical books are books that are unique to the Catholic Church. Jews and some Christians do not consider them a part of the inspired canon.

The stories in the book are color-coded:

> A story with a beige heading is from the Old Testament.

> A story with a brown heading is a deuterocanonical book.

> And a story with a blue heading is from the New Testament.

- Going Deeper sections include *Read It!* and *Do It!* sections that direct you to related readings with fun and educational family activities.

- Special Words teach meanings of unusual and unfamiliar biblical terms.

- Did You Know? sections will teach you fun facts.

- The Quote of the Day will share wisdom from important people.

- A list of resources can be found at http://extraordinarymomsnetwork. wordpress.com. Anytime there is a note to go online for directions or more information, check out this site and click the *My Big Book of Catholic Bible Stories* link.

To help you get the full context of stories, many have been keyed to the liturgical calendar in the "Going Deeper" section, listing first the season (or dedicated feast day)

and then the week and cycle associated with it. The main seasons are:

Advent (AD)
Christmas (CH)
Ordinary Time (OT)
Lent (LE), Easter (EA)

We have also included relevant passages of the Catechism (labeled "CCC") to help you better understand the meaning of a particular passage.

Family Prayer Time

The Benedictines have a simple rule, handed down to them by St. Benedict which is a useful mandate for us: *Ora et labora*, which means "pray and work." As we pray, we must be willing to work to understand all that God expects of us.

The benefits of drawing close to the Lord together, as a family, will bless you beyond measure. The next page starts with a favorite prayer of mine, one of the earliest Christian prayers that I hope will become one of your favorites too. May the Holy Spirit, to whom we offer this prayer, illuminate your mind as we begin the very first story!

God bless you!
Heidi Hess Saxton

PRAYER TO THE HOLY SPIRIT

A Twelfth Century Prayer

Holy Spirit, Font of light, Focus of God's glory bright,
Shed on us a shining ray.
Father of the fatherless, Giver of gifts limitless,
Come and touch our hearts today.
Source of strength and sure relief, Comforter in time of grief,
Enter in and be our Guest.
On our journey grant us aid, freshening breeze and cooling shade,
In our labors, inward rest.
Enter each aspiring heart, occupy its inmost part
With your dazzling purity.
All that gives to us our worth, all that benefits the earth
You bring to maturity.
With your soft, refreshing rains, break our draughts, remove
 our stains,
Bind up all our injuries.
Shake with rushing wind our will, melt with fire our icy chill,
Bring to light our perjuries.
As your promise we believe, make us ready to receive
Gifts from your unbounded store.
Grant enabling energy, courage in adversity,
Joys that last forever more.

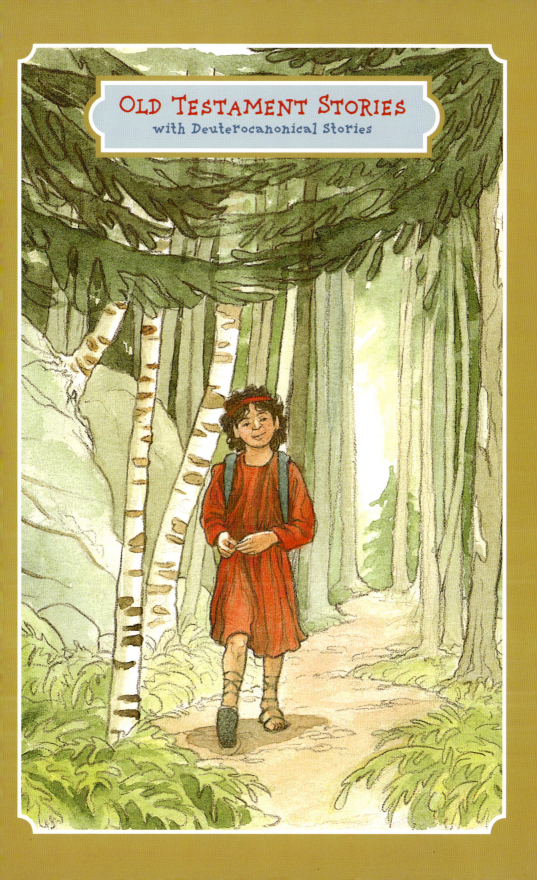

OLD TESTAMENT STORIES
with Deuterocanonical Stories

God Creates Light and Space

Genesis 1:1—8

God is eternal—that is, God has no beginning or end. And yet, the world and everything in it, even time itself, began when God spoke it into being. Let's read about God's amazing creative power in the very first book of the Bible, Genesis.

In the beginning when God created the heavens and the earth, ²the earth was a formless void and darkness covered the face of the deep, while a wind from God swept over the face of the waters. ³Then God said, "Let there be light"; and there was light. ⁴And God saw that the light was good; and God separated the light from the darkness. ⁵God called the light Day, and the darkness he called Night. And there was evening and there was morning, the first day.

6 And God said, "Let there be a dome in the midst of the waters, and let it separate the waters from the waters." ⁷So God made the dome and separated the waters that were under the dome from the waters that were above the dome. And it was so. ⁸God called the dome Sky. And there was evening and there was morning, the second day.

LET'S PRAY

The heavens tell the glory of God; the skies proclaim the work of his hands (from Psalm 19:1).

Thank you, God, for the beauty of your world. Help us to take good care of the beautiful things you have made and to treat creation with respect. In the name of the Father, and the Son, and the Holy Spirit, Amen!

GOING DEEPER

Read It! The creation of the world, which marks the beginning of "salvation history," is read every year at the Easter Vigil! See also CCC #279—89 (Religious instruction about the Creation is very important).

Do It! This week do something specific as a family to show respect for God's creation—take a load of recyclables to the recycling center or plant a tree.

SPECIAL WORDS:
A mighty wind is sometimes translated "a wind of God" or "Spirit of God."

DID YOU KNOW? There are volcanoes on Mars. The tallest, the Olympus Mons, stands eighteen miles high.

God Creates Sea and Sky

Genesis 1:9–19

Have you ever stood on the seashore and imagined how deep the water must be? Have you ever seen a mountain touch the sky? God created the world as a home for every fish that swims, every seagull that flies, and every bug that creeps. And then God entrusted it all to us! Let's listen to how God prepared a place for every living creature!

And God said, "Let the waters under the sky be gathered together into one place, and let the dry land appear." And it was so. ¹⁰God called the dry land Earth, and the waters that were gathered together he called Seas. And God saw that it was good. ¹¹Then God said, "Let the earth put forth vegetation: plants yielding seed, and fruit trees of every kind on earth that bear fruit with the seed in it." And it was so. ¹²The earth brought forth vegetation: plants yielding seed of every kind, and trees of every kind bearing fruit with the seed in it. And God saw that it was good. ¹³And there was evening and there was morning, the third day.

14.And God said, "Let there be lights in the dome of the sky to separate the day from the night; and let them be for signs and for seasons and for days and years, ¹⁵and let them be lights in the dome of the sky to give light upon the earth." And it was so. ¹⁶God made the two great lights—the greater light to rule the day and the lesser light to rule the night—and the stars. ¹⁷God set them in the dome of the sky to give light upon the earth, ¹⁸to rule over the day and over the night, and to separate the light from the darkness. And God saw that it was good. ¹⁹And there was evening and there was morning, the fourth day.

Let's Pray

Your mercy, Lord, is as deep as the deepest ocean; your love is greater than the highest mountain. Thank you for all the ways you take care of us! In the name of the Father, and the Son, and the Holy Spirit, Amen!

Going Deeper

Read It! This story is also from the Easter Vigil. See also CCC #299 (God's creation has order).

Do It! Together, go and watch the sun set tonight!

Special Words:
Vegetation refers to all the plant life on earth. The dome of the sky (v. 14), sometimes called the "firmament," refers to the vast space above the water.

God Creates All Living Creatures
Genesis 1:20–25

What's your favorite animal? Do you like puppies, giraffes, or majestic sea creatures? In today's reading, God created the birds, the fish, and all the other living creatures. Then he put them in the homes he had created just for them, until the whole world was filled with life!

And God said, "Let the waters bring forth swarms of living creatures, and let birds fly above the earth across the dome of the sky." [21]So God created the great sea monsters and every living creature that moves, of every kind, with which the waters swarm, and every winged bird of every kind. And God saw that it was good. [22]God blessed them, saying, "Be fruitful and multiply and fill the waters in the seas, and let birds multiply on the earth." [23]And there was evening and there was morning, the fifth day.

24 And God said, "Let the earth bring forth living creatures of every kind: cattle and creeping things and wild animals of the earth of every kind." And it was so. [25]God made the wild animals of the earth of every kind, and the cattle of every kind, and everything that creeps upon the ground of every kind. And God saw that it was good.

Let's Pray
Doxology by Thomas Ken
Praise God, from whom all blessings flow;
Praise Him, all creatures here below;
Praise Him above, ye heavenly host;
Praise Father, Son and Holy Ghost!
Amen.

Going Deeper
Read It! CCC #319 (God created the world to show his glory).
Do It! Visit a zoo this weekend!

Did You Know? The ordered beauty of Creation is proof that God exists. The world did not appear by accident, but by God's design. Before creating the birds and fish and animals, he created a home best suited to their needs. Before creating us, he made sure we'd have everything we need. What a wonderful God!

God Creates People

Genesis 1:26—31

After creating all those animals, God delighted in the infinite variety of the world. And yet something was still missing, someone who would take care of God's amazing creation. So God created the very first man, Adam.

Then God said, "Let us make humankind in our image, according to our likeness; and let them have dominion over the fish of the sea, and over the birds of the air, and over the cattle, and over all the wild animals of the earth, and over every creeping thing that creeps upon the earth."

27 So God created humankind in his image,
    in the image of God he created them;
    male and female he created them.

28 God blessed them, and God said to them, "Be fruitful and multiply, and fill the earth and subdue it; and have dominion over the fish of the sea and over the birds of the air and over every living thing that moves upon the earth." 29 God said, "See, I have given you every plant yielding seed that is upon the face of all the earth, and every tree with seed in its fruit; you shall have them for food. 30 And to every beast of the earth, and to every bird of the air, and to everything that creeps on the earth, everything that has the breath of life, I have given every green plant for food."

And it was so. 31 God saw everything that he had made, and indeed, it was very good. And there was evening and there was morning, the sixth day.

Let's Pray

Heavenly Father, thank you for loving us into the world.

Going Deeper

Read It! CCC #307 (We are fellow workers in God's kingdom).

Do It! Send a card today to someone for whom you are especially thankful!

Special Words:
One meaning of subdue is "to cultivate"; dominion refers to ownership.

Did You Know? There are more than three million varieties of animals on earth?

Adam and Eve

Genesis 2:18–24

Have you ever been to a wedding? In today's story, God brought Adam and Eve together to create the first human family. Adam waited for his partner until God made her just for him!

Then the LORD God said, "It is not good that the man should be alone; I will make him a helper as his partner." ¹⁹So out of the ground the LORD God formed every animal of the field and every bird of the air, and brought them to the man to see what he would call them; and whatever the man called every living creature, that was its name. ²⁰The man gave names to all cattle, and to the birds of the air, and to every animal of the field; but for the man there was not found a helper as his partner.

²¹So the LORD God caused a deep sleep to fall upon the man, and he slept; then he took one of his ribs and closed up its place with flesh. ²²And the rib that the LORD God had taken from the man he made into a woman and brought her to the man. ²³Then the man said,

"This at last is bone of my bones
and flesh of my flesh;

this one shall be called Woman,
for out of Man this one was taken."

²⁴Therefore a man leaves his father and his mother and clings to his wife, and they become one flesh.

Let's Pray

Prayer for the Family

A Traditonal Catholic Prayer

Blessed are you, loving Father, Ruler of the universe:
You have given us your Son,
And have made us temples of your Holy
Spirit.
Fill our family with your light and peace.
Have mercy on all who suffer,
And bring us to everlasting joy with you,
Father,
We bless your name forever and ever.
Amen.

Going Deeper

Read It! The gospel reading (OT 27B) is Mark 10:2–16; CCC #2207 (The family is the community where we learn things like moral values).

Do It! Plan a family night—something fun for the whole family to do together!

QUOTE OF THE DAY: "Perfect married life means the spiritual dedication of the parents for the benefit of their children."
—*St. Thomas Aquinas*

That Bad Snake!

Genesis 3:6, 9–15

*A*lone in the garden paradise, Adam and Eve enjoyed perfect happiness. God said they could eat from every tree in the garden except from the Tree of Knowledge of Good and Evil. So together they worked and played, took care of the animals, and marveled at the beauty all around them. Then the evil one, in the form of a snake, ruined it all. "Has God said . . . ?" the snake hissed, tempting Eve to doubt her Creator. "Surely God is afraid of your becoming as wise as he! Go on . . . take a bite!"

So when the woman saw that the tree was good for food, and that it was a delight to the eyes, and that the tree was to be desired to make one wise, she took of its fruit and ate; and she also gave some to her husband, who was with her, and he ate. . . .

⁹But the LORD God called to the man, and said to him, "Where are you?" ¹⁰He said, "I heard the sound of you in the garden, and I was afraid, because I was naked; and I hid myself." ¹¹He said, "Who told you that you were naked? Have you eaten from the tree of which I commanded you not to eat?" ¹²The man said, "The woman whom you gave to be with me, she gave me fruit from the tree, and I ate." ¹³Then the LORD God said to the woman, "What is this that you have done?" The woman said, "The serpent tricked me, and I ate." ¹⁴The LORD God said to the serpent,

"Because you have done this,
    cursed are you among all animals

and among all wild creatures;
upon your belly you shall go,
    and dust you shall eat
    all the days of your life.
¹⁵ I will put enmity between you and the
        woman,
    and between your offspring and hers;
    he will strike your head,
        and you will strike his heel."

LET'S PRAY

"God, whose mercy and compassion never fail, look kindly upon the sufferings of all mankind: the needs of the homeless; the anxieties of prisoners; the pains of the sick and the injured; the sorrows of the be- reaved; the helplessness of the aged and weak. Comfort and strengthen them for the sake of your Son, our Savior Jesus Christ."

—St. Anselm[1]

GOING DEEPER

Read It! This week (OT 10B), the gospel is Mark 3:20–35; CCC #324 (God would not permit an evil if he did not cause a good to come from it).

Do It! Look in magazines and newspapers for examples of people making good and bad choices. If the choice was a bad one, what should that person have done instead?

Cain and Abel
Genesis 4:3–5, 8–12

At first, Adam and Eve had two sons: Cain, who raised crops, and Abel, who tended flocks. Like most brothers, Cain and Abel didn't always get along! In this sad story, we read of a difference between the two brothers that brought about the first murder.

In the course of time Cain brought to the LORD an offering of the fruit of the ground, ⁴and Abel for his part brought of the firstlings of his flock, their fat portions. And the LORD had regard for Abel and his offering, ⁵but for Cain and his offering he had no regard. So Cain was very angry, and his countenance fell. . . .

8   Cain said to his brother Abel, "Let us go out to the field." And when they were in the field, Cain rose up against his brother Abel, and killed him. ⁹Then the LORD said to Cain, "Where is your brother Abel?" He said, "I do not know; am I my brother's keeper?" ¹⁰And the LORD said, "What have you done? Listen; your brother's blood is crying out to me from the ground! ¹¹And now you are cursed from the ground, which has opened its mouth to receive your brother's blood from your hand. ¹²When you till the ground, it will no longer yield to you its strength; you will be a fugitive and a wanderer on the earth."

LET'S PRAY
A Prayer for Vocations[2]

Lord, let me know clearly the work that you are calling me to do in life.

And grant me every grace I need to answer your call

With courage and love and lasting dedication to your will. Amen!

GOING DEEPER

Read It! CCC #2538 (The tenth commandment tells us not to envy).

Do It! Talk about a time when you were envious of someone. When we envy, we forget to be thankful! What would you like to thank God for today?

SPECIAL WORDS: Firstlings are the first animals to be born in a flock. The fat portions refer to the choicest and best parts of the animal.

Noah Builds an Ark

Genesis 6:5–8, 13, 18—22

*T*oo much water is a bad thing. When rivers and lakes spill over, or a storm whips up the ocean, water can destroy the homes or even lives of people and animals. In today's story, we hear about Noah, a good man who listened when God told him to build a big boat before he destroyed the whole world! His neighbors laughed, but Noah kept building the ark, and because he did, his family and all the animals on the boat stayed alive.

The LORD saw that the wickedness of humankind was great in the earth, and that every inclination of the thoughts of their hearts was only evil continually. ⁶And the LORD was sorry that he had made humankind on the earth, and it grieved him to his heart. ⁷So the LORD said, "I will blot out from the earth the human beings I have created— people together with animals and creeping things and birds of the air, for I am sorry that I have made them." ⁸But Noah found favor in the sight of the LORD. . . .

¹³And God said to Noah, "I have determined to make an end of all flesh, for the earth is filled with violence because of them; now I am going to destroy them along with the earth. . . . ¹⁸But I will establish my covenant with you; and you shall come into the ark, you, your sons, your wife, and your sons' wives with you. ¹⁹And of every living thing, of all flesh, you shall bring two of every kind into the ark, to keep them alive with you; they shall be male and female. ²⁰Of the birds according to their kinds, and of the animals according to their kinds, of every creeping thing of the ground according to its kind, two of every kind shall come in to you, to keep them alive. ²¹Also take with you every kind of food that is eaten, and store it up; and it shall serve as food for you and for them." ²²Noah did this; he did all that God commanded him.

LET'S PRAY

Father God, in you we live and move and have our being. Help us in times of trouble, and send us your Spirit to soften our hearts to do your will. Teach us to hear your voice, and follow it. In the name of the Father, and the Son, and the Holy Spirit, Amen!

GOING DEEPER

Read It! CCC #56–58 (God made a covenant with Noah).
Do It! Make animal cracker sandwiches with peanut butter or frosting. Be sure to eat them two by two!

QUOTE OF THE DAY: "After the unity of the human race was shattered by sin God at once sought to save humanity part by part. . . . 'in their lands, each with [its] own language, by their families, in their nations.'" —CCC #56

God Sends a Rainbow

Genesis 9:8–15

*P*oor Noah! All those animals and people crammed into such a tiny space! For forty days and forty nights it rained, and the ark floated on the water-covered earth. When dry land finally appeared, and the dove returned with the olive branch, Noah's family was finally able to leave their floating home. And as they did, they saw the most amazing sight: a rainbow, God's solemn promise that he would never flood the whole world again.

Then God said to Noah and to his sons with him, [9]"As for me, I am establishing my covenant with you and your descendants after you, [10]and with every living creature that is with you, the birds, the domestic animals, and every animal of the earth with you, as many as came out of the ark. [11]I establish my covenant with you, that never again shall all flesh be cut off by the waters of a flood, and never again shall there be a flood to destroy the earth. [12]God said, "This is the sign of the covenant that I make between me and you and every living creature that is with you, for all future generations:

[13]I have set my bow in the clouds, and it shall be a sign of the covenant between me and the earth. [14]When I bring clouds over the earth and the bow is seen in the clouds, [15]I will remember my covenant that is between me and you and every living creature of all flesh; and the waters shall never again become a flood to destroy all flesh."

Let's Pray:

O give thanks to the Lord, for he is good; for his steadfast love endures forever.

—Psalm 107:1

Going Deeper

Read It! The gospel reading (LE 1B) is Luke 1:26–38; CCC #1146–47 (God uses signs to communicate with us).

Do It! As a family, answer these questions: Why do you suppose God gave Noah and his family a visible reminder of his covenant with them? How do the sacraments do this for us?

Quote of the Day:
"God speaks to man through the visible creation. The material cosmos is so presented to man's intelligence that he can read there traces of its Creator."—CCC #1147

Abraham, Sarah, and Lot
Genesis 12:1–7

Have you ever moved to a new home? Was it hard to leave behind old friends or your old school or church? In Genesis 12, God calls Abram—later called Abraham—in order to establish a personal relationship with him. This "covenant of blessing" extended not only to Abram and his wife, Sarai, but to their children and future generations as well. But first, Abram had to leave everything behind and move to a place he had never seen. Imagine!

Now the LORD said to Abram, "Go from your country and your kindred and your father's house to the land that I will show you. ²I will make of you a great nation, and I will bless you, and make your name great, so that you will be a blessing. ³I will bless those who bless you, and the one who curses you I will curse; and in you all the families of the earth shall be blessed."

4 So Abram went, as the LORD had told him; and Lot went with him. Abram was seventy-five years old when he departed from Haran. ⁵Abram took his wife Sarai and his brother's son Lot, and all the possessions that they had gathered, and the persons whom they had acquired in Haran; and they set forth to go to the land of Canaan. When they had come to the land of Canaan, ⁶Abram passed through the land to the place at Shechem, to the oak of Moreh. At that time the Canaanites were in the land. ⁷Then the LORD appeared to Abram, and said, "To your offspring I will give this land." So he built there an altar to the LORD, who had appeared to him.

LET'S PRAY
A Prayer for Courage and Conversion
A Traditonal Catholic Prayer

Heavenly Father, just as Abram courageously put aside everything he knew to follow you, leaving behind even family and friends in obedience to your Word, help us to set aside everything that keeps us from loving you and serving you with all our hearts. In the name of the Father, and the Son, and the Holy Spirit, Amen!

GOING DEEPER

Read It! The gospel reading for today (LE 2A) is Matthew 17:1–9; CCC #145–47 (Abraham is the "father of all who believe").

Do It! Read CCC #1819 to help you find the answer to this question: What can we learn from Abram's willingness to leave everything behind at God's command?

Abraham Believes

Genesis 17:1–9, 15–16

When a child is adopted, or a woman gets married, her name may be legally changed to match her new family's. In the Bible, God sometimes changed a person's name too! (For example, Jesus changed Simon's name to Peter.) Here, Abram and Sarai became Abraham and Sarah; their friendship with God changed them inside and out!

When Abram was ninety-nine years old, the LORD appeared to Abram, and said to him, "I am God Almighty; walk before me, and be blameless. ²And I will make my covenant between me and you, and will make you exceedingly numerous." ³Then Abram fell on his face; and God said to him, ⁴"As for me, this is my covenant with you: You shall be the ancestor of a multitude of nations. ⁵No longer shall your name be Abram, but your name shall be Abraham; for I have made you the ancestor of a multitude of nations. ⁶I will make you exceedingly fruitful; and I will make nations of you, and kings shall come from you. ⁷I will establish my covenant between me and you, and your offspring after you throughout their generations, for an everlasting covenant, to be God to you and to your offspring after you. ⁸And I will give to you, and to your offspring after you, the land where you are now an alien, all the land of Canaan, for a perpetual holding; and I will be their God."

9 God said to Abraham, "As for you, you shall keep my covenant, you and your offspring after you throughout their generations. . . .

15 God said to Abraham, "As for Sarai your wife, you shall not call her Sarai, but Sarah shall be her name. ¹⁶I will bless her, and moreover I will give you a son by her. I will bless her, and she shall give rise to nations; kings of peoples shall come from her."

LET'S PRAY

"Blessed are those who fear the LORD, who walk in his ways!"   —Psalm 128:1

God, just like Abraham and Sarah, we want your love to change us from the inside out. In the name of the Father, and the Son, and the Holy Spirit, Amen.

GOING DEEPER:

Read It! CCC #762 (God called Abraham and began
preparing for the gathering of the People of God).

Do It! At confirmation, some people take the name of a
saint or other person they want to imitate. Did you or
your parents do this? If so, what name did you choose,
and why? What specific part of that person's life will
you follow?

Heavenly Guests
Genesis 18:1—15

Do you like having company at dinnertime? You get to hear some new stories, and you even get a special dessert! In today's story, Abraham welcomed three special visitors into his tent, and they turned out to be messengers of God, who had some very exciting news for Abraham and Sarah!

The Lord appeared to Abraham by the oaks of Mamre, as he sat at the entrance of his tent in the heat of the day. ²He looked up and saw three men standing near him. When he saw them, he ran from the tent entrance to meet them, and bowed down to the ground. ³He said, "My lord, if I find favor with you, do not pass by your servant. ⁴Let a little water be brought, and wash your feet, and rest yourselves under the tree. ⁵Let me bring a little bread, that you may refresh yourselves, and after that you may pass on—since you have come to your servant." So they said, "Do as you have said." ⁶And Abraham hastened into the tent to Sarah, and said, "Make ready quickly three measures of choice flour, knead it, and make cakes." ⁷Abraham ran to the herd, and took a calf, tender and good, and gave it to the servant, who hastened to prepare it. ⁸Then he took curds and milk and the calf that he had prepared, and set it before them; and he stood by them under the tree while they ate.

9 They said to him, "Where is your wife Sarah?" And he said, "There, in the tent." ¹⁰Then one said, "I will surely return to you in due season, and your wife Sarah shall have a son." And Sarah was listening at the tent entrance behind him. ¹¹Now Abraham and Sarah were old, advanced in age; it had ceased to be with Sarah after the manner of women. ¹²So Sarah laughed to herself, saying, "After I have grown old, and my husband is old, shall I have pleasure?" ¹³The Lord said to Abraham, "Why did Sarah laugh, and say, 'Shall I indeed bear a child, now that I am old?' ¹⁴Is anything too wonderful for the Lord? At the set time I will return to you, in due season, and Sarah shall have a son." ¹⁵But Sarah denied, saying, "I did not laugh"; for she was afraid. He said, "Oh yes, you did laugh."

Let's Pray

O Lord, who may abide in your tent?
Who may dwell on your holy hill?
Those who walk blamelessly, and do what is right, and speak truth from their heart.

—Psalm 15:1–2

GOING DEEPER

Read It! The gospel reading (OT 16C) is Luke 10:38–42;
CCC #706 (Against all human hope, God promises
descendents to Abraham).

Do It! Has there been a time when you were in a situation
that seemed impossible, that you turned over to God
and he helped you? Are you in such a situation right
now? Pray about it together, and watch those seeds of
faith grow!

Hagar and Ishmael
Genesis 21:1–3, 8–19

Have you ever wanted to do something, and had your parents tell you to clean your room first? Were you tempted to take a shortcut? When the Lord promised Abraham a son, he and Sarah did something sneaky: Sarah gave her servant Hagar to Abraham, to have a child. But once Sarah had Isaac, she wanted Hagar and her son Ishmael to disappear. What should Abraham do?

The LORD dealt with Sarah as he had said, and the LORD did for Sarah as he had promised. ²Sarah conceived and bore Abraham a son in his old age, at the time of which God had spoken to him. ³Abraham gave the name Isaac to his son whom Sarah bore him. . . .

8 The child grew, and was weaned; and Abraham made a great feast on the day that Isaac was weaned. ⁹But Sarah saw the son of Hagar the Egyptian, whom she had borne to Abraham, playing with her son Isaac. ¹⁰So she said to Abraham, "Cast out this slave woman with her son; for the son of this slave woman shall not inherit along with my son Isaac." ¹¹The matter was very distressing to Abraham on account of his son. ¹²But God said to Abraham, "Do not be distressed because of the boy and because of your slave woman; whatever Sarah says to you, do as she tells you, for it is through Isaac that offspring shall be named after you. ¹³As for the son of the slave woman, I will make a nation of him also, because he is your offspring." ¹⁴So Abraham rose early in the morning, and took bread and a skin of water, and gave it to Hagar, putting it on her shoulder, along with the child, and sent her away. And she departed, and wandered about in the wilderness of Beer-sheba.

15 When the water in the skin was gone, she cast the child under one of the bushes. ¹⁶Then she went and sat down opposite him a good way off, about the distance of a bow-shot; for she said, "Do not let me look on the death of the child." And as she sat opposite him, she lifted up her voice and wept. ¹⁷And God heard the voice of the boy; and the angel of God called to Hagar from heaven, and said to her, "What troubles you, Hagar? Do not be afraid; for God has heard the voice of the boy where he is. ¹⁸Come, lift up the boy and hold him fast with your hand, for I will make a great nation of him." ¹⁹Then God opened her eyes, and she saw a well of water. She went, and filled the skin with water, and gave the boy a drink.

LET'S PRAY

"Blessed is every one who fears the LORD, who walks in his ways!" —Psalm 128:1 RSV

Help us, Lord, to be a blessing to all those we meet, Christian and non-Christian alike.

GOING DEEPER:

Read It! Read Hebrews 11 to study the faith of Abraham
and other ancestors of Christ.

Do It! This Christmas and Advent season make a Jesse
Tree to honor and learn about the ancestry of Christ.
Search online to learn more.

God Tests Abraham
Genesis 22:1–3, 6–13

In the Bible, the wilderness is often a place of testing. During Lent we remember the forty days Christ was tested in the wilderness. Here the faith of Abraham was tested when God asked Abraham to sacrifice his only son, Isaac—the child God had promised him long ago.

After these things God tested Abraham. . . . ²He said, "Take your son, your only son Isaac, whom you love, and go to the land of Moriah, and offer him there as a burnt offering on one of the mountains that I shall show you." ³So Abraham rose early in the morning, saddled his donkey, and took two of his young men with him, and his son Isaac; he cut the wood for the burnt offering, and set out and went to the place in the distance that God had shown him. . . . ⁶Abraham took the wood of the burnt offering and laid it on his son Isaac, and he himself carried the fire and the knife. So the two of them walked on together. ⁷Isaac said to his father Abraham, . . ."The fire and the wood are here, but where is the lamb for a burnt offering?" ⁸Abraham said, "God himself will provide the lamb for a burnt offering, my son." So the two of them walked on together.

9 When they came to the place that God had shown him, Abraham built an altar there and laid the wood in order. He bound his son Isaac, and laid him on the altar, on top of the wood. ¹⁰Then Abraham reached out his hand and took the knife to kill his son. ¹¹But the angel of the LORD called to him from heaven, and said, "Abraham, Abraham!" And he said, "Here I am." ¹²He said, "Do not lay your hand on the boy or do anything to him; for now I know that you fear God, since you have not withheld your son, your only son, from me." ¹³And Abraham looked up and saw a ram, caught in a thicket by its horns. Abraham went and took the ram and offered it up as a burnt offering instead of his son.

LET'S PRAY

I love you, Lord, because you have heard my voice. Because you have inclined your ear toward me, I will call upon you as long as I live! (Adapted from Psalm 116:1–2.)

GOING DEEPER

Read It! (LE 2B Easter Vigil), the gospel reading is Mark 9:2–10; CCC #2572 (Abraham's faith was tested).

Do It! Talk about the similarities between Abraham's sacrificing Isaac and Christ's sacrifice for us. What small things can you sacrifice for your friends and family this week?

QUOTE OF THE DAY:
"The whole science of the saints consists in knowing and following the will of God."
—St. Isidore of Seville

A Wife for Isaac

Genesis 24:12—20

*D*o you think you'll get married when you grow up? Choosing a mate is one of the most important decisions in life, so it's important to pick someone who shares your faith! Abraham knew this, too. When Isaac became old enough to marry, Abraham wanted his son to find a good woman who would love the one true God, just as Isaac had been taught to do. So Abraham sent his trusted servant back to his hometown to find such a girl.

And he said, "O Lord, God of my master Abraham, please grant me success today and show steadfast love to my master Abraham. ¹³I am standing here by the spring of water, and the daughters of the townspeople are coming out to draw water. ¹⁴Let the girl to whom I shall say, 'Please offer your jar that I may drink,' and who shall say, 'Drink, and I will water your camels'—let her be the one whom you have appointed for your servant Isaac. By this I shall know that you have shown steadfast love to my master."

15 Before he had finished speaking, there was Rebekah, who was born to Bethuel son of Milcah, the wife of Nahor, Abraham's brother, coming out with her water jar on her shoulder. ¹⁶The girl was very fair to look upon, a virgin, whom no man had known. She went down to the spring, filled her jar, and came up. ¹⁷Then the servant ran to meet her and said, "Please let me sip a little water from your jar." ¹⁸"Drink, my lord," she said, and quickly lowered her jar upon her hand and gave him a drink. ¹⁹When she had finished giving him a drink, she said, "I will draw for your camels also, until they have finished drinking." ²⁰So she quickly emptied her jar into the trough and ran again to the well to draw, and she drew for all his camels.

Let's Pray

Lord, help us always to be as faithful as Abraham's servant, and as generous as Rebekah.

Going Deeper

Read It! Read the whole account in Genesis 24:52—67 and imagine what courage it must have taken for Rebekah to leave her family and go with the stranger to meet her future husband!

Do It! Parents, pray right now out loud with your children for their future vocation, whether to marriage or religious life.

Did You Know?
Camels drink eight to ten gallons a day, and can drink twenty-five to thirty gallons in ten minutes![4]

27

Jacob and Esau

Genesis 25:21, 24, 27–34; 27:1–4, 15–19

*D*o you ever boss around your brother or sister? When Rebekah was pregnant, God told her, "two nations are in your womb." Jacob was born moments after Esau, clutching his older brother's heel. This struggle went on throughout their lives. In today's story, Jacob stole not only his brother's inheritance, but their father's blessing as well.

Isaac prayed to the LORD for his wife, because she was barren; and the LORD granted his prayer, and his wife Rebekah conceived. . . . ²⁴When her time to give birth was at hand, there were twins in her womb. . . .

27 When the boys grew up, Esau was a skillful hunter, a man of the field, while Jacob was a quiet man, living in tents. ²⁸Isaac loved Esau, because he was fond of game; but Rebekah loved Jacob.

29 Once when Jacob was cooking a stew, Esau came in from the field, and he was famished. ³⁰Esau said to Jacob, "Let me eat some of that red stuff, for I am famished!" . . . ³¹Jacob said, "First sell me your birthright." ³²Esau said, "I am about to die; of what use is a birthright to me?" ³³Jacob said, "Swear to me first." So he swore to him, and sold his birthright to Jacob. ³⁴Then Jacob gave Esau bread and lentil stew, and he ate and drank, and rose and went his way. Thus Esau despised his birthright. . . .

27 When Isaac was old and his eyes were dim so that he could not see, he called his elder son Esau and said to him, "My son"; and he answered, "Here I am." ²He said, "See, I am old; I do not know the day of my death. ³Now then, take your weapons, your quiver and your bow, and go out to the field, and hunt game for me. ⁴Then prepare for me savory food, such as I

like, and bring it to me to eat, so that I may bless you before I die.". . .

¹⁵Then Rebekah took the best garments of her elder son Esau, which were with her in the house, and put them on her younger son Jacob; ¹⁶and she put the skins of the kids on his hands and on the smooth part of his neck. ¹⁷Then she handed the savory food, and the bread that she had prepared, to her son Jacob.

18 So he went in to his father, and said, "My father"; and he said, "Here I am; who are you, my son?" ¹⁹Jacob said to his father, "I am Esau your firstborn. I have done as you told me; now sit up and eat of my game, so that you may bless me."

LET'S PRAY

Lord, you have given us a rich inheritance. Make us worthy of your blessings.

SPECIAL WORDS: A birthright gave a double portion of a father's inheritance, usually to the eldest son, along with the designation as head of the family upon the father's death.

DID YOU KNOW? Esau's descendants, the Edomites, remained in conflict—yet subservient—to Israel throughout history (2 Kings 8:20–22), and they eventually disappeared altogether.

GOING DEEPER

Read It! CCC #2218 (The fourth commandment reminds adult children of their responsibilities toward parents).

Do It! Did Jacob "honor" his parents? Read the Catechism and discuss! Parents, share with your children how you currently honor your parents or did so in the past. Children, name ways you will show honor to your mom and dad this week.

A MORNING OFFERING

A Traditonal Catholic Prayer

God, please come to my assistance.

Lord make haste to help me.

Glory be to the Father, and to the Son,

and to the Holy Spirit:

As it was in the beginning, is now,

and ever shall be, world without end, Amen!

As morning breaks I look to you, O Lord,

to be my strength this day.

Jacob Marries Laban's Daughters

Genesis 29:16–28

Woo-eee! Was Esau ever mad at Jacob for stealing his birthright! To escape his brother's anger, Jacob ran away and went to work for his mother's relatives. He fell in love with Laban's younger daughter, Rachel, and agreed to work for his future father-in-law for seven years for the right to marry her. Sadly, Uncle Laban was not an honest man!

Now Laban had two daughters; the name of the elder was Leah, and the name of the younger was Rachel. [17]Leah's eyes were lovely, and Rachel was graceful and beautiful. [18]Jacob loved Rachel; so he said, "I will serve you seven years for your younger daughter Rachel." [19]Laban said, "It is better that I give her to you than that I should give her to any other man; stay with me." [20]So Jacob served seven years for Rachel, and they seemed to him but a few days because of the love he had for her.

21 Then Jacob said to Laban, "Give me my wife that I may go in to her, for my time is completed." [22]So Laban gathered together all the people of the place, and made a feast. [23]But in the evening he took his daughter Leah and brought her to Jacob; and he went in to her. [24](Laban gave his maid Zilpah to his daughter Leah to be her maid.) [25]When morning came, it was Leah! And Jacob said to Laban, "What is this you have done to me? Did I not serve with you for Rachel? Why then have you deceived me?" [26]Laban said, "This is not done in our country—giving the younger before the firstborn. [27]Complete the week of this one, and we will give you the other also in return for serving me for another seven years." [28]Jacob did so, and completed her week; then Laban gave him his daughter Rachel as a wife.

LET'S PRAY

The righteousness of the blameless keeps his way straight, but the wicked fall by their own wickedness.   —Proverbs 11:5

Lord, help us always to choose what is honest and good, and to avoid the trap of evil.

SPECIAL WORDS: "Lovely"
(rak in Hebrew) could also be
translated "dull" (eyes).

GOING DEEPER

Read It! CCC #2387 (Polygamy was not part of God's
plan for his people).

Do It! Talk about some important traits to look for
in a spouse when you are grown up. What are
your top five?

Jacob's Adventures

Genesis 32:1–7, 22–30

*T*he Bible is full of angel stories. Jacob was especially blessed, because he got to see angels twice! First he dreamed of angels going up and down a ladder (Genesis 28:10–13). And in this story, in which he is returning to his family to make up with his brother, Esau, Jacob encounters God's messengers again!

Jacob went on his way and the angels of God met him; ²and when Jacob saw them he said, "This is God's camp!" So he called that place Mahanaim.

3 Jacob sent messengers before him to his brother Esau in the land of Seir, the country of Edom, ⁴instructing them, "Thus you shall say to my lord Esau: Thus says your servant Jacob, 'I have lived with Laban as an alien, and stayed until now; ⁵and I have oxen, donkeys, flocks, male and female slaves; and I have sent to tell my lord, in order that I may find favor in your sight.'"

6 The messengers returned to Jacob, saying, "We came to your brother Esau, and he is coming to meet you, and four hundred men are with him." ⁷Then Jacob was greatly afraid and distressed; and he divided the people that were with him, and the flocks and herds and camels, into two companies, thinking, "If Esau comes to the one company and destroys it, then the company that is left will escape. . . .

22 The same night he got up and took his two wives, his two maids, and his eleven children, and crossed the ford of the Jabbok. ²³He took them and sent them across the stream, and likewise everything that he had.

24 Jacob was left alone; and a man wrestled with him until daybreak. ²⁵When the man saw that he did not prevail against Jacob, he struck him on the hip socket; and Jacob's hip was put out of joint as he wrestled with him. ²⁶Then he said, "Let me go, for the day is breaking." But Jacob said, "I will not let you go, unless you bless me." ²⁷So he said to him, "What is your name?" And he said, "Jacob." ²⁸Then the man said, "You shall no longer be called Jacob, but Israel, for you have striven with God and with humans, and have prevailed." ²⁹Then Jacob asked him, "Please tell me your name." But he said, "Why is it that you ask my name?" And there he blessed him. ³⁰So Jacob called the place Peniel, saying, "For I have seen God face to face, and yet my life is preserved."

Let's Pray

Psalm 91:11 tells us, "For he will command his angels concerning you to guard you in all your ways."

Dear Lord, we thank you for creating angels to watch over us. Amen.

SPECIAL WORDS: Israel means
"struggles with God." Peniel
means "face of God."

DID YOU KNOW? You have
a guardian angel!
(CCC #336).

GOING DEEPER

Read It! CCC #2573 (From Jacob's wrestling the angel,
the church has retained the symbol of prayer as a
battle of faith and as the triumph of perseverance).

Do It! Make angel cookies. As you eat them, hold up one
and name someone else in the Bible to whom angels
came. Why did the angels come, and what happened?

Joseph the Dreamer

Genesis 37:3–8, 12–14, 18–20

*W*hen you get something nice, like a birthday present, do you ever tease your brother or sister with it? Although Jacob (also called Israel) loved all his children, he was especially fond of Joseph, and gave him a beautiful coat that signaled to his older brothers how important Joseph was to their dad. No wonder they resented their little brother! And those seeds of envy bore dangerous fruit.

Now Israel loved Joseph more than any other of his children, because he was the son of his old age; and he had made him a long robe with sleeves. ⁴But when his brothers saw that their father loved him more than all his brothers, they hated him, and could not speak peaceably to him.

5 Once Joseph had a dream, and when he told it to his brothers, they hated him even more. ⁶He said to them, "Listen to this

dream that I dreamed. ⁷There we were, binding sheaves in the field. Suddenly my sheaf rose and stood upright; then your sheaves gathered around it, and bowed down to my sheaf." ⁸His brothers said to him, "Are you indeed to reign over us? Are you indeed to have dominion over us?" So they hated him even more because of his dreams and his words. . . .

12 Now his brothers went to pasture their father's flock near Shechem. ¹³And Israel said to Joseph, "Are not your brothers pasturing the flock at Shechem? Come, I will send you to them." He answered, "Here I am." ¹⁴So he said to him, "Go now, see if it is well with your brothers and with the flock; and bring word back to me." So he sent him from the valley of Hebron.

He came to Shechem. . . . ¹⁸They saw him from a distance, and before he came near to them, they conspired to kill him. ¹⁹They said to one another, "Here comes this dreamer. ²⁰Come now, let us kill him and throw him into one of the pits; then we shall say that a wild animal has devoured him, and we shall see what will become of his dreams."

LET'S PRAY

When I am tempted to envy, Lord Jesus, help me to love instead.

GOING DEEPER

Read It! CCC #2540 (Fight against envy by practicing good will.)

Do It! Family movie night! Rent and watch together the movie *Joseph and the Amazing Technicolor Dream Coat.*

Joseph Forgives
Genesis 41:46–49, 42:1–8, 45:3–5

Have you ever gotten in trouble for something you didn't do? Was it hard to forgive those who got you in trouble? Joseph was betrayed—first by his brothers who took him from the pit and sold him to slave-traders bound for Egypt. And then his owner's wife betrayed him, too, and he ended up in prison! Yet somehow Joseph never lost his trust in God, and ultimately God delivered Joseph, who became the second most powerful man in Egypt! In the end, not only did Joseph forgive his brothers, but he even took care of them!

Joseph was thirty years old when he entered the service of Pharaoh, king of Egypt. And Joseph went out from the presence of Pharaoh, and went through all the land of Egypt. 47During the seven plenteous years the earth produced abundantly. 48He gathered up all the food of the seven years when there was plenty in the land of Egypt, and stored up food in the cities; he stored up in every city the food from the fields around it. 49So Joseph stored up grain in such abundance—like the sand of the sea—that . . . it was beyond measure. . . .

42When Jacob learned that there was grain in Egypt, he said to his sons, ". . . 2I have heard that there is grain in Egypt; go down and buy grain for us there, that we may live and not die." 3So ten of Joseph's brothers went down to buy grain in Egypt. 4But Jacob did not send Joseph's brother Benjamin with his brothers, for he feared that harm might come to him. 5Thus the sons of Israel were among the other people who came to buy grain. . . .

6 Now Joseph was governor over the land; it was he who sold to all the people of the land. And Joseph's brothers came and bowed themselves before him with their faces to the ground. 7When Joseph saw his brothers, he recognized them, but he treated them like strangers and spoke harshly to them. "Where do you come from?" he said. They said, "From the land of Canaan, to buy food." 8Although Joseph had recognized his brothers, they did not recognize him. . . .

45Joseph said to his brothers, "I am Joseph. Is my father still alive?" But his brothers could not answer him, so dismayed were they at his presence.

4 Then Joseph said to his brothers, "Come closer to me." And they came closer. He said, "I am your brother, Joseph, whom you sold into Egypt. 5And now do not be distressed, or angry with yourselves, because you sold me here; for God sent me before you to preserve life."

LET'S PRAY
Prayer for Forgiveness[5]

Lord, hear the prayers of those who call on you, forgive the sins of those who confess to you, and in your merciful love give us your pardon and your peace.

GOING DEEPER

Read It! CCC #2844 (We must forgive).
Do It! "Love is stronger than sin" (CCC #2844). How do
we see this in the story of Joseph and his brothers?

Baby in the Basket
Exodus 2:1–10

*F*our hundred years ago, the first American colony was settled at Jamestown. Think of how much has changed since then! Four hundred years is a long time, and that's how long the Hebrew people remained in Egypt. Over time a new Pharaoh came to power who did not know Joseph. Because the Hebrew population had increased so much, Pharaoh decided every male Hebrew infant should be killed, so the slaves would stay weak and afraid. Then God began to reveal a plan to deliver his people. And it all began with a baby in a basket!

Now a man from the house of Levi went and married a Levite woman. ²The woman conceived and bore a son; and when she saw that he was a fine baby, she hid him three months. ³When she could hide him no longer she got a papyrus basket for him, and plastered it with bitumen and pitch; she put the child in it and placed it among the reeds on the bank of the river. ⁴His sister stood at a distance, to see what would happen to him.

5 The daughter of Pharaoh came down to bathe at the river, while her attendants walked beside the river. She saw the basket among the reeds and sent her maid to bring it. ⁶When she opened it, she saw the child. He was crying, and she took pity on him, "This must be one of the Hebrews' children," she said. ⁷Then his sister said to Pharaoh's daughter, "Shall I go and get you a nurse from the Hebrew women to nurse the child for you?" ⁸Pharaoh's daughter said to her, "Yes." So the girl went and called the child's mother. ⁹Pharaoh's daughter said to her, "Take this child and nurse it for me, and I will give you your wages." So the woman took the child and nursed it. ¹⁰When the child grew up, she brought him to Pharaoh's daughter, and she took him as her son. She named him Moses, "because," she said, "I drew him out of the water."

LET'S PRAY
A Prayer of Moses

Lord, you have been our dwelling place
   in all generations.
Before the mountains were brought forth,
   or ever you had formed the earth and
    the world
   from everlasting to everlasting
    you are God.

—Psalm 90:1

SPECIAL WORDS: *Levi was
the priestly tribe of Israel.
Bitumen is a tarlike substance
used for waterproofing.*

GOING DEEPER

Read It! Moses was adopted into Pharoah's family. Has
your family ever considered adoption? (CCC #2379).

Do It! Family Movie Night! Watch *Prince of Egypt* (for
younger kids) or *The Ten Commandments* (for older kids
and adults).

The Burning Bush
Exodus 3:1–8, 10

*D*id you ever do something wrong, then run away to avoid the consequences? As a young Egyptian prince, Moses fled Pharaoh's court and went to the wilderness because he had killed an Egyptian guard for mistreating a Hebrew slave. For forty years Moses tended his father-in-law's flocks in the wilderness of Sinai. Then one day, out on the mountain, a curious sight got Moses' attention.

Moses was keeping the flock of his father-in-law Jethro, the priest of Midian; he led his flock beyond the wilderness, and came to Horeb, the mountain of God. ²There the angel of the LORD appeared to him in a flame of fire out of a bush; he looked, and the bush was blazing, yet it was not consumed. ³Then Moses said, "I must turn aside and look at this great sight, and see why the bush is not burned up." ⁴When the LORD saw that he had turned aside to see, God called to him out of the bush, "Moses, Moses!" And he said, "Here I am." ⁵Then he said, "Come no closer! Remove the sandals from your feet, for the place on which you are standing is holy ground." ⁶He said further, "I am the God of your father, the God of Abraham, the God of Isaac, and the God of Jacob." And Moses hid his face, for he was afraid to look at God.

7 Then the LORD said, "I have observed the misery of my people who are in Egypt; I have heard their cry on account of their taskmasters. Indeed, I know their sufferings, ⁸and I have come down to deliver them from the Egyptians, and to bring them up out of that land to a good and broad land, a land flowing with milk and honey. . . . ¹⁰So come, I will send you to Pharaoh to bring my people, the Israelites, out of Egypt."

LET'S PRAY

Bless the LORD, O my soul,
   and all that is within me,
   bless his holy name.
Bless the LORD, O my soul,
   and do not forget all his benefits. . . .
The LORD is merciful and gracious,
   slow to anger and abounding in steadfast
     love. . . .
Bless the LORD, O my soul.
         —Psalm 103:1–2, 8, 22

GOING DEEPER

Read It! Today (LE 3C), the gospel is Mark 13:1–9; CCC #2574–2577 (Moses learns how to pray).

Do It! God called Moses to be a leader, first mediating between his people and Pharaoh, then between God and his people. How did this encounter prepare him? (Read Catechism passage for answer!) How is God preparing you for good work?

DID YOU KNOW? Moses was eighty years old when God sent him from the desert and placed him before Pharaoh! God can use us at any age if we let him!

"Let My People Go!"
Exodus 10:21–29, 11:1, 4–5, 7

In this story, when Moses and his brother, Aaron, went before the pharaoh, they had the power of God with them. Through these two men, God sent nine different warnings, from turning the Nile River to blood to covering the land in darkness. The pharaoh's heart was hard; he thought it was all trickery. He had to learn about God's power the hard way!

The LORD said to Moses, "Stretch out your hand toward heaven so that there may be darkness over the land of Egypt, a darkness that can be felt." ²²So Moses stretched out his hand toward heaven, and there was dense darkness in all the land of Egypt for three days. ²³People could not see one another, and for three days they could not move from where they were; but all the Israelites had light where they lived. ²⁴Then Pharaoh summoned Moses, and said, "Go, worship the LORD. Only your flocks and your herds shall remain behind. Even your children may go with you." ²⁵But Moses said, "You must also let us have sacrifices and burnt offerings to sacrifice to the LORD our God. ²⁶Our livestock also must go with us; not a hoof shall be left behind, for we must choose some of them for the worship of the LORD our God, and we will not know what to use to worship the LORD until we arrive there." ²⁷But the LORD hardened Pharaoh's heart, and he was unwilling to let them go.

²⁸Then Pharaoh said to him, "Get away from me! Take care that you do not see my face again, for on the day you see my face you shall die." ²⁹Moses said, "Just as you say! I will never see your face again." . . .

11 The LORD said to Moses, "I will bring one more plague upon Pharaoh and upon Egypt; afterwards he will let you go from here; indeed, when he lets you go, he will drive you away. . . .

⁴About midnight I will go out through Egypt. ⁵Every firstborn in the land of Egypt shall die, from the firstborn of Pharaoh . . . to the firstborn of the female slave . . . and all the firstborn of the livestock . . . ⁷But not a dog shall growl at any of the Israelites . . . so that you may know that the LORD makes a distinction between Egypt and Israel."

LET'S PRAY
Deliver us, O God, from every evil way. Keep us on the paths of righteousness.

44

GOING DEEPER

Read It! John 2 tells about the wedding at Cana, and we
see Christ as the "New Moses," and the Lord's first
miracle—turning water to wine, and later wine into his
precious blood—as complete fulfillment of the sign
Moses gave Pharaoh.

Do It! God took the children of Israel on a great
adventure. Plan a family vacation together and
prepare for your own adventure! Get out a map of the
United States or the region within your budget and let
everyone vote on where they would like to go.

Passover

Exodus 12:21—32

*N*ine times Moses said to Pharaoh, "Let my people go!" Pharaoh refused, but God was determined. And so, he sent the final, terrible plague, and the firstborn of each Egyptian family died. The Hebrew children were safe: at Moses' direction, each family killed a lamb and put some of its blood on the doorposts of their house. In this way, God knew to "pass over" that home.

Then Moses called all the elders of Israel and said to them, "Go, select lambs for your families, and slaughter the passover lamb. ²²Take a bunch of hyssop, dip it in the blood that is in the basin, and touch the lintel and the two doorposts with the blood in the basin. None of you shall go outside the door of your house until morning. ²³For the LORD will pass through to strike down the Egyptians; when he sees the blood on the lintel and on the two doorposts, the LORD will pass over that door and will not allow the destroyer to enter your houses to strike you down. ²⁴You shall observe this rite as a perpetual ordinance for you and your children. ²⁵When you come to the land that the LORD will give you, as he has promised, you shall keep this observance. ²⁶And when your children ask you, 'What do you mean by this observance?' ²⁷you shall say, 'It is the passover sacrifice to the LORD, for he passed over the houses of the Israelites in Egypt, when he struck down the Egyptians

but spared our houses.'" And the people bowed down and worshiped.

28 The Israelites went and did just as the LORD had commanded Moses and Aaron.

29 At midnight the LORD struck down all the firstborn in the land of Egypt, from the firstborn of Pharaoh who sat on his throne to the firstborn of the prisoner who was in the dungeon, and all the firstborn of the livestock. ³⁰Pharaoh arose in the night, he and all his officials and all the Egyptians; and there was a loud cry in Egypt, for there was not a house without someone dead. ³¹Then he summoned Moses and Aaron in the night, and said, "Rise up, go away from my people, both you and the Israelites! Go, worship the LORD, as you said. ³²Take your flocks and your herds, as you said, and be gone. And bring a blessing on me too!"

LET'S PRAY

Father, thank you for watching over and protecting us. Amen.

GOING DEEPER

Read It! Read about the full meaning of Passover for Christians (CCC #1096).

Do It! Have lamb chops and matzo bread for dinner tonight! This is what Jewish families eat when they celebrate the Passover. Find more information online.

DID YOU KNOW? Passover is still celebrated by Jewish families in honor of when God "passed over" the Israelite families in Egypt. It is a seven-day feast during Nisan (the first month in the Jewish calendar), which is around March and April.

Seaside Miracle

Exodus 14:5–10, 13–18, 21–22

*H*ave you ever been to a body of water that was so big you couldn't see from one side to the other? After the Israelites got away from Pharaoh, they had another challenge: they had to get across the Red Sea! That would have been hard enough, but then Pharaoh changed his mind and decided he was going to get those slaves back! Let's see what happens.

When the king of Egypt was told that the people had fled, the minds of Pharaoh and his officials were changed toward the people, and they said, "What have we done, letting Israel leave our service?" ⁶So he had his chariot made ready, and took his army with him; ⁷he took six hundred picked chariots and all the other chariots of Egypt with officers over all of them. ⁸The LORD hardened the heart of Pharaoh king of Egypt and he pursued the Israelites. . . . ⁹The Egyptians . . . overtook them camped by the sea. . . .

10 As Pharaoh drew near, the Israelites looked back, and there were the Egyptians advancing on them. In great fear the Israelites cried out to the LORD. . . . ¹³But Moses said to the people, "Do not be afraid, stand firm, and see the deliverance that the LORD will accomplish for you today; for the Egyptians whom you see today you shall never see again. ¹⁴The LORD will fight for you, and you have only to keep still."

15 Then the LORD said to Moses, "Why do you cry out to me? Tell the Israelites to go forward. ¹⁶But you lift up your staff, and stretch out your hand over the sea and divide it, that the Israelites may go into the sea on dry ground. ¹⁷Then I will harden the hearts of the Egyptians so that they will go in after them; and so I will gain glory for myself over Pharaoh and all his army, his chariots, and his chariot drivers. ¹⁸And the Egyptians shall know that I am the LORD, when I have gained glory for myself over Pharaoh, his chariots, and his chariot drivers." . . .

21 Then Moses stretched out his hand over the sea. The LORD drove the sea back by a strong east wind all night, and turned the sea into dry land; and the waters were divided. ²²The Israelites went into the sea on dry ground, the waters forming a wall for them on their right and on their left.

LET'S PRAY

"Lord, open the understanding of my unbelieving heart, so that I should recall my sins."—St. Patrick

GOING DEEPER

Read It! This passage is read each year at the Easter Vigil; CCC #1221 (The parting of the sea was an example of baptism).

Do It! The parting of the Red Sea was a major miracle, but even today God performs miracles all around us. Talk about the miracles you have experienced.

49

Bread from Heaven

Exodus 16:1–7, 13–15

Think of a time when you were very hungry and couldn't wait for dinner. Now imagine when suppertime came there wasn't anything to eat. When this happened to the Israelites, God provided once more in a very unique way.

The whole congregation of the Israelites . . . came to the wilderness of Sin, which is between Elim and Sinai, on the fifteenth day of the second month after they had departed from the land of Egypt. ²The whole congregation of the Israelites complained against Moses and Aaron in the wilderness. ³The Israelites said to them, "If only we had died by the hand of the LORD in the land of Egypt, when we sat by the fleshpots and ate our fill of bread; for you have brought us out into this wilderness to kill this whole assembly with hunger."

4 Then the LORD said to Moses, "I am going to rain bread from heaven for you, and each day the people shall go out and gather enough for that day. In that way I will test them, whether they will follow my instruction or not. ⁵On the sixth day, when they prepare what they bring in, it will be twice as much as they gather on other days." ⁶So Moses and Aaron said to all the Israelites, "In the evening you shall know that it was the LORD who brought you out of the land of Egypt, ⁷and in the morning you shall see the glory of the LORD, because he has heard your complaining against the LORD. For what are we, that you complain against us?" . . .

13 In the evening quails came up and covered the camp; and in the morning there was a layer of dew around the camp. ¹⁴When the layer of dew lifted, there on the surface of the wilderness was a fine flaky substance, as fine as frost on the ground. ¹⁵When the Israelites saw it, they said to one another, "What is it?" For they did not know what it was. Moses said to them, "It is the bread that the LORD has given you to eat.

LET'S PRAY

Dear God, thank you providing food for our bodies to grow healthy and strong. Please bless the people in the world who do not get enough to eat, and use me to make a difference for them. In your Son's name, Amen.

DID YOU KNOW? *Manna
resembled coriander seed
and tasted like honey.
Look in the pantry or at the
grocery store to see
what coriander seed
looks like!*

GOING DEEPER

Read It! The gospel reading this week (OT 18B) is John
6:24–35; CCC #2837 (Daily bread is necessary
for life; Jesus, our "daily bread," is necessary
for eternal life).

Do It! Go to daily Mass as a family this week!

Living Water
Exodus 17:1–6

*W*hen you get thirsty during a long trip, do you get cranky? So did the Israelites! No sooner had God provided the food they needed than they began to complain again. "Water . . . give us water!" And once again, God answered their prayers.

From the wilderness of Sin the whole congregation of the Israelites journeyed by stages, as the LORD commanded. They camped at Rephidim, but there was no water for the people to drink. ²The people quarreled with Moses, and said, "Give us water to drink." Moses said to them, "Why do you quarrel with me? Why do you test the LORD?" ³But the people thirsted there for water; and the people complained against Moses and said, "Why did you bring us out of Egypt, to kill us and our children and livestock with thirst?" ⁴So Moses cried out to the LORD, "What shall I do with this people? They are almost ready to stone me." ⁵The LORD said to Moses, "Go on ahead of the people, and take some of the elders of Israel with you; take in your hand the staff with which you struck the Nile, and go. ⁶I will be standing there in front of you on the rock at Horeb. Strike the rock, and water will come out of it, so that the people may drink." Moses did so, in the sight of the elders of Israel.

LET'S PRAY
Prayer of Adoration

"O God, we believe you are here, and most worthy of all our love. Flood our souls with your spirit and life. . . . Shine through us, and be so in us, that every soul we come in contact with may feel your spresence. Let them look up and see no longer us, but only Jesus!"

—Blessed Mother Teresa of Calcutta

GOING DEEPER

Read It! The gospel reading (LE 3A) is John 4:5–42.
   Just as Moses gave the people life-giving water,
   so Jesus is *our* Living Water (John 7:38)!
Do It! On a hot summer day. Open up a lemonade stand
   as a family. Instead of charging, share your refreshing
   beverages for free.

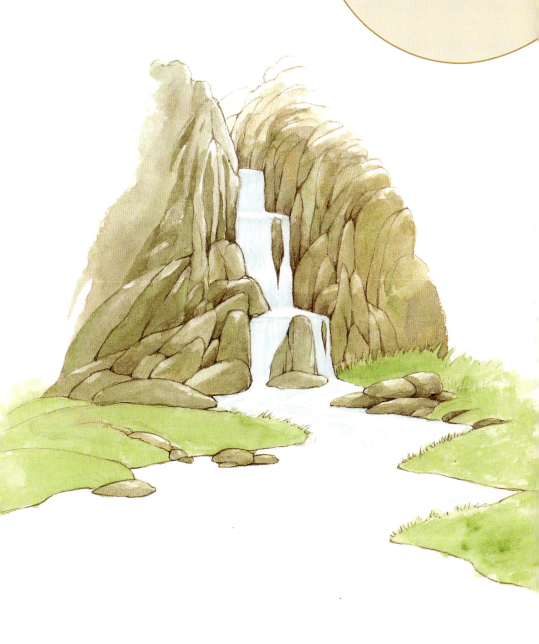

DID YOU KNOW? In the book of Numbers, we learn that Moses performed another "water miracle" and greatly displeased God. Read Numbers 20:1–13 and find out why.

God Gives the Law

Exodus 19:16–19; 20:1–4, 7–8, 12–17

*M*oses led the Israelites toward the Promised Land. For hundreds of years they had been under the rule of Pharaoh, but now God was calling them to be his people, following his rules. These rules were called the Ten Commandments (the Decalogue).

On the morning of the third day there was thunder and lightning, as well as a thick cloud on the mountain, and a blast of a trumpet so loud that all the people who were in the camp trembled. ¹⁷Moses brought the people out of the camp to meet God. They took their stand at the foot of the mountain. ¹⁸Now Mount Sinai was wrapped in smoke, because the LORD had descended upon it in fire; the smoke went up like the smoke of a kiln, while the whole mountain shook violently. ¹⁹As the blast of the trumpet grew louder and louder, Moses would speak and God would answer him in thunder. . . .

20 Then God spoke all these words: 2 I am the LORD your God, who brought you out of the land of Egypt, out of the house of slavery; ³you shall have no other gods before me.

4 You shall not make for yourself an idol, whether in the form of anything that is in heaven above, or that is on the earth beneath, or that is in the water under the earth. . . .

7 You shall not make wrongful use of the name of the LORD your God, for the LORD will not acquit anyone who misuses his name.

8 Remember the Sabbath day, and keep it holy. . . .

12 Honor your father and your mother, so that your days may be long in the land that the LORD your God is giving you.

13 You shall not murder.

14 You shall not commit adultery.

15 You shall not steal.

16 You shall not bear false witness against your neighbor.

17 You shall not covet your neighbor's house; you shall not covet your neighbor's wife, or male or female slave, or ox, or donkey, or anything that belongs to your neighbor.

LET'S PRAY

Lord, I love your commands. Help us to obey you in our thoughts, in our words, and in everything we do. In the name of the Father, and the Son, and the Holy Spirit, Amen!

GOING DEEPER

Read It! This is read at Pentecost (Vigil A). The gospel reading is John 7:37–39; CCC# 2056 (*Decalogue* means "ten words"); CCC #2085 (What we believe about God affects how we see ourselves).

Do It! Make a poster of the Ten Commandments to help you remember to obey them.

QUOTE OF THE DAY:
"Whoever doesn't have one master has many."
—St. Ambrose of Milan

A PRAYER FOR COURAGE
AND CONVERSION

A Traditonal Catholic Prayer

Heavenly Father, just as Abram courageously

put aside everything he knew to follow you,

leaving behind even family and friends in obedience

to your Word, help us to set aside everything

that keeps us from loving you and serving you

with all our hearts. In the name of the Father,

and the Son, and the Holy Spirit, Amen!

A Place to Worship

Exodus 25:1–11, 17–22

In Catholic churches, the "tabernacle" is where the Eucharist is reserved. We can go there to be with Jesus. God told the Israelites to build a tabernacle, too, a holy place of worship. The most beautiful and expensive materials were used to create this portable house of God—including the ark of the covenant, which contained the tablets of the Law, a jar of manna, and Aaron's staff (Numbers 17:1–11).

The LORD said to Moses: [2]Tell the Israelites to take for me an offering; from all whose hearts prompt them to give you shall receive the offering for me. [3]This is the offering that you shall receive from them: gold, silver, and bronze, [4]blue, purple, and crimson yarns and fine linen, goats' hair, [5]tanned rams' skins, fine leather, acacia wood, [6]oil for the lamps, spices for the anointing oil and for the fragrant incense, [7]onyx stones and gems to be set in the ephod and for the breastpiece. [8]And have them make me a sanctuary, so that I may dwell among them. [9]In accordance with all that I show you concerning the pattern of the tabernacle and of all its furniture, so you shall make it.

[10] They shall make an ark of acacia wood; it shall be two and a half cubits long, a cubit and a half wide, and a cubit and a half high. [11]You shall overlay it with pure gold, inside and outside you shall overlay it, and you shall make a molding of gold upon it all around. . . .

[17] Then you shall make a mercy seat of pure gold; two cubits and a half shall be its length, and a cubit and a half its width. [18]You shall make two cherubim of gold; you shall make them of hammered work, at the two ends of the mercy seat. [19]Make one cherub at the one end, and one cherub at the other; of one piece with the mercy seat you shall make the cherubim at its two ends. [20]The cherubim shall spread out their wings above, overshadowing the mercy seat with their wings. They shall face one to another; the faces of the cherubim shall be turned toward the mercy seat. [21]You shall put the mercy seat on the top of the ark; and in the ark you shall put the covenant that I shall give you. [22]There I will meet with you, and from above the mercy seat, from between the two cherubim that are on the ark of the covenant, I will deliver to you all my commands for the Israelites.

LET'S PRAY

Lord, just as you gave the Israelites a tabernacle, you have given us the Church. Thank you that no matter where we go, your presence is always with us. In the name of the Father and the Son and the Holy Spirit, Amen!

GOING DEEPER

Read It! CCC #2130 (The Scriptural mandate against "graven images" is to be understood in the context of God's use of tangible reminders of the story of Salvation, such as the ark.)

Do It! Study Hebrews 9–10 to see how the elements of the tabernacle of the Old Testament pointed to—and were perfectly fulfilled in—Christ. Mary is sometimes called the "ark of the covenant" because she carried within her the One who would be called the "Word of God," the "Bread of Life," and the "Rod of Jesse" (CCC #2676).

The Golden Calf
Exodus 32:1–7, 15–16, 19, 35

*D*o you ever forget to talk to God before you go to sleep at night? Are there times when you complain about going to Mass each week? When we forget to put God first in our lives, and forget the blessings he gives us every day, other things become like "gods" to us. In today's story, that's exactly what happened to the children of Israel—they bowed down to other gods!

When the people saw that Moses delayed to come down from the mountain, the people gathered around Aaron, and said to him, "Come, make gods for us, who shall go before us; as for this Moses, the man who brought us up out of the land of Egypt, we do not know what has become of him." ²Aaron said to them, "Take off the gold rings that are on the ears of your wives, your sons, and your daughters, and bring them to me." ³So all the people took off the gold rings from their ears, and brought them to Aaron. ⁴He took the gold from them, formed it in a mold, and cast an image of a calf; and they said, "These are your gods, O Israel, who brought you up out of the land of Egypt!" ⁵When Aaron saw this, he built an altar before it; and Aaron made proclamation and said, "Tomorrow shall be a festival to the LORD." ⁶They rose early the next day, and offered burnt offerings and brought sacrifices of well-being; and the people sat down to eat and drink, and rose up to revel.

7 The LORD said to Moses, "Go down at once! Your people, whom you brought up out of the land of Egypt, have acted perversely. . . .

15 Then Moses turned and went down from the mountain, carrying the two tablets of the covenant in his hands, tablets that were written on both sides, written on the front and on the back. ¹⁶The tablets were the work of God, and the writing was the writing of God, engraved upon the tablets. . . . ¹⁹As soon as he came near the camp and saw the calf and the dancing, Moses' anger burned hot, and he threw the tablets from his hands and broke them at the foot of the mountain. . . .

³⁵ Then the LORD sent a plague on the people, because they made the calf—the one that Aaron made.

Let's Pray

Dear Father, thank you for forgiving us when we sin; thank you for restoring our relationship even when we sometimes put other things before you.

GOING DEEPER

Read It! CCC #2132 (The Church's use of venerated images does not go against the first commandment).

Do It! Spend a Holy Hour this week in front of the Blessed Sacrament. In the Eucharist, Jesus is with us in a special way, both at Mass and in the Tabernacle. Unlike the golden calf, which was a graven image, the Tabernacle is full of the divine presence of Jesus.

Snakes in the Desert

Numbers 21:4–9

Many years after the golden calf, Miriam and Aaron, Moses' siblings, died. Moses was 120 years old. The people were tired of wandering around the desert. Once again they complained . . . and just as quickly, cried out for help when deadly snakes appeared.

From Mount Hor they set out by the way to the Red Sea, to go around the land of Edom; but the people became impatient on the way. ⁵The people spoke against God and against Moses, "Why have you brought us up out of Egypt to die in the wilderness? For there is no food and no water, and we detest this miserable food." ⁶Then the LORD sent poisonous serpents among the people, and they bit the people, so that many Israelites died. ⁷The people came to Moses and said, "We have sinned by speaking against the LORD and against you; pray to the LORD to take away the serpents from us." So Moses prayed for the people. ⁸And the LORD said to Moses, "Make a poisonous serpent, and set it on a pole; and everyone who is bitten shall look at it and live." ⁹So Moses made a serpent of bronze, and put it upon a pole; and whenever a serpent bit someone, that person would look at the serpent of bronze and live.

LET'S PRAY

Lord, help me to trust you in good times and bad. Thank you that when I sin, I can find healing if I only look to Jesus. In the name of the Father, and the Son, and the Holy Spirit, Amen!

GOING DEEPER

Read It! The gospel reading (Feast of the Holy Cross B) is John 3:13–17; CCC #2577 (God never forsakes his people, even when they complain).

Do It! Light a candle and pray for someone who is in need of healing.

SPECIAL WORDS: The caduceus, a symbol often worn by doctors and other medical staff, depicts two snakes entwined around a staff.

Moses Sees the Promised Land

Deuteronomy 32:48–52; 34:1, 4–7

> *S*ome mistakes stay with us for a lifetime. Because of disobedience, Moses never entered the Promised Land. But the Lord showed mercy, and took Moses high up on the mountain so he could see at a distance the land God had promised to give the chosen people. With a blessing on his lips and joy in his heart, Moses was "gathered to his fathers" knowing that God was pleased.

On that very day the LORD addressed Moses as follows: ⁴⁹"Ascend this mountain of the Abarim, Mount Nebo, which is in the land of Moab, across from Jericho, and view the land of Canaan, which I am giving to the Israelites for a possession; ⁵⁰you shall die there on the mountain that you ascend and shall be gathered to your kin, as your brother Aaron died on Mount Hor and was gathered to his kin; ⁵¹because both of you broke faith with me . . . by failing to maintain my holiness among the Israelites. ⁵²Although you may view the land from a distance, you shall not enter it—the land that I am giving to the Israelites."

34 Then Moses went up from the plains of Moab to Mount Nebo, to the top of Pisgah, which is opposite Jericho, and the LORD showed him the whole land. . . . ⁴The LORD said to him, "This is the land of which I swore to Abraham, to Isaac, and to Jacob, saying, 'I will give it to your descendants'; I have let you see it with your eyes, but you shall not cross over there." ⁵Then Moses, the servant of the LORD, died there in the land of Moab, at the Lord's command. ⁶He was buried in a valley in the land of Moab . . . but no one knows his burial place to this day. ⁷Moses was one hundred twenty years old when he died; his sight was unimpaired and his vigor had not abated.

LET'S PRAY

Ascribe greatness to our God! The Rock, his work is perfect . . . just and upright is he.
                    —Deuteronomy 32:3–4
    We bless you, almighty God!

GOING DEEPER

Read It! CCC #2816–17 (The kingdom of God is yet to come).
Do It! The apostles and early Christians believed that Christ would return in their lifetime. Like Moses, they worked hard to bring in the kingdom of God, and like Moses, they died without seeing that earthly kingdom. Share specific ways we should we live as though Christ will return tomorrow.

SPECIAL WORDS: Mount Nebo, the highest peak of Mount Pisgah, where Moses viewed the Promised Land, is eight miles east of the Jordan River, near the northeast end of the Dead Sea.⁸

Faithful Rahab
Joshua 2:1, 3–9, 12–14

After Moses died, Joshua sent spies ahead of the Israelites to scout out Canaan. One woman, Rahab, risked her life to keep them safe. She was a "nobody" in the city of Jericho . . . but she had faith in the one true God (Joshua 2:10–11). As the men escaped, she left a scarlet cord dangling out of her window in the city wall: a passage of safety for Rahab and her family.

Then Joshua son of Nun sent two men secretly from Shittim as spies, saying, "Go view the land, especially Jericho." So they went, and entered the house of a prostitute whose name was Rahab, and spent the night there. . . . ³Then the king of Jericho sent orders to Rahab, "Bring out the men who have come to you, who entered your house, for they have come only to search out the whole land." ⁴But the woman took the two men and hid them. Then she said, "True, the men came to me, but I did not know where they came from. ⁵And when it was time to close the gate at dark, the men went out. Where the men went I do not know. Pursue them quickly, for you can overtake them." ⁶She had, however, brought them up to the roof and hidden them with the stalks of flax that she had laid out on the roof. ⁷So the men pursued them on the way to the Jordan as far as the fords. As soon as the pursuers had gone out, the gate was shut.

8 Before they went to sleep, she came up to them on the roof ⁹and said to the men: "I know that the LORD has given you the land, and that dread of you has fallen on us, and that all the inhabitants of the land melt in fear before you. . . . ¹²Now then, since I have dealt kindly with you, swear to me by the LORD that you in turn will deal kindly with my family. Give me a sign of good faith ¹³that you will spare my father and mother, my brothers and sisters, and all who belong to them, and deliver our lives from death." ¹⁴The men said to her, "Our life for yours! If you do not tell this business of ours, then we will deal kindly and faithfully with you when the LORD gives us the land."

LET'S PRAY

When I am frightened, Lord, help me to have faith in you!

GOING DEEPER

Read It! Read Hebrews 11:31; Rahab is named among the "heroes of faith."

Do It! Movie night! Watch *The Hiding Place* or *The Diary of Anne Frank* and discuss the bravery of those who helped the Jews. What would you have done?

(Parents, note that these movies deal with serious themes that may not be appropriate for young children.)

DID YOU KNOW?
Archaeologists discovered that Jericho had an inner and outer wall, and that homes were built between the two!⁹

Miracle at the Jordan

Joshua 3:5–8, 14–17

Do you offer your day to God when you wake up every morning? When we offer our day to God, God helps us to make good choices. In today's story, the Israelites get to do something they had waited to do for more than forty years: cross over the Jordan River, into the promised land!

Then Joshua said to the people, "Sanctify yourselves; for tomorrow the LORD will do wonders among you." 6To the priests Joshua said, "Take up the ark of the covenant, and pass on in front of the people." So they took up the ark of the covenant and went in front of the people.

7 The LORD said to Joshua, "This day I will begin to exalt you in the sight of all Israel, so that they may know that I will be with you as I was with Moses. 8You are the one who shall command the priests who bear the ark of the covenant, 'When you come to the edge of the waters of the Jordan, you shall stand still in the Jordan.'" . . .

14 When the people set out from their tents to cross over the Jordan, the priests bearing the ark of the covenant were in front of the people. 15Now the Jordan overflows all its banks throughout the time of harvest. So when those who bore the ark had come to the Jordan, and the feet of the priests bearing the ark were dipped in the edge of the water, 16the waters flowing from above stood still, rising up in a single heap far off at Adam . . . while those flowing toward . . . the Dead Sea, were wholly cut off. Then the people crossed over opposite Jericho. 17While all Israel were crossing over on dry ground, the priests who bore the ark of the covenant of the LORD stood on dry ground in the middle of the Jordan, until the entire nation finished crossing over the Jordan.

LET'S PRAY

A Morning Offering[10]

God, please come to my assistance. Lord, make haste to help me.

Glory be to the Father, and to the Son, and to the Holy Spirit:

As it was in the beginning, is now and ever shall be, world without end, Amen!

As morning breaks I look to you, O Lord, to be my strength this day.

GOING DEEPER

Read It! CCC #2112 (Worshipping anything other than Jehovah insults the God "who gives life and intervenes in history").

Do It! The first thing God commanded was for the Israelites to "sanctify yourselves" before beginning their march around Jericho. Tell what you can do to sanctify yourselves as individuals and as a family this week.

69

Victory at Jericho

Joshua 6:8–12, 14–16, 20

*R*emember *when you were little, how you'd build a tower of blocks then crash them to the ground? In today's story, the Israelites prepared to attack the mighty city of Jericho, as God had commanded them. It took seven days of marching . . . and then those giant walls tumbled! Everyone saw the power of the mighty God of Israel!*

As Joshua had commanded the people, the seven priests carrying the seven trumpets of rams' horns before the LORD went forward, blowing the trumpets, with the ark of the covenant of the LORD following them. ⁹And the armed men went before the priests who blew the trumpets; the rear guard came after the ark, while the trumpets blew continually. ¹⁰To the people Joshua gave this command: "You shall not shout or let your voice be heard, nor shall you utter a word, until the day I tell you to shout. Then you shall shout." ¹¹So the ark of the LORD went around the city, circling it once; and they came into the camp, and spent the night in the camp.

12 Then Joshua rose early in the morning. . . . ¹⁴On the second day they marched around the city once and then returned to the camp. They did this for six days.

15 On the seventh day they rose early, at dawn, and marched around the city in the same manner seven times. It was only on that day that they marched around the city seven times. ¹⁶And at the seventh time, when the priests had blown the trumpets, Joshua said to the people, "Shout! For the LORD has given you the city. . . . ²⁰So the people shouted, and the trumpets were blown. As soon as the people heard the sound of the trumpets, they raised a great shout, and the wall fell down flat; so people charged straight ahead into the city and captured it.

LET'S PRAY

Praise the LORD . . . with trumpet sound; . . . Praise him with clanging cymbals; . . . Praise the LORD!   —Psalm 150:1, 3, 5, 6

GOING DEEPER

Read It! Joshua 6:22–25—Joshua kept Rahab and her family safe, as his men had promised, when the city of Jericho fell. However, Joshua pronounced a curse upon anyone who tried to rebuild the city, which was later fulfilled in 1 Kings 16:34.

Do It! Build a tower of blocks and retell the story of the march around Jericho!

DID YOU KNOW? At the time of Christ, the city of Jericho was about a mile south of the Old Testament ruins of this city."

Whom Will You Serve?

Joshua 24:1–5, 13–15

Confirmation provides a unique opportunity for young Catholics to "grow up" in their faith. Sealed with the Spirit, the confirmed receive gifts that enrich the Church and the world. But it all begins with a choice, a "Yes" to God. This intentional "yes" is echoed in today's story.

Then Joshua gathered all the tribes of Israel . . . and summoned the elders, the heads, the judges, and the officers of Israel; and they presented themselves before God. ²And Joshua said to all the people, "Thus says the LORD, the God of Israel: Long ago your ancestors . . . lived beyond the Euphrates and served other gods. Then I took your father Abraham from beyond the River and led him through all the land of Canaan and made his offspring many. I gave him Isaac; ⁴and to Isaac I gave Jacob and Esau. I gave Esau the hill country of Seir to possess, but Jacob and his children went down to Egypt. ⁵Then I sent Moses and Aaron, and I plagued Egypt with what I did in its midst; and afterwards I brought you out. . . . ¹³"I gave you a land on which you had not labored, and towns that you had not built, and you live in them; you eat the fruit of vineyards and oliveyards that you did not plant.

14 "Now therefore revere the LORD, and serve him in sincerity and in faithfulness; put away the gods that your ancestors served beyond the River and in Egypt, and serve the LORD. ¹⁵Now if you are unwilling to serve the LORD, choose this day whom you will serve, whether the gods your ancestors served in the region beyond the river or the gods of the Amorites in whose land you are living; but as for me and my household, we will serve the LORD."

LET'S PRAY

"O magnify the LORD with me, and let us exalt his name together."   —Psalm 34:3

DID YOU KNOW? The original site
of Joshua's stone monument,
which he and the Israelites built
to affirm their commitment
to God, can still be seen at
Shechem today![12]

GOING DEEPER

Read It! The gospel reading (OT 21B) is John 6:60–69,
when the Lord asks his disciples, "Will you also go
away?" and Peter answers, "Lord, to whom shall we
go? You have the words of eternal life."

Do It! Sacramentals are tangible reminders of faith. Do
you have any in your home? If not, this would be a
good opportunity to change that! Make or buy a cross
or religious picture and place it in a prominent place
as a reminder of your faith.

Deborah the Prophetess
Judges 4:4–10, 23

*A*fter Joshua's death, the Israelites were led by the "judges." Most of these judges were military heroes and other wise men. But one of them was a prophetess—a woman—who helped to deliver her people from foreign armies (Judges 4:4–14).

At that time Deborah, a prophetess, wife of Lappidoth, was judging Israel. 5She used to sit under the palm of Deborah between Ramah and Bethel in the hill country of Ephraim; and the Israelites came up to her for judgment. 6She sent and summoned Barak son of Abinoam from Kedesh in Naphtali, and said to him, "The LORD, the God of Israel, commands you, 'Go, take position at Mount Tabor, bringing ten thousand from the tribe of Naphtali and the tribe of Zebulun. 7I will draw out Sisera, the general of Jabin's army, to meet you by the Wadi Kishon with his chariots and his troops; and I will give him into your hand.'" 8Barak said to her, "If you will go with me, I will go; but if you will not go with me, I will not go." 9And she said, "I will surely go with you; nevertheless, the road on which you are going will not lead to your glory, for the LORD will sell Sisera into the hand of a woman." Then Deborah got up and went with Barak to Kedesh. 10Barak summoned Zebulun and Naphtali to Kedesh; and ten thousand warriors went up behind him; and Deborah went up with him. . . .

23 So on that day God subdued King Jabin of Canaan before the Israelites.

Let's Pray

Thank you, God, for creating holy heroes, men and women with the strength and wisdom to do your will. In the name of the Father, and the Son, and the Holy Spirit, Amen!

Going Deeper

Read It! Older children—especially boys—may enjoy listening to the gory account of how God used Jael to deliver her people from Sisera. Consider reading all of chapter four—after the younger children are in bed!

Do It! Just like Deborah encouraged the warriors, send an encouraging note to a soldier in your parish.

DID YOU KNOW?
Although Joshua had conquered the Canaanites, they were not completely driven out as God had commanded, possibly because of the Canaanites' discovery and use of iron weaponry and chariots (Deuteronomy 7:2–4).[13]

Samson and Delilah
Judges 16:23–25, 28–30

*D*id you ever tell a secret to a friend who couldn't be trusted to keep it? Samson was a man with superhuman strength and a weakness for a beautiful but greedy woman named Delilah. When wicked men wanted to capture Samson, they offered to pay her well to find the secret of Samson's strength. Soon she had coaxed him to tell her the source of his strength: his long hair. So Delilah gave Samson a haircut as he slept, and the Philistines quickly captured him and gouged out his eyes. In today's story, God gives Samson one more chance to be a hero.

Now the lords of the Philistines gathered to offer a great sacrifice to their god Dagon, and to rejoice; for they said, "Our god has given Samson our enemy into our hand." 24When the people saw him, they praised their god; for they said, "Our god has given our enemy into our hand, the ravager of our country, who has killed many of us." 25And when their hearts were merry, they said, "Call Samson, and let him entertain us." So they called Samson out of the prison, and he performed for them. They made him stand between the pillars. . . .

28 Then Samson called to the LORD and said, "Lord GOD, remember me and strengthen me only this once, O God, so that with this one act of revenge I may pay back the Philistines for my two eyes." 29And Samson grasped the two middle pillars on which the house rested, and he leaned his weight against them, his right hand on the one and his left hand on the other. 30Then Samson said, "Let me die with the Philistines." He strained with all his might; and the house fell on the lords and all the people who were in it. So those he killed at his death were more than those he had killed during his life.

LET'S PRAY
The LORD is my light and my salvation; whom shall I fear? The LORD is the stronghold of my life; of whom shall I be afraid?
—Psalm 27:1

GOING DEEPER
Read It! Samson's parents had dedicated their son to the Lord with a "nazirite vow"; an angel of the Lord had said Samson would deliver his people. For more about the nazirite vow read Numbers 6:2–8.

Do It! Today, make and eat dinner together as a family. As you work and eat, talk about Samson and his decisions. What were Samson's weaknesses? What are yours? How can you help each other overcome them?

Ruth and Boaz
Ruth 2:1–3, 5–12; 4:13, 16–17

*T*he story of Ruth is a beautiful example of love. When Ruth's first husband died and she went with Naomi to Judah, her mother-in-law's homeland, Ruth adopted Naomi's people and their traditions as her own. Ruth even became part of the lineage of Christ! But first, she had to meet her new husband as she worked to feed herself and Naomi.

Now Naomi had a kinsman on her husband's side, a prominent rich man, of the family of Elimelech, whose name was Boaz. ²And Ruth the Moabite said to Naomi, "Let me go to the field and glean among the ears of grain, behind someone in whose sight I may find favor." She said to her, "Go, my daughter." ³So she went. She came and gleaned in the field behind the reapers. As it happened, she came to the part of the field belonging to Boaz. . . . ⁵Then Boaz said to his servant who was in charge of the reapers, "To whom does this young woman belong?" ⁶The servant who was in charge of the reapers answered, "She is the Moabite who came back with Naomi . . . ⁷She said, 'Please, let me glean and gather among the sheaves behind the reapers.' So she came, and she has been on her feet from early this morning until now, without resting even for a moment."

8 Then Boaz said to Ruth, "Now listen, my daughter, do not go to glean in another field or leave this one, but keep close to my young women. ⁹Keep your eyes on the field that is being reaped, and follow behind them. I have ordered the young men not to bother you. If you get thirsty, go to the vessels and drink from what the young men have drawn." ¹⁰Then she fell prostrate, with her face to the ground, and said to him, "Why have I found favor in your sight, that you should take notice of me, when I am a foreigner?" ¹¹But Boaz answered her, "All that you have done for your mother-in-law since the death of your husband has been fully told me, and how you left your father and mother and your native land and came to a people that you did not know before. ¹²May the LORD reward you for your deeds, and may you have a full reward from the LORD, the God of Israel, under whose wings you have come for refuge!" . . .

4 So Boaz took Ruth and she became his wife. When they came together, the LORD made her conceive, and she bore a son. . . . ¹⁶Then Naomi took the child and laid him in her bosom, and became his nurse. ¹⁷The women of the neighborhood gave him a name, saying, "A son has been born to Naomi." They named him Obed; he became the father of Jesse, the father of David.

LET'S PRAY
Thank you, God, for making us all your adopted sons and daughters through your Son, Jesus. You are our loving Father.

Read It! Read Ephesians 1:5 and talk about what it means to be adopted.

Do It! Are you or anyone you know adopted? Is there a way you can "adopt" someone into your home? Whether it is legally adopting a new child or regularly inviting over a single parent or elderly neighbor, talk about how your family can share Christ's love through "adoption."

Hannah and Samuel

1 Samuel 1:9–20

*H*ave you ever prayed urgently for something, only to be disappointed when God didn't answer your prayer like you wanted? In today's story, Hannah wanted a baby. She had so much love to share and didn't understand why God wouldn't send her a child. One day Hannah went to the temple to pour out her unhappiness to God, and someone was listening!

After they had eaten and drunk at Shiloh, Hannah rose and presented herself before the LORD. Now Eli the priest was sitting on the seat beside the doorpost of the temple of the LORD. ¹⁰She was deeply distressed and prayed to the LORD, and wept bitterly. ¹¹She made this vow: "O LORD of hosts, if only you will look on the misery of your servant, and remember me, and not forget your servant, but will give to your servant a male child, then I will set him before you as a nazirite until the day of his death. . . .

12 As she continued praying before the LORD, Eli observed her mouth. ¹³Hannah was praying silently; only her lips moved, but her voice was not heard; therefore Eli thought she was drunk. ¹⁴So Eli said to her, "How long will you make a drunken spectacle of yourself? Put away your wine." ¹⁵But Hannah answered, "No, my lord, I am a woman deeply troubled; I have drunk neither wine nor strong drink, but I have been pouring out my soul before the LORD. ¹⁶Do not regard your servant as a worthless woman, for I have been speaking out of my great anxiety and vexation all this time." ¹⁷Then Eli answered, "Go in peace; the God of Israel grant the petition you have made to him." ¹⁸And she said, "Let your servant find favor in your sight." Then the woman went to her quarters, ate and drank with her husband, and her countenance was sad no longer.

19 They rose early in the morning and worshiped before the LORD; then they went back to their house at Ramah. Elkanah knew his wife Hannah, and the LORD remembered her. ²⁰In due time Hannah conceived and bore a son. She named him Samuel, for she said, "I have asked him of the LORD."

LET'S PRAY

Thank you, Lord, for listening to our prayers. Help us to trust you, and to remember that it is for our own good that sometimes you say, "Yes," sometimes you say, "No," and sometimes you say, "Not yet."
Amen.

GOING DEEPER

Read It! CCC #2578 (Samuel learned from his mother how to pray).

Do It! Take turns tonight at dinner praying for each other.

QUOTE OF THE DAY:
"God measures out affliction to our need."
—St. John Chrysostom

God Speaks to Samuel

1 Samuel 3:1–14

*D*id you know that little children sometimes hear God even better than grown-ups? When Samuel was very little, Hannah brought him to live at the temple to help the high priest, Eli. Eli took good care of Samuel, and Samuel loved Eli like his own father. In today's story, Eli helps Samuel recognize his calling to be a prophet—one who hears the voice of God and shares his message with other people.

Now the boy Samuel was ministering to the LORD under Eli. The word of the LORD was rare in those days; visions were not widespread.

2 At that time Eli, whose eyesight had begun to grow dim so that he could not see, was lying down in his room; ³the lamp of God had not yet gone out, and Samuel was lying down in the temple of the LORD, where the ark of God was. ⁴Then the LORD called, "Samuel! Samuel!" and he said, "Here I am!" ⁵and ran to Eli, and said, "Here I am, for you called me." But he said, "I did not call; lie down again." So he went and lay down. ⁶The LORD called again, "Samuel!" Samuel got up and went to Eli, and said, "Here I am, for you called me." But he said, "I did not call, my son; lie down again." ⁷Now Samuel did not yet know the LORD, and the word of the LORD had not yet been revealed to him. ⁸The LORD called Samuel again, a third time. And he got up and went to Eli, and said, "Here I am, for you called me." Then Eli perceived that the LORD was calling the boy. ⁹Therefore Eli said to Samuel, "Go, lie down; and if he calls you, you shall say, 'Speak, LORD, for your servant is listening.'" So Samuel went and lay down in his place.

10 Now the LORD came and stood there, calling as before, "Samuel! Samuel!" And Samuel said, "Speak, for your servant is listening." ¹¹Then the LORD said to Samuel, "See, I am about to do something in Israel that will make both ears of anyone who hears of it tingle. ¹²On that day I will fulfill against Eli all that I have spoken concerning his house, from beginning to end. ¹³For I have told him that I am about to punish his house forever, for the iniquity that he knew, because his sons were blaspheming God, and he did not restrain them. ¹⁴Therefore I swear to the house of Eli that the iniquity of Eli's house shall not be expiated by sacrifice or offering forever."

LET'S PRAY

Lord every day give me grace to pray, "Speak, Lord, your servant is listening!"

GOING DEEPER

Read It! The gospel reading (OT 2B) is John 1:35–42, in which a follower of John the Baptist, Andrew, began to follow Christ. He heard the Master speak, and he listened!

Do It! This week invite Jesus to speak to you just as Samuel did, with the words "Speak, Lord, your servant is listening." God speaks to us in many ways—through the Bible, through other people, and through our hearts. What is God saying to you this week?

A PRAYER FOR VOCATIONS

A Traditonal Catholic Prayer

Lord, let me know clearly the work that you

are calling me to do in life. And grant me every grace

I need to answer your call with courage and love

and lasting dedication to your will. Amen!

Samuel Anoints a King
1 Samuel 8:7; 9:15—17; 10:1

"Give us a king!" the elders of Israel insisted; they wanted to be like the other, surrounding nations. Samuel didn't want to do this. He knew that the people belonged to God alone. When Samuel took the people's request to the Lord, however, God gave the people what they wanted.

And the LORD said to Samuel, "Listen to the voice of the people in all that they say to you; for they have not rejected you, but they have rejected me from being king over them. . . ."

9 "Now the day before Saul came, the LORD had revealed to Samuel: 16"Tomorrow about this time I will send to you a man from the land of Benjamin, and you shall anoint him to be ruler over my people Israel. He shall save my people from the hand of the Philistines; for I have seen the suffering of my people, because their outcry has come to me." 17When Samuel saw Saul, the LORD told him, "Here is the man of whom I spoke to you. He it is who shall rule over my people." . . .

10 Samuel took a vial of oil and poured it on his head, and kissed him; he said, "The LORD has anointed you ruler over his people Israel. You shall reign over the people of the LORD and you will save them from the hand of their enemies all around. . . ."

LET'S PRAY

Dear Lord, help us to keep you as King all the days of our lives. In the name of the Father, the Son, and the Holy Spirit, Amen.

GOING DEEPER

Read It! First Samuel 13 tells the story of the downfall of Israel's first king, Saul. He started strong, but soon his pride caused God's favor to turn away from him and fall upon the man who would be the next and perhaps greatest king, David.

Do It! It's important to pray for those who rule over us, that they would be godly and make wise decisions. This week light a candle and say a prayer for our president and other government leaders.

SPECIAL WORDS: The word Christ *comes from the Greek translation of the Hebrew word* Messiah, *which means "anointed" (CCC #436).*

David and Goliath

1 Samuel 17:1, 4, 24–26, 31–32, 48–49

*D*avid was a young shepherd boy when the prophet Samuel secretly anointed David as Israel's future king (1 Samuel 16:13). However, God's spirit was strong in him, and when David was sent to bring supplies to his brothers, who were serving in King Saul's army, he heard the challenge of the Philistine's champion, Goliath. David volunteered to meet the giant armed with only a sling and five smooth stones—the same weapons he used to defend his father's sheep.

Now the Philistines gathered their armies for battle . . . and encamped between Socoh and Azekah, in Ephes-dammim. . . . ⁴And there came out from the camp of the Philistines a champion named Goliath, of Gath, whose height was six cubits and a span. . . .

24 All the Israelites, when they saw the man, fled from him and were very much afraid. ²⁵The Israelites said, "Have you seen this man who has come up? Surely he has come up to defy Israel. The king will greatly enrich the man who kills him, and will give him his daughter and make his family free in Israel." ²⁶David said to the men who stood by him, "What shall be done for the man who kills this Philistine, and takes away the reproach from Israel? For who is this uncircumcised Philistine that he should defy the armies of the living God?" . . .

31 When the words that David spoke were heard, they repeated them before Saul; and he sent for him. ³²David said to Saul, "Let no one's heart fail because of him; your servant will go and fight with this Philistine." . . .

48 When the Philistine drew nearer to meet David, David ran quickly toward the battle line to meet the Philistine. ⁴⁹David put his hand in his bag, took out a stone, slung it, and struck the Philistine on his forehead; the stone sank into his forehead, and he fell face down on the ground.

LET'S PRAY

Lord, give us the courage of David to stand up against evil. In the name of the Father, and the Son, and the Holy Spirit, Amen!

GOING DEEPER

Read It! CCC #2317 (There are times when war may be justified).

Do It! Peace starts at home. Make a point to be kind to one another today, and spread that kindness everywhere you go. Is there a bully on the playground? Make a point to be kind to the children that person is picking on, and even be kind to the bully!

SPECIAL WORDS: "Six cubits and a span" would have been about nine feet tall. Goliath's armor alone weighed about 120 pounds![14]

David Spares Saul

1 Samuel 26:2-3, 5, 7-12

*O*ver time King Saul became aware of the threat David posed to his own kingdom. Saul's heart toward God had become hardened, and soon the king was looking for ways to destroy David. Knowing his life was in danger, David fled King Saul's court, but he never lost his love and loyalty for Saul, God's anointed. In this story, spies tell King Saul where to find David, and they go to capture him. But God has other plans.

Saul rose and went down to the Wilderness of Ziph, with three thousand chosen men of Israel, to seek David. . . . ³Saul encamped on the hill of Hachilah, . . . But David remained in the wilderness. When he learned that Saul came after him into the wilderness, . . . ⁵then David set out and came to the place where Saul had encamped; and David saw the place where Saul lay, with Abner son of Ner, the commander of his army. . . .

⁷So David and Abishai went to the army by night; there Saul lay sleeping within the encampment, with his spear stuck in the ground at his head; and Abner and the army lay around him. ⁸Abishai said to David, "God has given your enemy into your hand today; now therefore let me pin him to the ground with one stroke of the spear; I will not strike him twice." ⁹But David said to Abishai, "Do not destroy him; for who can raise his hand against the Lord's anointed, and be guiltless?" ¹⁰David said, "As the LORD lives, the LORD will strike him down; or his day will come to die; or he will go down into battle and perish. ¹¹The LORD forbid that I should raise my hand against the LORD's anointed; but now take the spear that is at his head, and the water jar, and let us go." ¹²So David took the spear that was at Saul's head and the water jar, and they went away. No one saw it, or knew it, nor did anyone awake; for they were all asleep, because a deep sleep from the LORD had fallen upon them.

Let's Pray

Thank you, God, for your kindness toward us, even when we don't deserve it. Help us to also be kind to others. Amen.

Going Deeper

Read It! The gospel reading for today (OT 7C) is Luke 6:27-38, in which Christ teaches about loving one's enemies. How did David do these things for Saul?

Do It! Love your enemies this week! Is there someone at school who just isn't very nice? Is someone in your life mean to you? Make a point to be genuinely kind to them and see the difference it makes in their attitude toward you.

Quote for the Day:
"No one heals himself by wounding another."
—St. Ambrose of Milan

David Dances Before the Ark

2 Samuel 6:1–2, 5–7, 9–10, 12, 16–19

After the death of Saul (1 Samuel 31:1–6), David is made king. One of his first acts as king was to drive the Philistines from the area and capture Jerusalem—something Saul had been unable to do. David made Jerusalem his capital, and quickly made arrangements to bring the ark of the covenant back to the city. In all the excitement, one man made a fatal mistake, and King David was reminded to revere the God whose glory is greater than that of any earthly king.

David again gathered all the chosen men of Israel, thirty thousand. ²David and all the people with him set out and went from Baale-judah, to bring up from there the ark of God, which is called by the name of the LORD of hosts who is enthroned on the cherubim. . . . ⁵David and all the house of Israel were dancing before the LORD with all their might, with songs and lyres and harps and tambourines and castanets and cymbals.

6 When they came to the threshing floor of Nacon, Uzzah reached out his hand to the ark of God and took hold of it, for the oxen shook it. ⁷The anger of the LORD was kindled against Uzzah; and God struck him there because he reached out his hand to the ark; and he died there. . . . ⁹David was afraid of the LORD that day; he said, "How can the ark of the LORD come into my care?" ¹⁰So David was unwilling to take the ark of the LORD into his care in the city of David; instead David took it to the house of Obed-edom the Gittite. . . .

12 It was told King David, "The LORD has blessed the household of Obed-edom and all that belongs to him, because of the ark of God." So David went and brought up the ark of God from the house of Obed-edom to the city of David with rejoicing; . . .

16 As the ark of the LORD came into the city of David, Michal daughter of Saul looked out of the window, and saw King David leaping and dancing before the LORD; and she despised him in her heart.

17 They brought in the ark of the LORD, and set it in its place, inside the tent that David had pitched for it; and David offered burnt offerings and offerings of well-being before the LORD. ¹⁸When David had finished offering the burnt offerings and the offerings of well-being, he blessed the people in the name of the LORD of hosts, ¹⁹and distributed food among all the people, the whole multitude of Israel, both men and women, to each a cake of bread, a portion of meat, and a cake of raisins. Then all the people went back to their homes.

LET'S PRAY

Dear Father, thank you for your great glory and your presence. Help us to always be reverent toward you. Amen.

SPECIAL WORDS: Obed-edom was one of the chief "Levitical singers and doorkeepers." God permitted only the priestly tribe of Levi to touch the ark.
—1 Chronicles 15:14–15

GOING DEEPER

Read It! The passage from 1 Chronicles 15 is the first reading on the Feast of the Assumption, which is celebrated on August 15 (CCC # 966, 974).

Do It! Take a nature walk together as a family. Collect interesting rocks, twigs, leaves, and flowers, and praise God for his beautiful creation.

Solomon, a Wise King

1 Kings 3:16–20, 22–28

When David reached the end of his life, he passed his authority to his son Solomon, admonishing him to be a good king and to follow in the ways of the Lord. At the beginning of his reign, King Solomon was indeed a wise and mighty king, as this story shows.

Two women who were prostitutes came to the king and stood before him. ¹⁷The one woman said, "Please, my lord, this woman and I live in the same house; and I gave birth while she was in the house. ¹⁸Then on the third day after I gave birth, this woman also gave birth. We were together; there was no one else with us in the house, only the two of us were in the house. ¹⁹Then this woman's son died in the night, because she lay on him. ²⁰She got up in the middle of the night and took my son from beside me while your servant slept. . . ." ²²But the other woman said, "No, the living son is mine, and the dead son is yours." The first said, "No, the dead son is yours, and the living son is mine." So they argued before the king.

23 Then the king said, "The one says, 'This is my son that is alive, and your son is dead'; while the other says, 'Not so! Your son is dead, and my son is the living one.'" ²⁴So the king said, "Bring me a sword," and they brought a sword before the king. ²⁵The king said, "Divide the living boy in two; then give half to the one, and half to the other." ²⁶But the woman whose son was alive said to the king—because compassion for her son burned within her—"Please, my lord, give her the living boy; certainly do not kill him!" The other said, "It shall be neither mine nor yours; divide it." ²⁷Then the king responded: "Give the first woman the living boy; do not kill him. She is his mother." ²⁸All Israel heard of the judgment that the king had rendered; and they stood in awe of the king, because they perceived that the wisdom of God was in him, to execute justice.

LET'S PRAY

The LORD gives wisdom;
   from his mouth come knowledge and
      understanding.   —Proverbs 2:6
Lord, please bless us with wisdom to serve you better. Amen.

GOING DEEPER

Read It! CCC # 1303 (Wisdom is a gift from God).
Do It! Read one chapter a day from the book of Proverbs this month as a family.

DID YOU KNOW? King Solomon wrote three thousand proverbs, more than a thousand songs, and scientific works on botany and zoology (1 Kings 4:32–33).[5]

Elijah Hides from the King
1 Kings 16:29–34, 17:1–5

*H*ave you ever done something you knew was right—and got in trouble with those who wanted you to "go along with the crowd"? In today's story, Elijah brought a message to the wicked king Ahab, angering both the king and Queen Jezebel (a woman who had already killed many of God's prophets). Fleeing for his life, Elijah cried out to God, and God provided a place of safety: in a ravine where God sent ravens each day to bring food to his faithful prophet!

In the thirty-eighth year of King Asa of Judah, Ahab son of Omri began to reign over Israel. Ahab . . . reigned over Israel in Samaria twenty-two years. ³⁰Ahab . . . did evil in the sight of the LORD more than all who were before him.

31 And . . . he took as his wife Jezebel daughter of King Ethbaal of the Sidonians, and went and served Baal, and worshiped him. ³²He erected an altar for Baal in the house of Baal, which he built in Samaria. ³³Ahab also made a sacred pole. Ahab did more to provoke the anger of the LORD, the God of Israel, than had all the kings of Israel who were before him. ³⁴In his days Hiel of Bethel built Jericho; he laid its foundation at the cost of Abiram his firstborn, and set up its gates at the cost of his youngest son Segub, according to the word of the LORD, which he spoke by Joshua son of Nun.

17 Now Elijah the Tishbite, of Tishbe in Gilead, said to Ahab, "As the LORD the God of Israel lives, before whom I stand, there shall be neither dew nor rain these years, except by my word." ²The word of the LORD came to him, saying, ³"Go from here and turn eastward, and hide yourself by the Wadi Cherith, which is east of the Jordan. ⁴You shall drink from the wadi, and I have commanded the ravens to feed you there." ⁵So he went and did according to the word of the LORD; he went and lived by the Wadi Cherith, which is east of the Jordan.

LET'S PRAY
Prayer of Trust for God's Provision
Lord, just as you provided for Elijah in his time of need, we can count on you to provide for us, too. Thank you for your faithfulness. Amen.

SPECIAL WORDS: Sacred poles (sometimes called "Asherah poles") were expressly forbidden by God (Deuteronomy 16:21). A wadi is a dry riverbed that fills during times of rain.

GOING DEEPER

Read It! CCC #1857 (There are three conditions of
mortal sin: grave matter, full knowledge, and
deliberate consent). What does the story of Ahab
and Jezebel have to teach us about the soul-
deadening nature of deliberate sin?

Do It! Do you have any serious sin on your
conscience? Maybe you should go to
confession this week.

Elijah and the Widow
1 Kings 17:17–24

After the immediate danger of the king's wrath had passed, Elijah made his way from Cherith to Zarephath, where he encountered a widow and her young son who were suffering greatly from the drought. Asking for a little food and water, Elijah assured the widow that if she fed him, her flour and oil would last, and that God would not allow them to starve. The widow did as Elijah said, and sure enough, there was enough food for them all! How happy the widow must have been to know that God had not forgotten them. But then, just when the future looked bright, something sad happened.

After this the son of the woman, the mistress of the house, became ill; his illness was so severe that there was no breath left in him. ¹⁸She then said to Elijah, "What have you against me, O man of God? You have come to me to bring my sin to remembrance, and to cause the death of my son!" ¹⁹But he said to her, "Give me your son." He took him from her bosom, carried him up into the upper chamber where he was lodging, and laid him on his own bed. ²⁰He cried out to the LORD, "O LORD my God, have you brought calamity even upon the widow with whom I am staying, by killing her son?" ²¹Then he stretched himself upon the child three times, and cried out to the LORD, "O LORD my God, let this child's life come into him again." ²²The LORD listened to the voice of Elijah; the life of the child came into him again, and he revived. ²³Elijah took the child, brought him down from the upper chamber into the house, and gave him to his mother; then Elijah said, "See, your son is alive." ²⁴So the woman said to Elijah, "Now I know that you are a man of God, and that the word of the LORD in your mouth is truth."

LET'S PRAY

God, sometimes we are just like the widow—quick to doubt you when something bad happens, even after you have provided for us time and again. Help our faith to be like that jug of oil, never running out. In the name of the Father, and the Son, and the Holy Spirit, Amen!

GOING DEEPER

Read It! CCC #2582 (Elijah is the father of the prophets who St. James referred to when he wrote, "The prayers of the righteous are powerful and effective" (James 5:16).

Do It! Is there a single mother at your parish who could use a little extra help, either financially or in the way of friendship? Pray for her this week, and consider inviting her family for a "play date."

QUOTE OF THE DAY:
"They alone can truly feast,
who first have fasted."
—*John Cardinal Newman*

Elijah and the Prophets of Baal
1 Kings 18:25–26, 29–30, 33–39

*W*hen a terrible drought came, King Ahab became very angry and blamed Elijah. (In reality, the fault was Ahab's for his idolatrous ways.) To prove God's power once and for all, Elijah challenged the priests of Baal (the god of fertile crops) to a showdown: two altars, two offerings, and whichever deity responded by sending fire for the sacrifice would be the true God.

Then Elijah said to the prophets of Baal, "Choose for yourselves one bull and prepare it first, for you are many; then call on the name of your god, but put no fire to it." ²⁶So they took the bull that was given them, prepared it, and called on the name of Baal from morning until noon, crying, "O Baal, answer us!" But there was no voice, and no answer. They limped about the altar that they had made. . . . ²⁹As midday passed, they raved on until the time of the offering of the oblation, but there was no voice, no answer, and no response.

30 Then Elijah said to all the people, "Come closer to me"; and all the people came closer to him. First he repaired the altar of the LORD that had been thrown down. . . . ³³Next he put the wood in order, cut the bull in pieces, and laid it on the wood. He said, "Fill four jars with water and pour it on the burnt offering and on the wood." ³⁴Then he said, "Do it a second time"; and they did it a second time. Again he said, "Do it a third time"; and they did it a third time, ³⁵so that the water ran all around the altar, and filled the trench also with water.

36 At the time of the offering of the oblation, the prophet Elijah came near and said, "O LORD, God of Abraham, Isaac, and Israel, let it be known this day that you are God in Israel, that I am your servant, and that I have done all these things at your bidding. ³⁷Answer me, O LORD, answer me, so that this people may know that you, O LORD, are God, and that you have turned their hearts back." ³⁸Then the fire of the LORD fell and consumed the burnt offering, the wood, the stones, and the dust, and even licked up the water that was in the trench. ³⁹When all the people saw it, they fell on their faces and said, "The LORD indeed is God; the LORD indeed is God."

LET'S PRAY

God, thank you for showing yourself to us. Help us to live so that we show you to others. Amen.

GOING DEEPER

Read It! CCC #2766 (Referring to the story above, the Catechism reminds us that "Jesus does not give us a formula to repeat mechanically" in the Our Father. Rather, it is a cry of the heart that springs out of relationship with the one true God).

Do It! "Offer it up!" Have you ever heard this expression? In the Old Testament, God's people offered up sacrifices of animals. Today, we can offer up sacrifices of praise. Tonight, sing together and make music to praise the Lord!

Elijah Goes to Heaven
2 Kings 2:4–12

*F*or twenty-five years the prophet Elijah wandered the northern kingdom of Israel, trying to save it from total destruction. He advised kings, worked miracles, and urged the people to love the one true God and forsake idols. Toward the end of his life, Elijah was discouraged, for he had not been entirely successful in breaking the grip of Baal. Nevertheless, at God's command he anointed his successor, Elisha, and prepared to pass his authority on to the younger man when he died.

. . . So they came to Jericho. ⁵The company of prophets who were at Jericho drew near to Elisha, and said to him, "Do you know that today the Lᴏʀᴅ will take your master away from you?" And he answered, "Yes, I know; be silent."

6 Then Elijah said to him, "Stay here; for the Lᴏʀᴅ has sent me to the Jordan." But he said, "As the Lᴏʀᴅ lives, and as you yourself live, I will not leave you." So the two of them went on. ⁷Fifty men of the company of prophets also went, and stood at some distance from them, as they both were standing by the Jordan. ⁸Then Elijah took his mantle and rolled it up, and struck the water; the water was parted to the one side and to the other, until the two of them crossed on dry ground.

9 When they had crossed, Elijah said to Elisha, "Tell me what I may do for you, before I am taken from you." Elisha said, "Please let me inherit a double share of your spirit."

¹⁰He responded, "You have asked a hard thing; yet, if you see me as I am being taken from you, it will be granted you; if not, it will not." ¹¹As they continued walking and talking, a chariot of fire and horses of fire separated the two of them, and Elijah ascended in a whirlwind into heaven. ¹²Elisha kept watching and crying out, "Father, father! The chariots of Israel and its horsemen!" But when he could no longer see him, he grasped his own clothes and tore them in two pieces.

Lᴇᴛ's Pʀᴀʏ!
Hail Mary
A Traditonal Catholic Prayer

Hail Mary, full of grace, the Lord is with thee. Blessed are thou among women, and blessed is the fruit of your womb, Jesus. Holy Mary, Mother of God, pray for us sinners now and at the hour of our death.
Amen.

Gᴏɪɴɢ Dᴇᴇᴘᴇʀ

Read It! CCC #2684 (Charisms have been handed on from one believer to the next).

Do It! Sit together outside or around the table, and take turns talking about what you are thankful for.

Dɪᴅ Yᴏᴜ Kɴᴏᴡ?
Enoch (Genesis 5:24) and Elijah are two examples of friends of God who were taken to heaven without experiencing death. These events show the glory that is in store for all believers through the sacrifice of Christ.

Naaman Is Healed
2 Kings 5:1–15, 17

*A*though Elijah and Elisha were both holy men of God, they were very different. Elijah was a prophet of fire, like John the Baptist, zealous for the Lord and the utter destruction of every idol. Elisha was more like a gentle wind, a prophet who worked in people's hearts through kindness. The miracles of Elisha are recorded in 2 Kings 2 and 4–7.

Naaman, commander of the army of the king of Aram, was a great man and in high favor with his master, because by him the LORD had given victory to Aram. The man, though a mighty warrior, suffered from leprosy. ²Now the Arameans on one of their raids had taken a young girl captive from the land of Israel, and she served Naaman's wife. ³She said to her mistress, "If only my lord were with the prophet who is in Samaria! He would cure him of his leprosy." ⁴So Naaman went in and told his lord just what the girl from the land of Israel had said. ⁵And the king of Aram said, "Go then, and I will send along a letter to the king of Israel."

He went, taking with him ten talents of silver, six thousand shekels of gold, and ten sets of garments. ⁶He brought the letter to the king of Israel, which read, "When this letter reaches you, know that I have sent to you my servant Naaman, that you may cure him of his leprosy." ⁷When the king of Israel read the letter, he tore his clothes and said, "Am I God, to give death or life, that this man sends word to me to cure a man of his leprosy? Just look and see how he is trying to pick a quarrel with me."

8 But when Elisha the man of God heard that the king of Israel had torn his clothes, he sent a message to the king, ". . . Let him come to me, that he may learn that there is a prophet in Israel." ⁹So Naaman came with his horses and chariots, and halted at the entrance of Elisha's house. ¹⁰Elisha sent a messenger to him, saying, "Go, wash in the Jordan seven times, and your flesh shall be restored and you shall be clean." ¹¹But Naaman became angry and went away, saying, "I thought that for me he would surely come out, and stand and call on the name of the LORD his God, and would wave his hand over the spot, and cure the leprosy! ¹²Are not Abana and Pharpar, the rivers of Damascus, better than all the waters of Israel? Could I not wash in them, and be clean?" He turned and went away in a rage. ¹³But his servants approached and said to him, "Father, if the prophet had commanded you to do something difficult, would you not have done it? How much more, when all he said to you was, 'Wash, and be clean'?" ¹⁴So he went down and immersed himself seven times in the Jordan, according to the word of the man of God; his flesh was restored like the flesh of a young boy, and he was clean.

15 Then he returned to the man of God, he and all his company; he came and stood before him and said, "Now I know that there is no God in all the earth except in Israel . . . for your servant will no longer offer burnt offering or sacrifice to any god except the LORD."

SPECIAL WORDS: "Ten talents of silver, six thousand shekels of gold" would have had a combined weight of over eight hundred pounds![7]

LET'S PRAY

Sing to the LORD a new song,
   for he has done marvelous things. . . .
Make a joyful noise to the LORD, all the earth!

—Psalm 98:1, 4

   Thank you Lord for all you have done for us!

GOING DEEPER

Read It! The gospel reading (OT 28C) is Luke 17:11–19.

Do It! Naaman might never have received the healing he needed if that little servant girl hadn't suggested that her master go see Elisha. When someone you know is seriously ill, suggest they receive the anointing of the sick.

Hezekiah Prays for His People's Safety

2 Kings 19:14–19, 35–36

*H*ave *you ever encountered a bully, someone bigger and meaner than you could ever be, who always tries to push the smaller, weaker kids around? In today's story, we encounter a bully, the king of Assyria, who wanted to overthrow King Hezekiah, a good and godly king. But God had different plans. "Don't be afraid of what you've heard," the Lord told Hezekiah through his prophet Isaiah. God himself would see to the bully!*

Hezekiah received the letter from the hand of the messengers and read it; then Hezekiah went up to the house of the LORD and spread it before the LORD. ¹⁵And Hezekiah prayed before the LORD, and said: "O LORD the God of Israel, who are enthroned above the cherubim, you are God, you alone, of all the kingdoms of the earth; you have made heaven and earth. ¹⁶Incline your ear, O LORD, and hear; open your eyes, O LORD, and see; hear the words of Sennacherib, which he has sent to mock the living God. ¹⁷Truly, O LORD, the kings of Assyria have laid waste the nations and their lands, ¹⁸and have hurled their gods into the fire, though they were no gods but the work of human hands—wood and stone—and so they were destroyed. ¹⁹So now, O LORD our God, save us, I pray you, from his hand, so that all the kingdoms of the earth may know that you, O LORD, are God alone." . . .

35 That very night the angel of the LORD set out and struck down one hundred eighty-five thousand in the camp of the Assyrians; when morning dawned, they were all dead bodies. ³⁶Then King Sennacherib of Assyria left, went home, and lived at Nineveh.

LET'S PRAY

Father, we thank you for saving us. Help us to share your saving love with others. Amen.

GOING DEEPER

Read It! Second Chronicles 32 is another account of this story.

Do It! Make cookies for the priest or other leaders of your church. Visit as a family to thank them for their service.

DID YOU KNOW? In the 1970s a 650-foot section of the wall Hezekiah rebuilt in Jerusalem—ten feet high and twenty-three feet thick—was discovered by Professor Nahum Avigad[18]

Good King Josiah
2 Kings 23:1–4, 24–25

Can you think of a time when you made a big mistake and had to fix it? Josiah was only eight years old when he became king of Judah; at sixteen he came to know the God of David, and at twenty he began a long line of changes to return the people back to the true faith. Sadly, the people's idolatrous hearts were slow to turn. Josiah's efforts only delayed the destruction God had promised if the people did not turn from their evil ways, which they had learned under the previous king, Manasseh (2 Chronicles 33:1–20).

Then the king directed that all the elders of Judah and Jerusalem should be gathered to him. ²The king went up to the house of the LORD, and with him went all the people of Judah, all the inhabitants of Jerusalem, the priests, the prophets, and all the people, both small and great; he read in their hearing all the words of the book of the covenant that had been found in the house of the LORD. ³The king stood by the pillar and made a covenant before the LORD, to follow the LORD, keeping his commandments, his decrees, and his statutes, with all his heart and all his soul, to perform the words of this covenant that were written in this book. All the people joined in the covenant.

4 The king commanded the high priest Hilkiah, the priests of the second order, and the guardians of the threshold, to bring out of the temple of the LORD all the vessels made for Baal, for Asherah, and for all the host of heaven; he burned them outside Jerusalem in the fields of the Kidron, and carried their ashes to Bethel. . . .

24 Moreover Josiah put away the mediums, wizards, teraphim, idols, and all the abominations that were seen in the land of Judah and in Jerusalem, so that he established the words of the law that were written in the book that the priest Hilkiah had found in the house of the LORD. ²⁵Before him there was no king like him, who turned to the LORD with all his heart, with all his soul, and with all his might, according to all the law of Moses; nor did any like him arise after him.

LET'S PRAY
Dear God, there are many evil and sinful things in our land today. Please use us to bring healing to our land and to the people around us. In the name of the Father, and the Son, and the Holy Spirit, Amen!

GOING DEEPER

Read It! 2 Chronicles 34–35; CCC #1434–39 (There are different forms of penance in the Christian life).

Do It! Plan a random act of kindness for someone as a family. You could pay for the vehicle behind you in the drive-through, buy groceries for a stranger, or serve food at a shelter. Afterward, talk about how helping these people made you feel.

ACT OF CONTRITION

A Traditonal Catholic Prayer

O my God, I am heartily sorry for having
offended Thee, and I detest all my sins because
I dread the loss of Heaven and the pains of Hell;
but most of all because they offend Thee, my God,
Who art all-good and deserving of all my love.
I firmly resolve, with the help of Thy grace, to confess
my sins, to do penance, and to amend my life. Amen.

King Joash Repairs the Temple

2 Chronicles 24:1–14

For six years the land of Judah was ruled by the evil Queen Athaliah who, like her wicked mother Jezebel, promoted Baal and dishonored the God of Israel. She rose to power by killing the royal offspring of her predecessor, King Jehu; only the baby Joash was saved. At the age of seven, Joash began his forty-year reign by tearing down the altars to the false gods and repairing the temple.

Joash was seven years old when he began to reign... ²Joash did what was right in the sight of the LORD all the days of the priest Jehoiada. ³Jehoiada got two wives for him, and he became the father of sons and daughters.

4 Some time afterward Joash decided to restore the house of the LORD. ⁵He assembled the priests and the Levites and said to them, "Go out to the cities of Judah and gather money from all Israel to repair the house of your God, year by year; and see that you act quickly." But the Levites did not act quickly. ⁶So the king summoned Jehoiada the chief, and said to him, "Why have you not required the Levites to bring in from Judah and Jerusalem the tax levied by Moses, the servant of the LORD, on the congregation of Israel for the tent of the covenant?" ⁷For the children of Athaliah, that wicked woman, had broken into the house of God, and had even used all the dedicated things of the house of the LORD for the Baals.

8 So the king gave command, and they made a chest, and set it outside the gate of the house of the LORD. ⁹A proclamation was made throughout Judah and Jerusalem to bring in for the LORD the tax that Moses the servant of God laid on Israel in the wilderness. ¹⁰All the leaders and all the people rejoiced and brought their tax and dropped it into the chest until it was full. ¹¹Whenever the chest was brought to the king's officers by the Levites, when they saw that there was a large amount of money in it, the king's secretary and the officer of the chief priest would come and empty the chest and take it and return it to its place. So they did day after day, and collected money in abundance. ¹²The king and Jehoiada gave it to those who had charge of the work of the house of the LORD, and they hired masons and carpenters to restore the house of the LORD, and also workers in iron and bronze to repair the house of the LORD. ¹³So those who were engaged in the work labored, and the repairing went forward at their hands, and they restored the house of God to its proper condition and strengthened it. ¹⁴When they had finished, they brought the rest of the money to the king and Jehoiada, and with it were made utensils for the house of the LORD, utensils for the service and for the burnt offerings, and ladles, and vessels of gold and silver. They offered burnt offerings in the house of the LORD regularly all the days of Jehoiada.

SPECIAL WORDS: The "tent of
the covenant" in Moses'
day was the tabernacle; here
it refers to the temple.

DID YOU KNOW? Jehoiada was the
chief priest of the Lord who hid
Joash from the wicked Queen
Athaliah until he was
old enough to rule.

LET'S PRAY

Thank you, Lord, that we are never too young to serve you
faithfully. King Joash was only seven when he led the adults
around him to repair the temple. Give us the wisdom to know
what we ought to do, and the strength to do it. In the name of
the Father, and the Son, and the Holy Spirit, Amen!

GOING DEEPER

Read It! The story of Joash can also be found in
2 Kings 11—12:21.

Do It! Do you think it was hard for Joash to be
king when he was only seven years old?
Tell what *you* would have done if you
had been king (or queen).

113

King Uzziah Makes God Angry

2 Chronicles 26:1–3, 15–20

*H*ave you ever watched a little kid learning to ride a bike with his mom or dad holding on to the back? The kid gets going a little too fast, so his parents have to let go, and then the bike topples! Sometimes we get a little overconfident in our own abilities, and have to learn the hard way to slow down and stay safe! Just like King Uzziah, who ruled Judah a total of fifty-two years. As long as he followed God, Judah prospered and raised a huge army that defeated the Philistines, Arabs, and Ammonites. Sadly, King Uzziah grew too confident in his own abilities, and in time, God had to punish him!

All the people of Judah took Uzziah, who was sixteen years old, and made him king to succeed his father Amaziah. ²He rebuilt Eloth and restored it to Judah, after the king slept with his ancestors. ³Uzziah was sixteen years old when he began to reign, and he reigned fifty-two years in Jerusalem. His mother's name was Jecoliah of Jerusalem. . . .

¹⁵In Jerusalem he set up machines, invented by skilled workers, on the towers and the corners for shooting arrows and large stones. And his fame spread far, for he was marvelously helped until he became strong.

16 But when he had become strong he grew proud, to his destruction. For he was false to the LORD his God, and entered the temple of the LORD to make offering on the altar of incense. ¹⁷But the priest Azariah went in after him, with eighty priests of the LORD who were men of valor; ¹⁸they withstood King Uzziah, and said to him, "It is not for you, Uzziah, to make offering to the LORD, but for the priests the descendants of Aaron, who are consecrated to make offering. Go out of the sanctuary; for you have done wrong, and it will bring you no honor from the LORD God." ¹⁹Then Uzziah was angry. Now he had a censer in his hand to make offering, and when he became angry with the priests a leprous disease broke out on his forehead, in the presence of the priests in the house of the LORD, by the altar of incense. ²⁰When the chief priest Azariah, and all the priests, looked at him, he was leprous in his forehead. They hurried him out, and he himself hurried to get out, because the LORD had struck him.

LET'S PRAY

Thank you, Lord, for godly priests who are unafraid to tell the truth. Bless your Church with many such men, who will lead us faithfully. Amen.

GOING DEEPER

Read It! Read more about King Uzziah (also called Azariah) in 2 Kings 15:1–7.

Do It! Do you know someone who left the Church because of something hurtful someone said? Say a prayer for that person, and invite him or her to come back!

DID YOU KNOW? King Uzziah may have ruled Judah with his father, Amaziah, for the first twenty-four years of Uzziah's reign, possibly because the older man was captured in battle and taken to Israel (2 Kings 14:8–11).[19]

Tobias and Sarah

Tobit 6:11–16, 18; 7:9, 15; 8:4–5

*T*he archangel Raphael was sent to Tobias to give him a special message from God: he was to marry a distant relative named Sarah, who had been very unfortunate in love! Evil spirits had killed her previous husbands. Raphael reminded Tobias that God's power is greater than the power of any evil spirit. Once God had blessed their marriage, Tobias had no need to be afraid. This story is a lovely image of the sacrament of marriage, which binds two people together under the protective love of God.

Raphael said to the young man, "Brother Tobias[,] . . . we must stay this night in the home of Raguel. He is your relative, and he has a daughter named Sarah. ¹²He has no male heir and no daughter except Sarah only, and you, as next of kin to her, have before all other men a hereditary claim on her. Also it is right for you to inherit her father's possessions. Moreover, the girl is sensible, brave, and very beautiful, and her father is a good man. ¹³. . . Indeed he knows that you, rather than any other man, are entitled to marry his daughter. So now listen to me, brother, and tonight we shall speak concerning the girl and arrange her engagement to you. And when we return from Rages we will take her and bring her back with us to your house."

14 Then Tobias said in answer to Raphael, "Brother Azariah, I have heard that she already has been married to seven husbands and that they died in the bridal chamber. . . . ¹⁵. . . I am afraid that I may die and bring my father's and mother's life down to their grave, grieving for me—and they have no other son to bury them."

16But Raphael said to him, ". . . Say no more about this demon. . . . ¹⁸ . . . Now when you are about to go to bed with her, both of you must first stand up and pray, imploring the Lord of heaven that mercy and safety may be granted to you. Do not be afraid, for she was set apart for you before the world was made. You will save her, and she will go with you. I presume that you will have children by her, and they will be as brothers to you. Now say no more!" When Tobias heard the words of Raphael and learned that she was his kinswoman, related through his father's lineage, he loved her very much, and his heart was drawn to her. . . .

7 . . . When they had bathed and washed themselves and reclined to dine, Tobias said to Raphael, "Brother Azariah, ask Raguel to give me my kinswoman Sarah." . . .

15 Raguel called his wife Edna and said to her, "Sister, get the other room ready, and take her there." . . .

8 When the parents had gone out and shut the door of the room, Tobias got out of bed and said to Sarah, "Sister, get up, and let us pray and implore our Lord that he grant us mercy and safety." ⁵So she got up, and they began to pray and implore that they might be kept safe.

Raguel's Prayer of Thanksgiving

Blessed are you, O God, with every pure blessing;

let all your chosen ones bless you.

Let them bless you forever.

Blessed are you because you have made me glad.

It has not turned out as I expected,

but you have dealt with us according to your great mercy.

—Tobit 8:15–16

GOING DEEPER

Read It! Read Tobit 8 and the beautiful prayers regarding marriage.

Do It! Weddings are so much fun, but they are also a lot of work!

Do you know a young couple or family who could use your help preparing for a wedding? Offer your assistance.

Esther

Esther 5:3–4; 7:1–7, 10

The story of Esther is an important one about the deliverance of the Jewish people following the Babylonian captivity, five hundred years before the time of Christ. The great Persian king Xerxes noticed Esther. She was brought to court by her cousin Mordecai, who raised her and had advised her not to tell anyone she was Jewish. Enchanted with her beauty and intelligence, Xerxes made Esther his wife. Meanwhile, Mordecai's life, and the lives of every Jew in the kingdom, was endangered when he angered the king's closest advisor, Haman. As the story opens, lovely Esther has embarked on the dangerous task of saving her people, by inviting her husband and Haman to dinner!

The king said to her, "What is it, Queen Esther? What is your request? It shall be given you, even to the half of my kingdom." ⁴Then Esther said, "If it pleases the king, let the king and Haman come today to a banquet that I have prepared for the king."

7 So the king and Haman went in to feast with Queen Esther. ²On the second day, as they were drinking wine, the king . . . said to Esther, "What is your petition, Queen Esther? It shall be granted you. And what is your request? Even to the half of my kingdom, it shall be fulfilled." ³Then Queen Esther answered, "If I have won your favor, O king, and if it pleases the king, let my life be given me—that is my petition—and the lives of my people—that is my request. ⁴For we have been sold, I and my people, to be destroyed, to be killed, and to be annihilated. If we had been sold merely as slaves, men and women, I would have held my peace; but no enemy can compensate for this damage to the king." ⁵Then King Ahasuerus said to Queen Esther, "Who is he, and where is he, who has presumed to do this?" ⁶Esther said, "A foe and enemy, this wicked Haman!" Then Haman was terrified before the king and the queen. ⁷The king rose from the feast in wrath and went into the palace garden, but Haman stayed to beg his life from Queen Esther, for he saw that the king had determined to destroy him. . . . ¹⁰ So they hanged Haman on the gallows that he had prepared for Mordecai. Then the anger of the king abated.

LET'S PRAY

When people look at us, Lord Jesus, may they be attracted to your Spirit within us. In the name of the Father, and the Son, and the Holy Spirit, Amen!

GOING DEEPER

Read It! Read the whole book of Esther this week!

Do It! Make Hamantaschen cookies—a favorite Purim treat. Get online for directions.

DID YOU KNOW? The Jews celebrate "Purim" each year to commemorate this event. It is so festive, with costumes and treats, that some call it "Jewish Mardi Gras"!

The Maccabees Decide to Revolt
1 Maccabees 1:11–15; 2:1, 6, 14, 29–31, 38–41 RSV

*T*he story of the Maccabees helps us understand the New Testament, particularly in how the Jews' thought of salvation (connected with earthly deliverance) differed from what Christ taught, and, consequently, why the two were often in conflict. In this story we are introduced to Mattathias, the first leader of the Jewish revolt.

In those days lawless men came forth from Israel, and misled many, saying, "Let us go and make a covenant with the Gentiles round about us, for since we separated from them many evils have come upon us." ¹²This proposal pleased them, ¹³and some of the people eagerly went to the king. He authorized them to observe the ordinances of the Gentiles. ¹⁴So they built a gymnasium in Jerusalem, according to Gentile custom, ¹⁵ . . . and abandoned the holy covenant. They joined with the Gentiles and sold themselves to do evil. . . .

2 In those days Mattathias . . . [and his five sons] moved from Jerusalem and settled in Modein. . . . ⁶He saw the blasphemies being committed in Judah and Jerusalem. . . .

14 And Mattathias and his sons rent their clothes, put on sackcloth, and mourned greatly. . . .

29 Then many who were seeking righteousness and justice went down to the wilderness to dwell there, ³⁰they, their sons, their wives, and their cattle, because evils pressed heavily upon them. ³¹And it was reported to the king's officers, and to the troops in Jerusalem the city of David, that men who had rejected the king's command had gone down to the hiding places in the wilderness. . . . ³⁸So they attacked them on the sabbath, and they died, with their wives and children and cattle, to the number of a thousand persons.

39 When Mattathias and his friends learned of it, they mourned for them deeply. ⁴⁰And each said to his neighbor: "If we all do as our brethren have done and refuse to fight with the Gentiles for our lives and for our ordinances, they will quickly destroy us from the earth." ⁴¹So they made this decision that day: "Let us fight against every man who comes to attack us on the sabbath day; let us not all die as our brethren died in their hiding places."

LET'S PRAY!

Father, we thank you for the men and women in our military who have devoted their lives to protecting us. Today we ask for your hand of blessing and protection on them and their families. In the name of the Father, and of the Son, and the Holy Spirit, Amen.

GOING DEEPER:

Read It! CCC #2308 (We should work to avoid war).

Do It! Mattathias and his friends chose to fight the enemy
forces after they saw their peace-loving neighbors
being destroyed. In light of the Catechism passage
above, tell how it is possible to work for peace by
fighting.

Judas Dedicates the Temple

1 Maccabees 4:36–60

Judas was the son of Mattathias and led the revolt after the death of Mattathias. Judas believed with all his heart that he had been called by God to bring the people back to the faith, starting with the temple, which over the years had been made unholy by pagan worship. Full of zeal and confidence, Judas and his brothers worked hard to restore the temple.

Then Judas and his brothers said, "See, our enemies are crushed; let us go up to cleanse the sanctuary and dedicate it." So all the army assembled and went up to Mount Zion. ³⁸There they saw the sanctuary desolate, the altar profaned, and the gates burned. In the courts they saw bushes sprung up as in a thicket, or as on one of the mountains. They saw also the chambers of the priests in ruins. ³⁹Then they tore their clothes and mourned with great lamentation; they sprinkled themselves with ashes ⁴⁰and fell face down on the ground. And when the signal was given with the trumpets, they cried out to Heaven.

41 Then Judas detailed men to fight against those in the citadel until he had cleansed the sanctuary. ⁴²He chose blameless priests devoted to the law, ⁴³and they cleansed the sanctuary and removed the defiled stones to an unclean place. ⁴⁴They deliberated what to do about the altar of burnt offering, which had been profaned. ⁴⁵And they thought it best to tear it down, so that it would not be a lasting shame to them that the Gentiles had defiled it. So they tore down the altar, ⁴⁶and stored the stones in a convenient place on the temple hill until a prophet should come to tell what to do with them. ⁴⁷Then they took unhewn stones, as the law directs, and built a new altar like the former one. ⁴⁸They also

rebuilt the sanctuary and the interior of the temple, and consecrated the courts. ⁴⁹They made new holy vessels, and brought the lampstand, the altar of incense, and the table into the temple. ⁵⁰Then they offered incense on the altar and lit the lamps on the lampstand, and these gave light in the temple. ⁵¹They placed the bread on the table and hung up the curtains. Thus they finished all the work they had undertaken.

52 Early in the morning on the twenty-fifth day of the ninth month, which is the month of Chislev, in the one hundred and forty-eighth year [164 BC], ⁵³they rose and offered sacrifice, as the law directs, on the new altar of burnt offering that they had built. ⁵⁴At the very season and on the very day that the Gentiles had profaned it, it was dedicated with songs and harps and lutes and cymbals. ⁵⁵All the people fell on their faces and worshiped and blessed Heaven, who had prospered them. ⁵⁶So they celebrated the dedication of the altar for eight days, and joyfully offered burnt offerings with gladness; they offered a sacrifice of well-being and a thanksgiving offering. ⁵⁷They decorated the front of the temple with golden crowns and small shields; they restored the gates and the chambers for the priests, and fitted them with doors. ⁵⁸There was very great joy among the people, and

the disgrace brought by the Gentiles was removed.

59 Then Judas and his brothers and all the assembly of Israel determined that every year at that season the days of dedication of the altar should be observed with joy and gladness for eight days. . . .

60 At that time they fortified Mount Zion with high walls and strong towers all around, to keep the Gentiles from coming and trampling them down as they had done before.

SPECIAL WORDS:
Unhewn *means "whole."*

LET'S PRAY!

Thank you, Lord, for our church. Help us always to treat it with the respect your house deserves. In the name of the Father, and the Son, and the Holy Spirit, Amen!

GOING DEEPER:

Read It! A parallel account of this story of the rededication of the temple may be found in 2 Maccabees 10:1–8.

Do It! Two Jewish festivals are associated with this passage: the Feast of Tabernacles (which is to remember the rebuilding of the temple) and the Feast of Lights (also known as Hanukkah). This week, go to the library and learn more about these Jewish feast days.

A Story of Seven Brothers

2 Maccabees 7:1, 20–29, 40

When someone we love is suffering, it hurts! In today's sad story, a poor but faith-filled woman had to watch as each of her seven sons, one after the other, was murdered by an unjust king. Yet her faith gave her courage and strength. She knew that if her children remained faithful to the truth, they would all be together again one day.

It happened also that seven brothers and their mother were arrested and were being compelled by the king, under torture with whips and thongs, to partake of unlawful swine's flesh. . . .

20 The mother was especially admirable and worthy of honorable memory. Although she saw her seven sons perish within a single day, she bore it with good courage because of her hope in the Lord. [21]She encouraged each of them in the language of their ancestors. Filled with a noble spirit, she reinforced her woman's reasoning with a man's courage. [She said,] [23]" . . . The Creator of the world, who shaped the beginning of humankind and devised the origin of all things, will in his mercy give life and breath back to you again, since you now forget yourselves for the sake of his laws."

24 Antiochus felt that he was being treated with contempt, and he was suspicious of her reproachful tone. The youngest brother being still alive, Antiochus not only appealed to him in words, but promised with oaths that he would make him rich and enviable if he would turn from the ways of his ancestors, and that he would take him for his friend and entrust him with public affairs. [25]Since the young man would not listen to him at all, the king called the mother to him and urged her to advise the youth to save himself. [26]After much urging on his part, she undertook to persuade her son. [27]But, leaning close to him, she spoke in their native language as follows, deriding the cruel tyrant: "My son, have pity on me. I carried you nine months in my womb, and nursed you for three years, and have reared you and brought you up to this point in your life, and have taken care of you. [28]I beg you, my child, to look at the heaven and the earth and see everything that is in them, and recognize that God did not make them out of things that existed. And in the same way the human race came into being. [29]Do not fear this butcher, but prove worthy of your brothers. Accept death, so that in God's mercy I may get you back again along with your brothers." . . . [40]So he died in his integrity, putting his whole trust in the Lord.

LET'S PRAY!

Prayer for Dangerous Moments

God, come to my assistance, make haste to help me! In the name of the Father, and the Son, and the Holy Spirit, Amen!

GOING DEEPER:

Read It! Today's reading (OT 32C) is placed alongside the gospel story of Jesus' teaching of the Resurrection (Luke 20:27–38). It is in light of these teachings that the church honors the martyrs, including the seven brothers in today's story (CCC #2474).

Do It! Read aloud some of the stories of the martyrs and how brave they were for Jesus!

DID YOU KNOW? Antiochus Epiphanes, who lived about 215–164 BC, started the Maccabean revolt in 167 BC when he outlawed Jewish religious practices, including all Jewish feasts, sacrifices, and the rite of circumcision.

Job

Job 1:1–3; 2:1–10; 42:10, 12

The name "Job" is associated with someone who has endured great suffering. In this story, Job is a man who has enjoyed tremendous blessing—great wealth, large family, and many friends. But one day, everything was taken away from him. God allowed Job's faith to be tested, confident that Job would trust him no matter what. What do you think happened? Let's see.

There was once a man in the land of Uz whose name was Job. That man was blameless and upright, one who feared God and turned away from evil. ²There were born to him seven sons and three daughters. ³He had seven thousand sheep, three thousand camels, five hundred yoke of oxen, five hundred donkeys, and very many servants; so that this man was the greatest of all the people of the east. . . .

2 One day the heavenly beings came to present themselves before the LORD, and Satan also came among them to present himself before the LORD. ²The LORD said to Satan, "Where have you come from?" Satan answered the LORD, "From going to and fro on the earth, and from walking up and down on it." ³The LORD said to Satan, "Have you considered my servant Job? There is no one like him on the earth, a blameless and upright man who fears God and turns away from evil." . . . ⁴Then Satan answered the LORD, ". . . ⁵Stretch out your hand now and touch his bone and his flesh, and he will curse you to your face." ⁶The

LORD said to Satan, "Very well, he is in your power; only spare his life."

7 So Satan went out from the presence of the LORD, and inflicted loathsome sores on Job from the sole of his foot to the crown of his head. ⁸Job took a potsherd with which to scrape himself, and sat among the ashes.

9 Then his wife said to him, "Do you still persist in your integrity? Curse God, and die." ¹⁰But he said to her, "You speak as any foolish woman would speak. Shall we receive the good at the hand of God, and not receive the bad?" In all this Job did not sin with his lips. . . .

42 And the LORD restored the fortunes of Job . . . and . . . gave Job twice as much as he had before. . . . ¹²The LORD blessed the latter days of Job more than his beginning.

LET'S PRAY

Father, thank you that even when bad things happen, you can bring good out of them. Amen.

GOING DEEPER:

Read It! Read Romans 8:28 and talk about how that might relate to Job's story.

Do It! Let God use you to bring good to others. Do you know someone who is sick or lonely and could use some cheering this week?

The Shepherd Psalm
Psalm 23

*A*s a boy, long before he played his harp for King Saul, David spent hours roaming the countryside, tending his father's sheep. In this psalm, that shepherd boy's experiences combined with his love for God and his creatures to create this most familiar and comforting of all David's writings.

The LORD is my shepherd, I shall not want.
2 He makes me lie down in
      green pastures;
  he leads me beside still waters;
3   he restores my soul.
  He leads me in right paths
      for his name's sake.
4 Even though I walk through the
      darkest valley,
    I fear no evil;
  for you are with me;
      your rod and your staff—they
    comfort me.
5 You prepare a table before me
      in the presence of my enemies;
  you anoint my head with oil;
      my cup overflows.
6 Surely goodness and mercy shall
      follow me
    all the days of my life,
  and I shall dwell in the house of the LORD
      my whole life long.

LET'S PRAY
Traditional Bedtime Prayer

Now I lay me down to sleep, I pray the Lord my soul to keep.

God, be with me through the night, and wake me with the morning light. Amen.

GOING DEEPER
Read It! CCC #1293 (Anointing with oil, especially at Confirmation, has a special meaning).
Do It! Memorize Psalm 23 as a family.

QUOTE OF THE DAY:
"I am the good shepherd.
The good shepherd lays
down his life for the sheep."
—Jesus, John 10:11

129

We Worship You, Lord
Psalm 32

It is such a blessing to be forgiven of our sin. When we are not forgiven, it is as if we are carrying around heavy, dirty bags of garbage in our lives. They pull us down and make us tired; it's no fun carrying around these gross and heavy bags! When we ask for forgiveness, Jesus takes them away and makes us clean!

A Prayer of Penitence

Happy are those whose transgression is
    forgiven,
      whose sin is covered.
2 Happy are those to whom the LORD
      imputes no iniquity,
    and in whose spirit there is no deceit.
3 While I kept silence, my body wasted
      away
    through my groaning all day long.
4 For day and night your hand was heavy
      upon me;
    my strength was dried up as by the
      heat of summer. *Selah*
5 Then I acknowledged my sin to you,
    and I did not hide my iniquity;
I said, "I will confess my transgressions
    to the LORD,"
    and you forgave the guilt of my sin.
      Selah
6 Therefore let all who are faithful
    offer prayer to you;
at a time of distress, the rush of mighty
      waters
    shall not reach them.
7 You are a hiding place for me;
    you preserve me from trouble;
    you surround me with glad cries of
      deliverance. *Selah*
8 I will instruct you and teach you the way
      you should go;
    I will counsel you with my eye upon
      you.
9 Do not be like a horse or a mule, without
      understanding,
    whose temper must be curbed with bit
      and bridle,
    else it will not stay near you.
10 Many are the torments of the wicked,
    but steadfast love surrounds those
      who trust in the LORD.
11 Be glad in the LORD and rejoice,
    O righteous,
    and shout for joy, all you upright in
      heart.

Let's Pray

You are my hiding place, O Lord. You always fill my heart with songs of deliverance when I am afraid. Jesus, I will trust in you! In the name of the Father, and the Son, and the Holy Spirit, Amen!

GOING DEEPER

Read It! Have you read the story of David and Bathsheba?
   Read it in 2 Samuel 11–12.

Do It! Examine yourself daily to keep sin from forming a
   deep habit in your life.

Praise the Lord!

Psalm 148:1—12

This is one of the five "Hallelujah Psalms" that is echoed in the very last book of the Bible, the book of Revelation. Let the angels, and the sun and moon and stars, and all the heavens shout, "Hallelujah!"

Praise the LORD!
Praise the LORD from the heavens;
   praise him in the heights!
2 Praise him, all his angels;
   praise him, all his host!
3 Praise him, sun and moon;
   praise him, all you shining stars!
4 Praise him, you highest heavens,
   and you waters above the heavens!
5 Let them praise the name of the LORD,
   for he commanded and they were
     created.
6 He established them forever and ever;
   he fixed their bounds, which cannot
     be passed.
7 Praise the LORD from the earth,
   you sea monsters and all deeps,

8 fire and hail, snow and frost,
   stormy wind fulfilling his command!
9 Mountains and all hills,
   fruit trees and all cedars!
10 Wild animals and all cattle,
   creeping things and flying birds!
11 Kings of the earth and all peoples,
   princes and all rulers of the earth!
12 Young men and women alike,
   old and young together!

LET'S PRAY!

Today, Father, we lift up our praise to you!
Praise Father, Son, and Holy Spirit. Amen!

GOING DEEPER:

Read It! CCC #2637—38 (Thanksgiving is part of the prayers of the Church).

Do It! What's your favorite way to praise the Lord? Do you like to sing, dance, draw, or pray? Make up your own special way to thank God today, and share it with your family.

DID YOU KNOW?
The word Eucharist *means "thanksgiving."*

Solomon's Wisdom

Proverbs 3:1–6

*T*he book of Proverbs was written by King Solomon. Both he and his father, King David, were special friends of God, and their writings form a large part of the Bible that is called "Wisdom Literature."

Shortly after Solomon became king of Israel, he decided to build a temple in Jerusalem dedicated to the one true God. This pleased the Lord so much that he appeared to Solomon in a dream and offered him a reward—anything King Solomon wanted. What would you have asked for? Let's see what King Solomon said (1 Kings 3:6–9):

"You have shown great and steadfast love to your servant my father David, because he walked before you in faithfulness, in righteousness, and in uprightness of heart toward you; and you have kept for him this great and steadfast love, and have given him a son to sit on his throne today. [7]And now, O LORD my God, you have made your servant king in place of my father David, although I am only a little child; I do not know how to go out or come in. [8]And your servant is in the midst of the people whom you have chosen, a great people, so numerous they cannot be numbered or counted. [9]Give your servant therefore an understanding mind to govern your people, able to discern between good and evil; for who can govern this your great people?"

God was pleased with King Solomon's response, and promised him not only great wisdom, but wealth and power as well. In the following passage, King Solomon shares some of that great storehouse of wisdom with each of us!

My child, do not forget my teaching,
but let your heart keep my
commandments;
[2] for length of days and years of life
and abundant welfare they will
give you.
[3] Do not let loyalty and faithfulness
forsake you;
bind them around your neck,
write them on the tablet of your heart.
[4] So you will find favor and good repute
in the sight of God and of people.
[5] Trust in the LORD with all your heart,
and do not rely on your own insight.
[6] In all your ways acknowledge him,
and he will make straight your paths.

LET'S PRAY!

Thank you, Lord, for the gift of parents who share their wisdom with us. In the name of the Father, and the Son, and the Holy Spirit, Amen!

GOING DEEPER:

Read It! CCC #1831 (Wisdom is one of the gifts of the Holy Spirit).

Do It! Name the seven gifts of the Holy Spirit. (See the Catechism passage).

A Good Wife

Proverbs 31:10–12, 20–22, 27–30

This chapter of Proverbs tells us how valuable godly women are and describes important traits they have. Let's read it and find what character traits and habits are pleasing to God.

A capable wife who can find?
>   She is far more precious than jewels.
11 The heart of her husband trusts in her,
>   and he will have no lack of gain.
12 She does him good, and not harm,
>   all the days of her life. . . .
20 She opens her hand to the poor,
>   and reaches out her hands to the
>   needy.
21 She is not afraid for her household when
>   it snows,
>   for all her household are clothed in
>   crimson.
22 She makes herself coverings;
>   her clothing is fine linen and
>   purple. . . .

27 She looks well to the ways of her
>   household,
>   and does not eat the bread of idleness.
28 Her children rise up and call her happy;
>   her husband too, and he praises her:
29 "Many women have done excellently,
>   but you surpass them all."
30 Charm is deceitful, and beauty is vain,
>   but a woman who fears the LORD is to
>   be praised.

LET'S PRAY!

Thank you, God, for the gift of mothers and wives. Today we remember especially the Blessed Mother, who raised the Lord Jesus and through him became our spiritual mother. Amen.

GOING DEEPER:

Read It! CCC #963 (Mary is Mother of the Church).

Do It! Tonight at dinner, talk about Mary and how she showed great feminine virtue. Then pray a "Hail, Mary" together.

Good Friends

Sirach 6:14–17

*D*o not acquire friends too quickly, Sirach warns us, but be cautious; be sure those friends won't get us in trouble! The best friends are those who also share friendship with God! Have you talked with a friend about God lately?

Faithful friends are a sturdy shelter;
    whoever finds one has found a
        treasure.
¹⁵ Faithful friends are beyond price;
    no amount can balance their worth.
¹⁶ Faithful friends are life-saving
        medicine;
    and those who fear the Lord will find
        them.
¹⁷ Those who fear the Lord direct their
        friendship aright,
    for as they are, so are their
        neighbors also.

LET'S PRAY!

Lord, help me to be a faithful friend and to choose my friends wisely. Amen!

GOING DEEPER:

Read It! CCC #1468 (Reconciliation is a way to reestablish our friendship with God).

Do It! Get out some paper and craft supplies and make a card for a friend. Let that friend know how important he or she is to you. It will really make that person's day!

DID YOU KNOW? The Book of Sirach was written by a Jewish scholar in 180 BC. It was translated into Greek by his grandson about fifty years later. This too is not included in Jewish and some Christian Bibles.

Wisdom Speaks

Sirach 24:1–12, 17, 19–21, RSV

In the Scriptures "Wisdom" is portrayed as a woman sent from God, yet separate from him. In the liturgy, Wisdom is associated with the Blessed Virgin Mary.

Wisdom will praise herself,
  and will glory in the midst of her people.
2 In the assembly of the Most High she
      will open her mouth,
    and in the presence of his host she will
      glory:
3 "I came forth from the mouth of the
      Most High,
    and covered the earth like a mist.
4 I dwelt in high places,
    and my throne was in a pillar of cloud.
5 Alone I have made the circuit of the vault
      of heaven
    and have walked in the depths of the
      abyss.
6 In the waves of the sea, in the whole earth,
    and in every people and nation I have
      gotten a possession.
7 Among all these I sought a resting place;
    I sought in whose territory I might
      lodge.
8 Then the Creator of all things gave me a
      commandment,
    and the one who created me assigned
      a place for my tent.
  And he said, 'Make your dwelling in Jacob,
    and in Israel receive your inheritance.'
9 From eternity, in the beginning, he
      created me,

and for eternity I shall not cease to
      exist.
10 In the holy tabernacle I ministered
      before him,
    and so I was established in Zion.
11 In the beloved city likewise he gave me a
      resting place,
    and in Jerusalem was my dominion.
12 So I took root in an honored people,
    in the portion of the Lord, who is their
      inheritance. . . .
17 Like a vine I caused loveliness to bud,
    and my blossoms became glorious and
      abundant fruit. . . .
19 "Come to me, you who desire me,
    and eat your fill of my produce.
20 For the remembrance of me is sweeter
      than honey,
    and my inheritance sweeter than the
      honeycomb.
21 Those who eat me will hunger for more,
    and those who drink me will thirst for
      more."

LET'S PRAY!

Lord, make me hungry for Wisdom! In the name of the Father, and the Son, and the Holy Spirit, Amen!

GOING DEEPER:

Read It! CCC #771 (The Church, an embodiment of Wisdom, is both visible and spiritual).
Do It! Who are your favorite wise people from the Bible and from history?

EMMAUS PRAYER FOR PRIESTS

A Traditonal Catholic Prayer

Lord Jesus, hear our prayer

For the spiritual renewal of priests.

We praise you for giving their ministry to the Church.

In these days renew them with the gifts of your Spirit.

You once opened the Scriptures

To the disciples on the road to Emmaus.

Now renew your ordained ministers

With the truth and power of your Word.

In the Eucharist you gave the Emmaus disciples

Renewed life and hope.

Nourish priests with your own Body and Blood.

Help them to imitate in their lives

The death and resurrection they celebrate at your altar.

Isaiah's Vision

Isaiah 6:1—8

*H*ave you ever wondered what heaven is like? The prophet Isaiah, who was considered the "messianic prophet" and is quoted more often in the New Testament than any other prophet, had a beautiful vision of heaven that we remember each week in the Mass during the Liturgy of the Eucharist.

In the year that King Uzziah died, I saw the Lord sitting on a throne, high and lofty; and the hem of his robe filled the temple. ²Seraphs were in attendance above him; each had six wings: with two they covered their faces, and with two they covered their feet, and with two they flew. ³And one called to another and said:

"Holy, holy, holy is the LORD of hosts;
the whole earth is full of his glory."

⁴The pivots on the thresholds shook at the voices of those who called, and the house filled with smoke. ⁵And I said: "Woe is me! I am lost, for I am a man of unclean lips, and I live among a people of unclean lips; yet my eyes have seen the King, the LORD of hosts!"

6 Then one of the seraphs flew to me, holding a live coal that had been taken from the altar with a pair of tongs. ⁷The seraph touched my mouth with it and said: "Now that this has touched your lips, your guilt has departed and your sin is blotted out." ⁸Then I heard the voice of the Lord saying, "Whom shall I send, and who will go for us?" And I said, "Here am I; send me!"

LET'S PRAY!

Dear God, thank you for being holy and good. I want to be willing to serve you and go for you. Here am I; send me! Amen.

GOING DEEPER:

Read It! CCC #1370—71 (The Pascal banquet attended by the angels and saints).

Do It! This week at Mass, when you hear the "Sanctus," remember the angels who are singing it to God!

SPECIAL WORDS: The "seraphim" are the highest order of angels, or those closest to God.

Jeremiah

Jeremiah 1:4—15

One hundred years after Isaiah, God raised up another prophet named Jeremiah, to urge his people to turn from their idols to avoid total destruction. Sadly, he was unable to accomplish this task, and Jerusalem was totally destroyed by the Babylonians.

Now the word of the LORD came to me saying,
5 "Before I formed you in the womb I
  knew you,
  and before you were born I
  consecrated you;
  I appointed you a prophet to the
  nations."
⁶Then I said, "Ah, Lord GOD! Truly I do not know how to speak, for I am only a boy." ⁷But the LORD said to me,
  "Do not say, 'I am only a boy';
  for you shall go to all to whom I send
  you,
  and you shall speak whatever I
  command you,
8 Do not be afraid of them,
  for I am with you to deliver you,
  says the LORD."
⁹Then the LORD put out his hand and touched my mouth; and the LORD said to me,
  "Now I have put my words in your
  mouth.
¹⁰ See, today I appoint you over nations
  and over kingdoms,
  to pluck up and to pull down,
  to destroy and to overthrow,

to build and to plant."

11 The word of the LORD came to me, saying, "Jeremiah, what do you see?" And I said, "I see a branch of an almond tree." ¹²Then the LORD said to me, "You have seen well, for I am watching over my word to perform it." ¹³The word of the LORD came to me a second time, saying, "What do you see?" And I said, "I see a boiling pot, tilted away from the north."

14 Then the LORD said to me: Out of the north disaster shall break out on all the inhabitants of the land. ¹⁵For now I am calling all the tribes of the kingdoms of the north, says the LORD; and they shall come and all of them shall set their thrones at the entrance of the gates of Jerusalem, against all its surrounding walls and against all the cities of Judah.

LET'S PRAY!

Thank you, Lord, for the gifts you have given me to share with the world. Help me to be courageous and wise in knowing when to use them. In the name of the Father, and the Son, and the Holy Spirit, Amen!

GOING DEEPER:

Read It! CCC #2270 (Life begins at conception. Before you were born, God knew you).

Do It! Make a stained glass window! Ask your parents to get online and find out how to make them with crayons and wax paper. Be sure to have your parents help you.

147

Jerusalem Captured
Jeremiah 52:4–16

The Israelites were stunned when Nebuchadnezzar captured the temple. They never imagined God would allow such a thing! But because of their unfaithfulness, God permitted his people to endure seventy years of exile in Babylon. This is the story of how it happened.

And in the ninth year of his reign, in the tenth month, on the tenth day of the month, King Nebuchadnezzar of Babylon came with all his army against Jerusalem, and they laid siege to it; they built siegeworks against it all around. ⁵So the city was besieged until the eleventh year of King Zedekiah. ⁶On the ninth day of the fourth month the famine became so severe in the city that there was no food for the people of the land. ⁷Then a breach was made in the city wall; and all the soldiers fled and went out from the city by night by the way of the gate between the two walls, by the king's garden, though the Chaldeans were all around the city. They went in the direction of the Arabah. ⁸But the army of the Chaldeans pursued the king, and overtook Zedekiah in the plains of Jericho; and all his army was scattered, deserting him. ⁹Then they captured the king, and brought him up to the king of Babylon at Riblah in the land of Hamath, and he passed sentence on him. ¹⁰The king of Babylon killed the sons of Zedekiah before his eyes, and also killed all the officers of Judah at Riblah. ¹¹He put out the eyes of Zedekiah, and bound him in fetters, and the king of Babylon took him to Babylon, and put him in prison until the day of his death.

12 In the fifth month, on the tenth day of the month—which was the nineteenth year of King Nebuchadnezzar, king of Babylon—Nebuzaradan the captain of the bodyguard who served the king of Babylon, entered Jerusalem. ¹³He burned the house of the LORD, the king's house, and all the houses of Jerusalem; every great house he burned down. ¹⁴All the army of the Chaldeans, who were with the captain of the guard, broke down all the walls around Jerusalem. ¹⁵Nebuzaradan the captain of the guard carried into exile some of the poorest of the people and the rest of the people who were left in the city and the deserters who had defected to the king of Babylon, together with the rest of the artisans. ¹⁶But Nebuzaradan the captain of the guard left some of the poorest people of the land to be vinedressers and tillers of the soil.

LET'S PRAY!

"Lord, I am yours, and I must belong to no one but you. My soul is yours, and must live only by you. My will is yours, and must love only for you. I must love you as my first cause, since I am from you. I must love you as my end and rest, since I am for you. I must love you more than my own being, since my being subsists by you. I must love you more than myself, since I am all yours and all in you." —St. Francis de Sales

GOING DEEPER:

Read It! Read about the Babylonian destruction of the temple in Jerusalem in 2 Kings 24:18–25:21.

Do It! Get Lincoln Logs or your favorite kind of blocks and build a castle!

Baruch on Wisdom
Baruch 3:9–21, 32, 35–37; 4:1

*B*aruch was Jeremiah's scribe; that means he wrote what Jeremiah told him. He knew very well of the prophet's struggle and the devastating consequences of the people's disregard for the prophet's message. Although Jeremiah's book is in all biblical texts, Baruch is unique to the Catholic text.

Hear the commandments of life, O Israel;
    give ear, and learn wisdom!
¹⁰ Why is it, O Israel, why is it that you are
      in the land of your enemies,
        that you are growing old in a foreign
        country,
that you are defiled with the dead,
¹¹   that you are counted among those in
      Hades?
¹² You have forsaken the fountain of wisdom.
¹³ If you had walked in the way of God,
      you would be living in peace forever.
¹⁴ Learn where there is wisdom,
      where there is strength,
      where there is understanding,
    so that you may at the same time
      discern
      where there is length of days, and life,
      where there is light for the eyes, and
      peace.
¹⁵ Who has found her place?
    And who has entered her
      storehouses?
¹⁶ Where are the rulers of the nations,
      and those who lorded it over the
      animals on earth;
¹⁷ those who made sport of the birds of the
      air,
    and who hoard up silver and gold,
  in which people trust,
    and there is no end to their getting;

¹⁸ those who schemed to get silver, and
      were anxious,
    but there is no trace of their works?
¹⁹ They have vanished and gone down to
      Hades,
    and others have arisen in their place.
²⁰ Later generations have seen the light of
      day,
    and have lived upon the earth;
    but they have not learned the way to
      knowledge,
      nor understood her paths,
      nor laid hold of her.
²¹ Their descendants have strayed far from
      her way . . .
³² But the one who knows all things knows
      her,
    he found her by his understanding,
The one who prepared the earth for all
      time. . . .
³⁵ This is our God;
      no other can be compared to him.
³⁶ He found the whole way to
      knowledge. . . .
³⁷ Afterward she appeared on earth and
    lived with humankind.

4 She is the book of the commandments
    of God,
    the law that endures forever.
All who hold her fast will live,
    and those who forsake her will die.

GOING DEEPER:

Read It! "The beginning of wisdom is the most sincere desire for instruction" (Wisdom 6:17).

Do It! Learn a valuable life skill together as a family. For example, why not plant a garden together this spring?

DID YOU KNOW? The book of Baruch is a collection of short writings composed around the time of the fall of Jerusalem and the destruction of Solomon's temple in 587 BC.

Ezekiel's Challenge
Ezekiel 3:16–21

The prophet Ezekiel was taken into captivity in Babylon several years before the fall of Jerusalem; he may have been a student of Jeremiah's.

At the end of seven days, the word of the LORD came to me: [17]Mortal, I have made you a sentinel for the house of Israel; whenever you hear a word from my mouth, you shall give them warning from me. [18]If I say to the wicked, "You shall surely die," and you give them no warning, or speak to warn the wicked from their wicked way, in order to save their life, those wicked persons shall die for their iniquity; but their blood I will require at your hand. [19]But if you warn the wicked, and they do not turn from their wickedness, or from their wicked way, they shall die for their iniquity; but you will have saved your life. [20]Again, if the righteous turn from their righteousness and commit iniquity, and I lay a stumbling block before them, they shall die; because you have not warned them, they shall die for their sin, and their righteous deeds that they have done shall not be remembered; but their blood I will require at your hand. [21]If, however, you warn the righteous not to sin, and they do not sin, they shall surely live, because they took warning; and you will have saved your life.

LET'S PRAY!
Prayer of Intercession
A Traditonal Catholic Prayer

God, today I offer all my sufferings, large and small, joyfully to you.
Unite them with the merits of Your Son, that they might
Purify your love in me, and become an intercessory offering
for souls who do not yet know you.
In your mercy, Lord Jesus, hear my prayer.Amen.

GOING DEEPER:
Read It! CCC #1137 (Some of the imagery in Ezekiel is seen in Revelation and in the liturgy).
Do It! Pray for missionaries and church leaders all over the world who are delivering God's Word.

DID YOU KNOW?
Several images from the book of Ezekiel appear again in Revelation: the cherubim (Ezekiel 1), the scroll (Ezekiel 3), Gog and Magog (Ezekiel 38), New Jerusalem (Ezekiel 40–48), and the river of the water of life (Ezekiel 47).[20]

Shadrach, Meshach, and Abednego

Daniel 3:8–12, 19–23, (1, 24, 26–28) RSV

This story reminds us that God protects the faithful. Even when bad things happen, we can entrust ourselves to God, knowing that the soul, which lasts forever, is safe in his hands.

Therefore at that time certain Chaldeans came forward and maliciously accused the Jews. ⁹They said to King Nebuchadnezzar, "O king, live for ever! ¹⁰You, O king, have made a decree, that every man who hears the sound of the horn, pipe, lyre, trigon, harp, bagpipe, and every kind of music, shall fall down and worship the golden image; ¹¹and whoever does not fall down and worship shall be cast into a burning fiery furnace. ¹²There are certain Jews whom you have appointed over the affairs of the province of Babylon: Shadrach, Meshach, and Abednego. These men, O king, pay no heed to you; they do not serve your gods or worship the golden image which you have set up." . . .

19 Then Nebuchadnezzar was full of fury, and the expression of his face was changed against Shadrach, Meshach, and Abednego. He ordered the furnace heated seven times more. . . . ²⁰And he ordered certain mighty men of his army to bind Shadrach, Meshach, and Abednego, and to cast them into the burning fiery furnace. ²¹Then these men were bound in their mantles, their tunics, their hats, and their other garments, and they were cast into the burning fiery furnace. ²²Because the king's order was strict and the furnace very hot, the flame of the fire slew those men who took up Shadrach, Meshach, and Abednego. ²³And these three men, Shadrach, Meshach, and Abednego, fell bound into the burning fiery furnace.

1 *And they walked about in the midst of the flames, singing hymns to God and blessing the Lord. . . .*

²⁴*And the flame streamed out above the furnace. . . . ²⁶But the angel of the Lord came down into the furnace . . . and drove the fiery flame out of the furnace, ²⁷and made the midst of the furnace like a moist whistling wind, so that the fire did not touch them at all or hurt them or trouble them.*

28 *Then the three, as with one mouth, praised and glorified and blessed God in the furnace.*

LET'S PRAY!

"You, O God, are a fire that takes away the coldness, illuminates the mind with light, and causes me to know Your truth. And I know that You are wisdom and beauty itself. The food of angels, You give Yourself to us in the fire of Your love."²¹

GOING DEEPER:

Read It! The "Prayer of Azariah" (Daniel 3) is a beautiful prayer of thanksgiving.

Do It! Toast marshmallows together and talk about how God has protected your family!

The Hand of God
Daniel 5:1–2, 4–9, 17, 25–29

*O*n *the night of the fall of Babylon, King Belshazzar held a great feast. The prophet Daniel, who had been Nebuchadnezzar's advisor for many years, was now an old man. But his zeal for the Lord was strong. When Babylon fell to Persia, and Darius the Mede became king, Daniel was made one of three presidents. The hand of the Lord was upon Daniel; in this story, that hand had a message for everyone!*

King Belshazzar made a great festival for a thousand of his lords, and he was drinking wine in the presence of the thousand.

2 Under the influence of the wine, Belshazzar commanded that they bring in the vessels of gold and silver that his father Nebuchadnezzar had taken out of the temple in Jerusalem, so that the king and his lords, his wives, and his concubines might drink from them. . . . ⁴They drank the wine and praised the gods of gold and silver, bronze, iron, wood, and stone.

5 Immediately the fingers of a human hand appeared and began writing on the plaster of the wall of the royal palace, next to the lampstand. The king was watching the hand as it wrote. ⁶Then the king's face turned pale, and his thoughts terrified him. His limbs gave way, and his knees knocked together. ⁷The king cried aloud to bring in the enchanters, the Chaldeans, and the diviners; and the king said to the wise men of Babylon, "Whoever can read this writing and tell me its interpretation shall be clothed in purple, have a chain of gold around his neck, and rank third in the kingdom." ⁸Then all the king's wise men came in, but they could not read the writing or tell the king the interpretation.

⁹Then King Belshazzar became greatly terrified and his face turned pale, and his lords were perplexed. . . .

17 Then Daniel answered in the presence of the king, "Let your gifts be for yourself, or give your rewards to someone else! Nevertheless I will read the writing to the king and let him know the interpretation. . . .

²⁵And this is the writing that was inscribed: MENE, MENE, TEKEL, and PARSIN. ²⁶This is the interpretation of the matter: MENE, God has numbered the days of your kingdom and brought it to an end; ²⁷TEKEL, you have been weighed on the scales and found wanting; ²⁸PERES, your kingdom is divided and given to the Medes and Persians."

29 Then Belshazzar gave the command, and Daniel was clothed in purple, a chain of gold was put around his neck, and a proclamation was made concerning him that he should rank third in the kingdom.

LET'S PRAY!
Lord, in your mercy, hear us. You who cause princes to rise and fall, make us worthy to take our place in your kingdom. In the name of the Father, and the Son, and the Holy Spirit, Amen!

SPECIAL WORDS: The expression "the writing is on the wall" comes from this story, referring to a situation in which the outcome is easily anticipated.

GOING DEEPER:

Read It! CCC #67 ("Private" revelations or messages helped individuals live more fully in certain periods of history).

Do It! Write your grandparents letters this week, telling them how much you love them!

Daniel in the Lions' Den
Daniel 6:13–23

Do you ever feel lonely because of your faith? Daniel did. After seventy years in Babylon, he was still an "outsider" when Darius, king of Persia, made Daniel one of three presidents. Darius's men resented Daniel and plotted to get rid of him. They could not accuse Daniel of wrongdoing—so they trapped him with an unjust law: Whoever prayed to anyone but the king had to spend the night in a den with lions! Yet Daniel refused to deny his God; he continued to pray beside his open window three times every day. He was determined to honor God rather than man!

Then they responded to the king, "Daniel, one of the exiles from Judah, pays no attention to you, O king, or to the interdict you have signed, but he is saying his prayers three times a day."

14 When the king heard the charge, he was very much distressed. He was determined to save Daniel, and until the sun went down he made every effort to rescue him. ¹⁵Then the conspirators came to the king and said to him, "Know, O king, that it is a law of the Medes and Persians that no interdict or ordinance that the king established can be changed."

16 Then the king gave the command, and Daniel was brought and thrown into the den of lions. The king said to Daniel, "May your God, whom you faithfully serve, deliver you!" ¹⁷A stone was brought and laid on the mouth of the den, and the king sealed it with his own signet and with the signet of his lords, so that nothing might be changed concerning Daniel. ¹⁸Then the king went to his palace and spent the night fasting; no food was brought to him, and sleep fled from him.

19 Then, at break of day, the king got up and hurried to the den of lions. ²⁰When he came near the den where Daniel was, he cried out anxiously to Daniel, "O Daniel, servant of the living God, has your God whom you faithfully serve been able to deliver you from the lions?" ²¹Daniel then said to the king, "O king, live forever! ²²My God sent his angel and shut the lions' mouths so that they would not hurt me, because I was found blameless before him; and also before you, O king, I have done no wrong." ²³Then the king was exceedingly glad and commanded that Daniel be taken up out of the den. So Daniel was taken up out of the den, and no kind of harm was found on him, because he had trusted in his God.

LET'S PRAY!
Pray the "Our Father" together.

GOING DEEPER:
Read It! John 12:23–26 speaks of the grain that is buried, then bears fruit. This may be why many early Christians saw the stories of the fiery furnace and the lion's den as images of resurrection!²²

Do It! Get some crayons and draw a picture of Daniel in the lions' den.

Susanna

Daniel 13:1–2, 31–32, 34, 36–37, 39–43, 51–54, 56–62 RSV

Were you ever blamed for something you didn't do? The story of Susanna is a parable about resisting evil. When the virtuous Susanna resisted two wicked men, leaders in the city who had tried to harm her, they falsely accused her of wrongdoing. Frightened, she cried out to the Lord, and God sent a good man to deliver her.

There was a man living in Babylon whose name was Joakim. ²And he took a wife named Susanna, the daughter of Hilkiah, a very beautiful woman and one who feared the Lord. . . .

31 Now Susanna was a woman of great refinement, and beautiful in appearance. ³²As she was veiled, the wicked men ordered her to be unveiled, that they might feed upon her beauty. . . .

34 Then the two elders stood up in the midst of the people, and laid their hands upon her head. . . . ³⁶The elders said, "As we were walking in the garden alone, this woman came in with two maids, shut the garden doors, and dismissed the maids. ³⁷Then a young man, who had been hidden, came to her. . . . ³⁹We saw them embracing, but we could not hold the man, for he was too strong for us, and he opened the doors and dashed out. ⁴⁰So we seized this woman and asked her who the young man was, but she would not tell us. These things we testify."

41 The assembly believed them, because they were elders of the people and judges; and they condemned her to death.

42 Then Susanna cried out with a loud voice, and said, "O eternal God, who dost discern what is secret, who art aware of all things before they come to be, ⁴³thou knowest that these men have borne false witness against me. And now I am to die! Yet I have done none of the things that they have wickedly invented against me!" . . .

⁵¹And Daniel said to them, "Separate them [the witnesses] far from each other, and I will examine them."

52 When they were separated from each other, he summoned one of them and said to him, . . . ⁵⁴ "Now then, if you really saw her, tell me this: Under what tree did you see them being intimate with each other?" He answered, "Under a mastic tree." . . .

56 Then he put him aside, and commanded them to bring the other. And he said to him, ⁵⁸" . . . Tell me: Under what tree did you catch them . . . ?" He answered, "Under an evergreen oak." ⁵⁹And Daniel said to him, "Very well! You also have lied against your own head, for the angel of God is waiting with his sword to saw you in two, that he may destroy you both."

60 Then all the assembly shouted loudly and blessed God, who saves those who hope in him. ⁶¹And they rose against the two elders, for out of their own mouths Daniel had convicted them of bearing false witness; ⁶²and they did to them as they had wickedly planned to do to their neighbor; acting in accordance with the law of Moses, they put them to death. Thus innocent blood was saved that day.

LET'S PRAY!

Lord, you are my shield and my fortress. When I am in
trouble, Jesus I will trust in you! In the name of the Father,
and the Son, and the Holy Spirit, Amen!

GOING DEEPER:

Read It! CCC #572 (Jesus was betrayed by religious leaders).

Do It! When someone we love is sick or suffering, it helps
  our loved one to know that we are praying for him or her.
  Make a card or special treat for someone you know who
  needs a reminder of God's love this week.

Hosea and Gomer

Hosea 1:2–10

Hosea was from the northern kingdom (Israel) and ministered around the time of the fall of the northern capital, Samaria (about 721 BC). Idolatry was commonplace; the national god was a golden calf![24] But God sent Hosea to remind the people of his love for them—a love that did not cease even when they turned away from God, just as Hosea's wife turned away from her husband until his love for her drew her back to him.

When the LORD first spoke through Hosea, the LORD said to Hosea, "Go, take for yourself a wife of whoredom and have children of whoredom, for the land commits great whoredom by forsaking the LORD." ³So he went and took Gomer daughter of Diblaim, and she conceived and bore him a son.

4 And the LORD said to him, "Name him Jezreel; for in a little while I will punish the house of Jehu for the blood of Jezreel, and I will put an end to the kingdom of the house of Israel. ⁵On that day I will break the bow of Israel in the valley of Jezreel."

6 She conceived again and bore a daughter. Then the LORD said to him, "Name her Lo-ruhamah, for I will no longer have pity on the house of Israel or forgive them. ⁷But I will have pity on the house of Judah, and I will save them by the LORD their God; I will not save them by bow, or by sword, or by war, or by horses, or by horsemen."

8 When she had weaned Lo-ruhamah, she conceived and bore a son. ⁹Then the LORD said, "Name him Lo-ammi, for you are not my people and I am not your God."

10 Yet the number of the people of Israel shall be like the sand of the sea, which can be neither measured nor numbered; and in the place where it was said to them, "You are not my people," it shall be said to them, "Children of the living God."

LET'S PRAY!

Bless the LORD, O my soul,
    and all that is within me,
    bless his holy name.
² Bless the LORD, O my soul,
    and do not forget all his benefits—
³ who forgives all your iniquity,
    who heals all your diseases,
⁴ who redeems your life from the Pit,
    who crowns you with steadfast love
        and mercy,
⁵ who satisfies you with good as long as
        you live
    so that your youth is renewed like the
    eagle's.   —Psalm 103:1–5

SPECIAL WORDS: The names
of Hosea's children were
part of the prophetic message
of how God was going to deal
with Israel. Jezreel means "God
scatters." Lo-Ruhama means
"unloved." And Lo-Ammi
means "not my people."

GOING DEEPER:

Read It! In Hosea 2:16–22, we discover that the
relationship of Hosea and Gomer is very similar to
the relationship between God and His people at that
time.

Do It! Time and again God's people were unfaithful to
him just as we are sometimes unfaithful. Today as a
family, offer a prayer of thanksgiving for God's love,
which never fails.

Jonah

Jonah 1:1–7, 15–17

*I*n today's story, a man named Jonah tried to run away from God and from the job God had given him to do. God wanted Jonah to give the people of Nineveh a chance to repent of their sinful ways, and Jonah thought it would be better if God just destroyed them all! Instead of sailing for Nineveh, Jonah went the other way, until God caught up with him, that is!

Now the word of the LORD came to Jonah son of Amittai, saying, ²"Go at once to Nineveh, that great city, and cry out against it; for their wickedness has come up before me." ³But Jonah set out to flee to Tarshish from the presence of the LORD. He went down to Joppa and found a ship going to Tarshish; so he paid his fare and went on board, to go . . . away from the presence of the LORD.

4 But the LORD hurled a great wind upon the sea, and such a mighty storm came upon the sea that the ship threatened to break up. ⁵Then the mariners were afraid, and each cried to his god. They threw the cargo that was in the ship into the sea, to lighten it for them. Jonah, meanwhile, had gone down into the hold of the ship and had lain down, and was fast asleep. ⁶The captain came and said to him, "What are you doing sound asleep? Get up, call on your god! Perhaps the god will spare us a thought so that we do not perish."

7 The sailors said to one another, "Come, let us cast lots, so that we may know on whose account this calamity has come upon us." So they cast lots, and the lot fell on Jonah. . . .

¹⁵So they picked Jonah up and threw him into the sea; and the sea ceased from its raging. ¹⁶Then the men feared the LORD even more, and they offered a sacrifice to the LORD and made vows.

17 But the LORD provided a large fish to swallow up Jonah; and Jonah was in the belly of the fish three days and three nights.

LET'S PRAY!

Some went down to the sea in ships,
   doing business on the mighty waters;
²⁴ they saw the deeds of the LORD,
   his wondrous works in the deep.
²⁵ For he commanded and raised the
      stormy wind,
   which lifted up the waves of the sea. . . .
²⁸ Then they cried to the LORD in their
      trouble,
   and he brought them out from their
      distress;
²⁹ he made the storm be still,
   and the waves of the sea were hushed.
³⁰ Then they were glad because they had
      quiet,
   and he brought them to their desired
      haven. —Psalm 107:23–25, 28–30
Thank you, God, for saving us.

GOING DEEPER:

Read It! CCC #29 (God will not leave us, but we can leave God).
Do It! Family Movie Night! Watch the VeggieTales® movie *Jonah*.

Zechariah's Chariots
Zechariah 6:1–15

In this dramatic story, the four chariots represent the angelic hosts God sends to the four ends of the earth. The chariot with the black horses brings the Lord's anger to the land of Babylon for keeping his people so long in captivity and their idolatry. This vision comes before the Messianic prophecies of Zechariah 9; it is frequently associated with Palm Sunday.[25]

I looked up and saw four chariots coming out from between two mountains—mountains of bronze. [2]The first chariot had red horses, the second chariot black horses, [3]the third chariot white horses, and the fourth chariot dappled gray horses. [4]Then I said to the angel who talked with me, "What are these, my lord?" [5]The angel answered me, "These are the four winds of heaven going out, after presenting themselves before the Lord of all the earth. [6]The chariot with the black horses goes toward the north country, the white ones go toward the west country, and the dappled ones go toward the south country." [7]When the steeds came out, they were impatient to get off and patrol the earth. And he said, "Go, patrol the earth." So they patrolled the earth. [8]Then he cried out to me, "Lo, those who go toward the north country have set my spirit at rest in the north country."

[9] The word of the Lord came to me: [10]Collect silver and gold from the exiles—from Heldai, Tobijah, and Jedaiah—who have arrived from Babylon; and go the same day to the house of Josiah son of Zephaniah. [11]Take the silver and gold and make a crown, and set it on the head of the high priest Joshua son of Jehozadak; [12]say to him: Thus says the Lord of hosts: Here is a man whose name is Branch: for he shall branch out in his place, and he shall build the temple of the Lord. [13]It is he that shall build the temple of the Lord; he shall bear royal honor, and shall sit and rule on his throne. There shall be a priest by his throne, with peaceful understanding between the two of them. [14]And the crown shall be in the care of Heldai, Tobijah, Jedaiah, and Josiah son of Zephaniah, as a memorial in the temple of the Lord.

[15] Those who are far off shall come and help to build the temple of the Lord; and you shall know that the Lord of hosts has sent me to you. This will happen if you diligently obey the voice of the Lord your God.

Let's Pray!

Rejoice greatly, O daughter Zion!
Shout aloud, O daughter Jerusalem!
Lo, your king comes to you;
triumphant and victorious is he,
humble and riding on a donkey,
on a colt, the foal of a donkey.
—Zechariah 9:9

Going Deeper:

Read It! CCC #336 (The believer has an angel as protector and shepherd).
Do It! Make fancy paper crowns to celebrate the Prince of Peace!

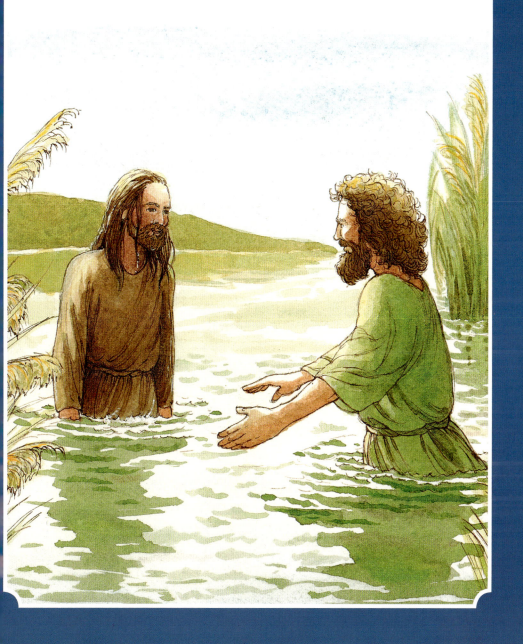

The Annunciation

Luke 1:26–38 RSV

*G*od's messenger, the angel Gabriel, was sent to Mary to tell her she was about to become the mother of the Word made flesh, the holy Son of God! The Lord had prepared Mary from all eternity for this special task, and her simple yes set in motion God's eternal plan to restore the human race, making us his adopted children. We call the miracle of Jesus' birth the "Incarnation" and the angel's appearance, the "Annunciation."

In the sixth month the angel Gabriel was sent from God to a city of Galilee named Nazareth, 27to a virgin betrothed to a man whose name was Joseph, of the house of David; and the virgin's name was Mary. 28And he came to her and said, "Hail, full of grace, the Lord is with you!" 29But she was greatly troubled at the saying, and considered in her mind what sort of greeting this might be. 30And the angel said to her, "Do not be afraid, Mary, for you have found favor with God. 31And behold, you will conceive in your womb and bear a son, and you shall call his name Jesus.

32 He will be great, and will be called the
   Son of the Most High;
  and the Lord God will give to him the
   throne of his father David,

33 and he will reign over the house of Jacob
   for ever;
  and of his kingdom there will be no end."

34And Mary said to the angel, "How shall this be, since I have no husband?" 35And the angel said to her,

"The Holy Spirit will come upon you,
  and the power of the Most High will
   overshadow you;
 therefore the child to be born will be
   called holy,
 the Son of God.

36And behold, your kinswoman Elizabeth in her old age has also conceived a son; and this is the sixth month with her who was called barren. 37For with God nothing will be impossible." 38AndMary said, "Behold, I am the handmaid of the Lord; let it be to me according to your word." And the angel departed from her.

Let's Pray!

Hail Mary

A Traditonal Catholic Prayer

Hail Mary, full of grace, the Lord is with thee! Blessed are thou among women, and blessed is the fruit of thy womb, Jesus. Holy Mary, Mother of God, pray for us sinners, now and at the hour of our death, Amen!

DID YOU KNOW? Mary's title
"Mother of God" (Theotokos)
was declared at the Council
of Ephesus (432 AD). The
Feast of Mary, Mother
of God is January 1.

GOING DEEPER:

Read It! This is the reading for AD 4B and the Feast
   of the Annunciation (March 25). CCC #488 (Mary
   was chosen from the beginning to be mother of
   Jesus); CCC #490–94 (These readings tell about the
   Immaculate Conception of Mary).

Do It! Make some angel sugar cookies!

THE ANGELUS

A Traditonal Catholic Prayer

The angel of the Lord declared unto Mary,
And she conceived of the Holy Spirit. Hail Mary . . .
Behold the handmaid of the Lord.
Be it done unto me as you have said. Hail Mary . . .
And the Word was made flesh
And dwelt among us. Hail Mary . . .
Pray for us, O Holy Mother of God,
That we may be made worthy of the promises of Christ.
Let us pray. "Pour forth, we beseech Thee, O Lord, Thy grace into
our hearts, that we to whom the Incarnation of Christ Thy Son
was made known by the message of an angel, may by His Passion
and Cross be brought to the glory of His Resurrection. Through
the same Christ Our Lord, Amen!"

Mary Visits Elizabeth
Luke 1:39–56

When the angel visited Mary, he also told her that her relative Elizabeth, even in her old age, was going to have a child as well. Mary went to visit Elizabeth. At long last, Elizabeth and Zechariah were going to have a child! And even more miraculous, so was she!

In those days Mary set out and went with haste to a Judean town in the hill country, ⁴⁰where she entered the house of Zechariah and greeted Elizabeth. ⁴¹When Elizabeth heard Mary's greeting, the child leaped in her womb. And Elizabeth was filled with the Holy Spirit ⁴²and exclaimed with a loud cry, "Blessed are you among women, and blessed is the fruit of your womb. ⁴³And why has this happened to me, that the mother of my Lord comes to me? ⁴⁴For as soon as I heard the sound of your greeting, the child in my womb leaped for joy. ⁴⁵And blessed is she who believed that there would be a fulfillment of what was spoken to her by the Lord."

46 And Mary said,
  "My soul magnifies the Lord,
⁴⁷ and my spirit rejoices in God my Savior,
⁴⁸ for he has looked with favor on the
    lowliness of his servant.
  Surely, from now on all generations
    will call me blessed;
⁴⁹ for the Mighty One has done great things
    for me,
  and holy is his name.
⁵⁰ His mercy is for those who fear him
    from generation to generation.
⁵¹ He has shown strength with his arm;
  he has scattered the proud in the
    thoughts of their hearts.

⁵² He has brought down the powerful from
    their thrones,
  and lifted up the lowly;
⁵³ he has filled the hungry with good things,
  and sent the rich away empty.
⁵⁴ He has helped his servant Israel,
  in remembrance of his mercy,
⁵⁵ according to the promise he made to our
    ancestors,
  to Abraham and to his descendants
    forever."

56 And Mary remained with her about three months and then returned to her home.

Let's Pray!
The Angelus
A Traditonal Catholic Prayer

The angel of the Lord declared unto Mary,
  And she conceived of the Holy Spirit.
Hail Mary . . .
  Behold the handmaid of the Lord.
  Be it done unto me as you have said. Hail Mary . . .
  And the Word was made flesh
  And dwelt among us. Hail Mary . . .
  Pray for us, O Holy Mother of God,
  That we may be made worthy of the promises of Christ.
  Let us pray. "Pour forth, we beseech Thee, O Lord, Thy grace into our hearts, that we

to whom the Incarnation of Christ Thy Son was made known by the message of an angel, may by His Passion and Cross be brought to the glory of His Resurrection. Through the same Christ Our Lord, Amen!"

GOING DEEPER:

Read It! This is the gospel reading for the Feast of the Assumption B, on August 15 and AD 4C. The first reading is Revelation 12:1–6, 10. See also CCC #2676 (The "Hail Mary").

Do It! Create your own Rosary Book, with pictures cut from cards or magazines, or hand drawn, to illustrate the Joyful, Sorrowful, Luminous, and Glorious Mysteries.

Joseph Sees an Angel
Matthew 1:18–25

Mary was a teenager, not yet married, when the angel appeared. Her future husband's name was Joseph. How surprised he must have been when he heard that Mary was going to have a child! But the angel came to him and assured him that this child was from God.

Now the birth of Jesus the Messiah took place in this way. When his mother Mary had been engaged to Joseph, but before they lived together, she was found to be with child from the Holy Spirit. [19] Her husband Joseph, being a righteous man and unwilling to expose her to public disgrace, planned to dismiss her quietly. [20] But just when he had resolved to do this, an angel of the Lord appeared to him in a dream and said, "Joseph, son of David, do not be afraid to take Mary as your wife, for the child conceived in her is from the Holy Spirit. [21] She will bear a son, and you are to name him Jesus, for he will save his people from their sins." [22] All this took place to fulfill what had been spoken by the Lord through the prophet:

[23] "Look, the virgin shall conceive and
        bear a son,
    and they shall name him Emmanuel,"
which means, "God is with us."
[24] When Joseph awoke from sleep, he did as the angel of the Lord commanded him; he took her as his wife, [25] but had no marital relations with her until she had borne a son; and he named him Jesus.

Let's Pray!

Lord Jesus, all Your life You honored St. Joseph, who taught You by his own example to be a man. Help us to do the right thing, even when it is hard—just as St. Joseph did. In the name of the Father, and the Son, and the Holy Spirit, Amen!

Going Deeper:

Read It! This is the gospel on the Feast of St. Joseph (March 19); the first reading is 2 Samuel 7:4–16. It is also read during Christmas Vigil (A–C); CCC #510. (With her whole being, Mary was always a handmaid of the Lord).

Do It! St. Joseph is the patron saint of families, fathers, carpenters, and the nation of China! Order some Chinese take-out tonight (with chopsticks!) in honor of St. Joseph.

The Birth of Jesus
Luke 2:1–16 RSV

O little town of Bethlehem, how still we see thee lie." Each year at Christmas we celebrate the birthday of Jesus, the divine Child who made angels sing, stars shine, and shepherds leave their sheep. Let's listen to the story of the very first Christmas.

In those days a decree went out from Caesar Augustus that all the world should be enrolled. ²This was the first enrollment, when Quirinius was governor of Syria. ³And all went to be enrolled, each to his own city. ⁴And Joseph also went up from Galilee, from the city of Nazareth, to Judea, to the city of David, which is called Bethlehem, because he was of the house and lineage of David, ⁵to be enrolled with Mary his betrothed, who was with child. ⁶And while they were there, the time came for her to be delivered. ⁷And she gave birth to her firstborn son and wrapped him in swaddling cloths, and laid him in a manger, because there was no place for them in the inn.

8 And in that region there were shepherds out in the field, keeping watch over their flock by night. ⁹And an angel of the Lord appeared to them, and the glory of the Lord shone around them, and they were filled with fear. ¹⁰And the angel said to them, "Be not afraid; for behold, I bring you good news of a great joy which will come to all the people; ¹¹for to you is born this day in the city of David a Savior, who is Christ the Lord. ¹²And this will be a sign for you: you will find a babe wrapped in swaddling cloths and lying in a manger." ¹³And suddenly there was with the angel a multitude of the heavenly host praising God and saying,

¹⁴ "Glory to God in the highest,
   and on earth peace among men with
      whom he is pleased!"

15 When the angels went away from them into heaven, the shepherds said to one another, "Let us go over to Bethlehem and see this thing that has happened, which the Lord has made known to us." ¹⁶And they went with haste, and found Mary and Joseph, and the babe lying in a manger.

Let's Pray!

Dear Jesus, thank you for being born into our world as one of us. Help us to be like the shepherds and come with haste to worship you. Amen.

GOING DEEPER:

Read It! This is the gospel reading for the Christmas Midnight Mass (A, B, C); the first reading is Isaiah 9:1–6; CCC #426 (To catechize is to put people in communion with Christ).

Do It! Make Christmas cookies, even if it's July!

Simeon and Anna

Luke 2:25–38

Most Catholic children are baptized when they are very small. In the time of Christ, male infants were circumcised at eight days of age. Forty days after the birth, parents went to the temple and offered a sacrifice according to what they could afford. Poor families offered two turtledoves. When Mary and Joseph brought Jesus to the temple, the elderly Simeon and Anna were there, as they had been every day for decades, and they rejoiced that they were finally seeing God's promise fulfilled.

Now there was a man in Jerusalem whose name was Simeon; this man was righteous and devout, looking forward to the consolation of Israel, and the Holy Spirit rested on him. 26It had been revealed to him by the Holy Spirit that he would not see death before he had seen the Lord's Messiah. 27Guided by the Spirit, Simeon came into the temple; and when the parents brought in the child Jesus, to do for him what was customary under the law, 28Simeon took him in his arms and praised God, saying,

29 "Master, now you are dismissing your
　　　　servant in peace,
　　according to your word;
30 for my eyes have seen your salvation,
31　　which you have prepared in the
　　　　presence of all peoples,
32 a light for revelation to the Gentiles
　　and for glory to your people Israel."

33 And the child's father and mother were amazed at what was being said about him. 34Then Simeon blessed them and said to his mother Mary, "This child is destined for the falling and the rising of many in Israel, and to be a sign that will be opposed 35so that the inner thoughts of many will be revealed—and a sword will pierce your own soul too."

36 There was also a prophet, Anna the daughter of Phanuel, of the tribe of Asher. She was of a great age, having lived with her husband seven years after her marriage, 37then as a widow to the age of eighty-four. She never left the temple but worshiped there with fasting and prayer night and day. 38At that moment she came, and began to praise God and to speak about the child to all who were looking for the redemption of Jerusalem.

LET'S PRAY!
Nunc Dimittis
Canticle of Simeon, Fourth Century

"Now dismiss Thy servant, Lord, in peace, according to Thy word.

For mine eyes have seen Thy salvation, which Thou hast prepared

Which Thou hast prepared in the sight of all peoples

A light to reveal to the nations and the glory of Thy people Israel. Amen."

GOING DEEPER:

Read It! This passage is read on the Feast of the Presentation (B), with the first reading of Malachi 3:1–4; CCC #527–29 (Circumcision is a sign of baptism to come; Jesus is seen to be the long-expected Messiah).

Do It! Light a candle in church this week and ask God to bless your family in the coming year.

The Magi

Matthew 2:1–5, 7–12

Sometime between the age of forty days and two years old, the Christ child received some very special visitors at the Holy Family's home in Nazareth: Wise men brought gifts, including gold (for royalty), incense (for priesthood), and myrrh (foretelling Jesus' death).

In the time of King Herod, after Jesus was born in Bethlehem of Judea, wise men from the East came to Jerusalem, ²asking, "Where is the child who has been born king of the Jews? For we observed his star at its rising, and have come to pay him homage." ³When King Herod heard this, he was frightened, and all Jerusalem with him; ⁴and calling together all the chief priests and scribes of the people, he inquired of them where the Messiah was to be born. ⁵They told him, "In Bethlehem of Judea. . . ."

7 Then Herod secretly called for the wise men and learned from them the exact time when the star had appeared. ⁸Then he sent them to Bethlehem, saying, "Go and search diligently for the child; and when you have found him, bring me word so that I may also go and pay him homage." ⁹When they had heard the king, they set out; and there, ahead of them, went the star that they had seen at its rising, until it stopped over the place where the child was. ¹⁰When they saw that the star had stopped, they were overwhelmed with joy. ¹¹On entering the house, they saw the child with Mary his mother; and they knelt down and paid him homage. Then, opening their treasure chests, they offered him gifts of gold, frankincense, and myrrh. ¹²And having been warned in a dream not to return to Herod, they left for their own country by another road.

LET'S PRAY!

As the Magi brought gifts to Jesus, so do we bring the gifts in our lives to your service. Please use us that others may come and know you. Amen.

SPECIAL WORDS: Magi were a Persian priestly class, who were regarded to have supernatural knowledge. The men in this story—traditionally three but likely more than that were in the entourage—were astrologers.[28]

GOING DEEPER:

Read It! This is the gospel for the Feast of Epiphany, with a first reading of Isaiah 60:1–6. See also CCC #528 (The feast of Epiphany celebrates the adoration of Jesus by the wise men).

Do It! In some homes, gifts are exchanged on Epiphany rather than Christmas, to celebrate the arrival of the Magi. Bake a special "King's Cake" that is made with little gold coins hidden inside.

Flight into Egypt
Matthew 2:13–16, 19–23

*W*hen Israel was a child, I loved him, and out of Egypt I called my son" (Hosea 11:1). These words from the prophet Hosea remind us that God had control over the life story of his Son long before the Incarnation. Wicked kings, wise visitors, dreams and visions—everything came together to create a real-life drama, a way of escape for the Holy Family.

Now after they had left, an angel of the Lord appeared to Joseph in a dream and said, "Get up, take the child and his mother, and flee to Egypt, and remain there until I tell you; for Herod is about to search for the child, to destroy him." ¹⁴Then Joseph got up, took the child and his mother by night, and went to Egypt, ¹⁵and remained there until the death of Herod. This was to fulfill what had been spoken by the Lord through the prophet, "Out of Egypt I have called my son."

16 When Herod saw that he had been tricked by the wise men, he was infuriated, and he sent and killed all the children in and around Bethlehem who were two years old or under, according to the time that he had learned from the wise men. . . .

19 When Herod died, an angel of the Lord suddenly appeared in a dream to Joseph in Egypt and said, ²⁰"Get up, take the child and his mother, and go to the land of Israel, for those who were seeking the child's life are dead." ²¹Then Joseph got up, took the child and his mother, and went to the land of Israel. . . . And after being warned in a dream, he went away to the district of Galilee. ²³There he made his home in a town called Nazareth, so that what had been spoken through the prophets might be fulfilled, "He will be called a Nazorean."

LET'S PRAY!
Prayer for Charity
A Traditonal Catholic Prayer

O my Jesus, Thou who art very Love,
 enkindle in my heart that Divine Fire
 which consumes the Saints and
 transforms them into Thee.
O Lord our God,
 we offer Thee our hearts
 united in the strongest and most sincere
 love of brotherhood;
we pray that Jesus in the Blessed
 Sacrament may be the daily food of our
 souls and bodies;
that Jesus may be established as the center
 of our affections, even as He was for
 Mary and Joseph.
Finally, O Lord, may sin never disturb our
 union on earth; and may we be eternally
 united in heaven with Thee and Mary
 and Joseph and with all Thy Saints.
Amen.

Read It! This is the gospel for the Feast of the Holy Family (A, B, C), with a first reading of Genesis 15:1–6. See also CCC #530 (Joseph and Mary's trip into Egypt and Herod's killing of innocent children shows the difference between good and evil).

Do It! God created families to take care of one another. Have each family member choose a way to care for other members of the family this week.

DID YOU KNOW? Egypt was a traditional place of refuge for those escaping persecution in Palestine; the journey of the Holy Family recalled the trail of the Exodus.[29]

Joseph and Mary Find Jesus
Luke 2:39–52

*A*fter a year in Egypt, the Holy Family returned to Nazareth. We don't know much about the life of Jesus, Mary, and Joseph during the years that followed. Jesus may have helped Joseph in his carpenter's shop and played with children in the village. The Scriptures say very little except for one incident in the life of Christ, when he was twelve and his parents took him to the temple in Jerusalem.

When they had finished everything required by the law of the Lord, they returned to Galilee, to their own town of Nazareth. 40The child grew and became strong, filled with wisdom; and the favor of God was upon him.

41 Now every year his parents went to Jerusalem for the festival of the Passover. 42And when he was twelve years old, they went up as usual for the festival. 43When the festival was ended and they started to return, the boy Jesus stayed behind in Jerusalem, but his parents did not know it. 44Assuming that he was in the group of travelers, they went a day's journey. Then they started to look for him among their relatives and friends. 45When they did not find him, they returned to Jerusalem to search for him. 46After three days they found him in the temple, sitting among the teachers, listening to them and asking them questions. 47And all who heard him were amazed at his understanding and his answers. 48When his parents saw him they were astonished; and his mother said to him, "Child, why have you treated us like this? Look, your father and I have been searching for you in great anxiety." 49He said to them, "Why were you searching for me? Did you not know that I must be in my Father's house?" 50But they did not understand what he said to them. 51Then he went down with them and came to Nazareth, and was obedient to them. His mother treasured all these things in her heart.

52 And Jesus increased in wisdom and in years, and in divine and human favor.

LET'S PRAY!
Thank you, God, that even when we feel lost, we are never far from your love. Thank you for parents who care enough to keep us on the straight and narrow way. In the name of the Father, and the Son, and the Holy Spirit, Amen!

QUOTE OF THE DAY: "Obedience
is the only virtue that
implants the other virtues in the
heart and preserves them after
they are so implanted."
—Pope Gregory the Great

GOING DEEPER:

Read It! CCC #533–34 (The hidden life of Jesus in
  Nazareth lets everyone have fellowship with him in
  ordinary daily life).

Do It! Do you have trouble obeying Mom and Dad, the
  first time they ask? Create a jar labeled "Make Mom
  Smile!" Have her drop a coin in it each time you make
  a good choice and obey the first time. At the end of the
  week, if there is enough money, go out for a treat so you
  can smile together!

John Baptizes Jesus
Matthew 3:13–17

John the Baptist, Elizabeth's son, who jumped for joy at the sound of Mary's voice even before he was born, grew up to be a great prophet of God. His job was to "prepare the way," to get the people ready to receive the message of Jesus. "I baptize you with water," John told his followers, "but one who is more powerful than I is coming. . . . He will baptize you with the Holy Spirit and fire" (Luke 3:16). In today's story, this prophecy came true!

Then Jesus came from Galilee to John at the Jordan, to be baptized by him. ¹⁴John would have prevented him, saying, "I need to be baptized by you, and do you come to me?" ¹⁵But Jesus answered him, "Let it be so now; for it is proper for us in this way to fulfill all righteousness." Then he consented. ¹⁶And when Jesus had been baptized, just as he came up from the water, suddenly the heavens were opened to him and he saw the Spirit of God descending like a dove and alighting on him. ¹⁷And a voice from heaven said, "This is my Son, the Beloved, with whom I am well pleased."

LET'S PRAY!

Just as John the Baptist obeyed God even when he didn't understand the reason for it, we pray that we might be willing to and able to obey God without questioning why.

GOING DEEPER:

Read It! This is the gospel for the Feast of the Presentation of the Lord (OT 1A, B, C); the first reading is Isaiah 42:1–7. See also CCC #535–37 (Jesus' public life begins with his baptism by John in the Jordan River).

Do It! Look at your baptism pictures with your parents, and let them tell you what they remember about that day.

Temptation in the Desert

Matthew 4:1—11

I dare you!" Have you ever said this to another kid, when you wanted to get him to do something you both knew he shouldn't? In today's story, Satan waited until Jesus was hungry and tired, after Jesus had been fasting in the wilderness for forty days. Then he tempted the Lord, daring him to do things they both knew he shouldn't. Three times the evil one attacked, and three times Jesus responded with the truth: "It is written!"

Then Jesus was led up by the Spirit into the wilderness to be tempted by the devil. ²He fasted forty days and forty nights, and afterwards he was famished. ³The tempter came and said to him, "If you are the Son of God, command these stones to become loaves of bread." ⁴But he answered, "It is written,

'One does not live by bread alone,
but by every word that comes from the mouth of God.'"

5   Then the devil took him to the holy city and placed him on the pinnacle of the temple, ⁶saying to him, "If you are the Son of God, throw yourself down; for it is written,

'He will command his angels concerning you,'
and 'On their hands they will bear you up,
so that you will not dash your foot against a stone.'"

⁷Jesus said to him, "Again it is written, 'Do not put the Lord your God to the test.'"

8   Again, the devil took him to a very high mountain and showed him all the kingdoms of the world and their splendor; ⁹and he said to him, "All these I will give you, if you will fall down and worship me." ¹⁰Jesus said to him, "Away with you, Satan! for it is written,

'Worship the Lord your God,
and serve only him.'"

¹¹Then the devil left him, and suddenly angels came and waited on him.

LET'S PRAY!

Pray the "Our Father." Take a moment to think about the end of the prayer after you say, "Lead us not into temptation, but deliver us from evil."

GOING DEEPER:

Read It! See CCC #538–40 (By not giving in to the temptations, Jesus showed himself as God's servant, totally obedient to God).

Do It! Lent begins with Ash Wednesday. Go as a family to receive ashes! If it isn't Lent yet, make this a day of prayer and fasting and providing for those who are hungry. Take canned goods to a local food bank or serve as a family at a local soup kitchen.

Sermon on the Mount

Matthew 5:3–12

As Jesus and his followers traveled from Galilee throughout Judea, the crowds began to grow as word spread about Jesus' miracles and his wisdom. The following is from the "Sermon on the Mount," a series of teachings that the Lord gave to his followers during this early period of his ministry. These "Beatitudes," as they are called, are a map for basic Christian living.

"Blessed are the poor in spirit, for theirs is the kingdom of heaven.

4 Blessed are those who mourn, for they will be comforted.

5 Blessed are the meek, for they will inherit the earth.

6 Blessed are those who hunger and thirst for righteousness, for they will be filled.

7 Blessed are the merciful, for they will receive mercy.

8 Blessed are the pure in heart, for they will see God.

9 Blessed are the peacemakers, for they will be called children of God.

10 Blessed are those who are persecuted for righteousness' sake, for theirs is the kingdom of heaven.

11 Blessed are you when people revile you and persecute you and utter all kinds of evil against you falsely on my account. 12 Rejoice and be glad, for your reward is great in heaven, for in the same way they persecuted the prophets who were before you."

LET'S PRAY!

Light rises in the darkness for the upright;
  the LORD is gracious, merciful, and
    righteous.
5 It is well with the man who deals
    generously and lends,
  who conducts his affairs with justice.
6 For the righteous will never be moved;
  he will be remembered for ever.
7 He is not afraid of evil tidings;
  his heart is firm, trusting in the LORD.
—Psalm 112:4–7 RSV

Father, we thank you for your grace. Help us to be righteous and trust you.

GOING DEEPER:

Read It! See CCC #1720 (This is about the Christian Beatitude). (Note: This is also the gospel reading for the Feasts of All Saints and All Souls).

Do It! Is there someone who "persecutes you for righteousness' sake"? What can you do this week to bless that person?

A Light on a Hill

Matthew 5:13—22

*J*esus challenged his followers to do everything out of love for God. He didn't want Christians to just go through the motions, doing things just to win the approval of other people. "Let your light shine before others," Jesus reminds us today, "so that they may see your good works and give glory to your Father in heaven! (Matthew 5:16)." This light is the love of God, which warms our hearts and helps us to care even for the people who are hardest to love.

"You are the salt of the earth; but if salt has lost its taste, how can its saltiness be restored? It is no longer good for anything, but is thrown out and trampled under foot. 14 "You are the light of the world. A city built on a hill cannot be hid. ¹⁵No one after lighting a lamp puts it under the bushel basket, but on the lampstand, and it gives light to all in the house. ¹⁶In the same way, let your light shine before others, so that they may see your good works and give glory to your Father in heaven.

17 "Do not think that I have come to abolish the law or the prophets; I have come not to abolish but to fulfill. ¹⁸For truly I tell you, until heaven and earth pass away, not one letter, not one stroke of a letter, will pass from the law until all is accomplished. ¹⁹Therefore, whoever breaks one of the least of these commandments, and teaches others to do the same, will be called least in the kingdom of heaven; but whoever does them and teaches them will be called great in the kingdom of heaven. ²⁰For I tell you, unless your righteousness exceeds that of the scribes and Pharisees, you will never enter the kingdom of heaven.

21 "You have heard that it was said to those of ancient times, 'You shall not murder'; and 'whoever murders shall be liable to judgment.' ²²But I say to you that if you are angry with a brother or sister, you will be liable to judgment; and if you insult a brother or sister, you will be liable to the council; and if you say, 'You fool,' you will be liable to the hell of fire."

LET'S PRAY!

Glory Be

A Traditonal Catholic Prayer

Glory be to the Father, and to the Son, and to the Holy Spirit! As it was in the beginning, is now and shall be forever, world without end. Amen.

Did You Know? Just like
our bodies need water
and oxygen to survive,
they also need salt!

GOING DEEPER:

Read It! This is the gospel reading for OT 5A; the first
reading is Isaiah 58:7–10. Read CCC #551 (Jesus chose
twelve men to help him in his mission).

Do It! Can you name all of the apostles? (There are
fourteen, including the apostle to the Gentiles and the
one who replaced Judas.)

Wedding at Cana

John 2:1–12

Once upon a time, there was a beautiful bride and a happy groom. Their families had prepared a great feast that would last for many days. They invited Jesus, his mother, Mary, and his disciples. For days everyone had a great time, eating and drinking and laughing. Then suddenly the man in charge of the party looked very serious. When Mary heard what the problem was, she knew just what to do.

On the third day there was a wedding in Cana of Galilee, and the mother of Jesus was there. 2Jesus and his disciples had also been invited to the wedding. 3When the wine gave out, the mother of Jesus said to him, "They have no wine." 4And Jesus said to her, "Woman, what concern is that to you and to me? My hour has not yet come." 5His mother said to the servants, "Do whatever he tells you." 6Now standing there were six stone water jars for the Jewish rites of purification, each holding twenty or thirty gallons. 7Jesus said to them, "Fill the jars with water." And they filled them up to the brim. 8He said to them, "Now draw some out, and take it to the chief steward." So they took it. 9When the steward tasted the water that had become wine, and did not know where it came from (though the servants who had drawn the water knew), the steward called the bridegroom 10and said to him, "Everyone serves the good wine first, and then the inferior wine after the guests have become drunk. But you have kept the good wine until now." 11Jesus did this, the first of his signs, in Cana of Galilee, and revealed his glory; and his disciples believed in him.

12 After this he went down to Capernaum with his mother, his brothers, and his disciples; and they remained there a few days.

LET'S PRAY!

You are our Bridegroom, we are your bride. Lord Jesus, help us to get ready for that great wedding feast of heaven! In the name of the Father, and the Son, and the Holy Spirit, Amen!

GOING DEEPER:

Read It! The corresponding reading for this passage (OT 2C) is Isaiah 62:1–5; CCC #2618 (Mary intercedes in faith).

Do It! Look at your parents' wedding album, and listen to stories about their wedding. Did any "small miracles" happen that day for them?

GLORY BE

A Traditonal Catholic Prayer

Glory be to the Father, and to the Son,

and to the Holy Spirit

As it was in the beginning,

is now and ever shall be,

world without end, Amen.

HAIL MARY

A Traditonal Catholic Prayer

Hail Mary, full of grace, the Lord is with thee.

Blessed are thou among women, and blessed

is the fruit of thy womb, Jesus.

Holy Mary, Mother of God, pray for us sinners,

now and at the hour of our death, Amen!

Jesus Clears the Temple
John 2:13–25

God commanded that we "remember the sabbath day and keep it holy" (Exodus 20:8). We keep the sabbath by going to Mass each week—dressing neatly, praying and singing with the rest of God's people, and listening carefully to the readings and the homily. In today's story, Jesus saw a group of people misusing God's house, dishonoring his heavenly Father. What do you suppose he did?

The Passover of the Jews was near, and Jesus went up to Jerusalem. [14]In the temple he found people selling cattle, sheep, and doves, and the money changers seated at their tables. [15]Making a whip of cords, he drove all of them out of the temple, both the sheep and the cattle. He also poured out the coins of the money changers and overturned their tables. [16]He told those who were selling the doves, "Take these things out of here! Stop making my Father's house a marketplace!" [17]His disciples remembered that it was written, "Zeal for your house will consume me." [18]The Jews then said to him, "What sign can you show us for doing this?" [19]Jesus answered them, "Destroy this temple, and in three days I will raise it up." [20]The Jews then said, "This temple has been under construction for forty-six years, and will you raise it up in three days?" [21]But he was speaking of the temple of his body. [22]After he was raised from the dead, his disciples remembered that he had said this; and they believed the scripture and the word that Jesus had spoken.

23 When he was in Jerusalem during the Passover festival, many believed in his name because they saw the signs that he was doing. [24]But Jesus on his part would not entrust himself to them, because he knew all people [25]and needed no one to testify about anyone; for he himself knew what was in everyone.

LET'S PRAY!

The law of the LORD is perfect,
 reviving the soul;
The decrees of the LORD are sure,
  making wise the simple . . .
[9] the fear of the LORD is pure,
 enduring forever;
the ordinances of the LORD are true,
 and righteous altogether.
[10] More to be desired are they than gold,
 even much fine gold;
sweeter also than honey,
 and drippings of the honeycomb.
—Psalm 19:7, 9–11

SPECIAL WORDS:
Money changers were there to exchange Roman currency (which had the image of Caesar and could not be used to pay the temple tax). Every Jewish male over nineteen had to pay the half shekel in Tyrian currency.[30]

GOING DEEPER:

Read It! The corresponding reading for this story (LE 3B) is Exodus 20:1–17; also read CCC #583–86 (Jesus showed respect for the temple).

Do It! How can we show greater respect for God's house this week?

A Nighttime Visit
John 3:1–12

Although Jesus had many people following him, hoping for a miracle, not everyone believed Jesus was the Messiah God had promised. Almost from the beginning of his ministry Jesus had powerful enemies among the Jewish leaders. And yet, he also had a handful of "secret believers." These men, for some reason, did not publicly follow Christ, yet they admired him and thought about what he said. Today's story is about one such man.

Now there was a Pharisee named Nicodemus, a leader of the Jews. ²He came to Jesus by night and said to him, "Rabbi, we know that you are a teacher who has come from God; for no one can do these signs that you do apart from the presence of God." ³Jesus answered him, "Very truly, I tell you, no one can see the kingdom of God without being born from above." ⁴Nicodemus said to him, "How can anyone be born after having grown old? Can one enter a second time into the mother's womb and be born?" ⁵Jesus answered, "Very truly, I tell you, no one can enter the kingdom of God without being born of water and Spirit. ⁶What is born of the flesh is flesh, and what is born of the Spirit is spirit. ⁷Do not be astonished that I said to you, 'You must be born from above.' ⁸The wind blows where it chooses, and you hear the sound of it, but you do not know where it comes from or where it goes. So it is with everyone who is born of the Spirit." ⁹Nicodemus said to him, "How can these things be?" ¹⁰Jesus answered him, "Are you a teacher of Israel, and yet you do not understand these things?

11 "Very truly, I tell you, we speak of what we know and testify to what we have seen; yet you do not receive our testimony. ¹²If I have told you about earthly things and you do not believe, how can you believe if I tell you about heavenly things?"

Let's Pray!

Lord, it was Nicodemus who first heard the famous words "God so loved the world that he gave his only Son, so that everyone who believes in him may not perish but may have eternal life" (John 3:16). Jesus, I believe in you! Amen.

GOING DEEPER:

Read It! Please read CCC #505 (Jesus is our brother through adoption).

Do It! Talk together about some ways you can share your faith with someone who doesn't know Jesus.

The Woman at the Well

John 4:3–14

*I*n the summertime, as the sun creeps high in the sky, people often try to stay cool by going inside or seeking out a shady spot. When it's very hot, we tend to slow down, drink lots of water, and cover up to prevent sunburn. But in today's story, a Samaritan woman chose the very hottest part of the day to lug her water pitcher down to the village well. She was trying to avoid the crowds since the people weren't very kind to her. Then she met Jesus, and she couldn't wait to tell everyone what had happened!

[Jesus] left Judea and started back to Galilee. 4But he had to go through Samaria. 5So he came to a Samaritan city called Sychar, near the plot of ground that Jacob had given to his son Joseph. 6Jacob's well was there, and Jesus, tired out by his journey, was sitting by the well. It was about noon.

7 A Samaritan woman came to draw water, and Jesus said to her, "Give me a drink." 8(His disciples had gone to the city to buy food.) 9The Samaritan woman said to him, "How is it that you, a Jew, ask a drink of me, a woman of Samaria?" (Jews do not share things in common with Samaritans.) 10Jesus answered her, "If you knew the gift of God, and who it is that is saying to you, 'Give me a drink,' you would have asked him, and he would have given you living water." 11The woman said to him, "Sir, you have no bucket, and the well is deep. Where do you get that living water? 12Are you greater than our ancestor Jacob, who gave us the well, and with his sons and his flocks drank from it?" 13Jesus said to her, "Everyone who drinks of this water will be thirsty again, 14but those who drink of the water that I will give them will never be thirsty. The water that I will give will become in them a spring of water gushing up to eternal life."

LET'S PRAY!

Prayer of an Indian Christian

O tree of Calvary, send your roots deep
    down into my heart.
Gather together the soil of my heart,
The sands of my fickleness,
The mud of my desires.
Bind them all together, O tree of Calvary,
Interlace them with thy strong roots,
Entwine them with the network of thy
    love.[32]

SPECIAL WORDS: "Living water"
refers to the Holy Spirit.

DID YOU KNOW? Jacob's Well
remains the center of Samaritan
worship today. At one hundred
feet deep and nine feet across,
it is one of the few places in
the life of Jesus that can be
readily identified.[33]

GOING DEEPER:

Read It! Read CCC #2652 (The Holy Spirit is living water).

Do It! The Samaritans believed they were worshipping
the same God as the Jews, even though some of their
beliefs were very different. Notice that Jesus did not
criticize the woman at the well for her beliefs; he
simply spoke to her about what she needed. What can
we learn from this in our dealings with other brothers
and sisters in Christ?

Jesus Teaches His Disciples to Pray

Matthew 6:5–18

Do you talk to God in prayer before you go to bed at night or when you wake up each morning or before meals? Some people just rattle through their prayers quickly without really thinking about what they are saying, or to whom they are speaking. Imagine driving to your grandma's house, running inside to her favorite chair, shouting "Hi, Grandma! How are you? I'm fine. Bye!" and then running back to your car again. She would wonder what was wrong!

We show our love for Grandma by taking time to speak from the heart, and listening for her answer. We show God we love him when we think about what we are saying to him and when we sit quietly in his presence to give him a chance to speak to our hearts. Whether the words are our own (extemporaneous prayer), or whether we borrow someone else's (rote prayer), it's important to make the words our own by thinking about the One who hears them. This is what Jesus had in mind when he warned the people about "empty phrases."

"And whenever you pray, do not be like the hypocrites; for they love to stand and pray in the synagogues and at the street corners, so that they may be seen by others. Truly I tell you, they have received their reward. ⁶But whenever you pray, go into your room and shut the door and pray to your Father who is in secret; and your Father who sees in secret will reward you.

7 "When you are praying, do not heap up empty phrases as the Gentiles do; for they think that they will be heard because of their many words. ⁸Do not be like them, for your Father knows what you need before you ask him.

9 "Pray then in this way:
Our Father in heaven,
hallowed be your name.
¹⁰ Your kingdom come.
Your will be done,
on earth as it is in heaven.
¹¹ Give us this day our daily bread.

¹² And forgive us our debts,
as we also have forgiven our debtors.
¹³ And do not bring us to the time of trial,
but rescue us from the evil one.
¹⁴For if you forgive others their trespasses, your heavenly Father will also forgive you; ¹⁵but if you do not forgive others, neither will your Father forgive your trespasses.

16 "And whenever you fast, do not look dismal, like the hypocrites, for they disfigure their faces so as to show others that they are fasting. Truly I tell you, they have received their reward. ¹⁷But when you fast, put oil on your head and wash your face, ¹⁸so that your fasting may be seen not by others but by your Father who is in secret; and your Father who sees in secret will reward you."

LET'S PRAY!

Father, thank you for teaching us to pray. Help us to enter into this time of communion with you daily. Amen.

GOING DEEPER:

Read It! CCC #2779–2803 (Conversion is necessary for the true prayer of faith).

Do It! Rote prayers are prayers that you "borrow" from someone else. What is your favorite rote prayer? The Hail Mary? The Our Father? The Prayer to the Holy Spirit? Today, turn your favorite prayer into a card, and send it to your grandma or other relative. (Don't forget to add your own little message from the heart!)

Don't Worry!

Matthew 6:24–33

Can you think of a time when you were worried, about a test perhaps? Were you so afraid you wouldn't do well, that you couldn't think of anything else? When we let fear take over our lives like this, we miss out on the happiness God wants us to have. However, if we practice common sense and do our best to study for that test, for example, and leave the outcome in God's hands, nothing can take away our joy!

"No one can serve two masters; for a slave will either hate the one and love the other, or be devoted to the one and despise the other. You cannot serve God and wealth.

25"Therefore I tell you, do not worry about your life, what you will eat or what you will drink, or about your body, what you will wear. Is not life more than food, and the body more than clothing? 26Look at the birds of the air; they neither sow nor reap nor gather into barns, and yet your heavenly Father feeds them. Are you not of more value than they? 27And can any of you by worrying add a single hour to your span of life? 28And why do you worry about clothing? Consider the lilies of the field, how they grow; they neither toil nor spin, 29yet I tell you, even Solomon in all his glory was not clothed like one of these. 30But if God so clothes the grass of the field, which is alive today and tomorrow is thrown into the oven, will he not much more clothe you—you of little faith? 31Therefore do not worry, saying, 'What will we eat?' or 'What will we drink?' or 'What will we wear?' 32For it is the Gentiles who strive for all these things; and indeed your heavenly Father knows that you need all these things. 33But strive first for the kingdom of God and his righteousness, and all these things will be given to you as well."

LET'S PRAY!

Thank you Father, for taking care of our every need. When we are tempted to worry, remind us of your faithfulness. Amen.

SPECIAL WORDS: "Gentiles"
in this passage refers to those
who don't know God.

QUOTE OF THE DAY: "By the
anxieties and worries of this
life Satan tries to dull man's
heart and make a dwelling
for himself there."
—St. Francis of Assisi

GOING DEEPER:

Read It! The reading today (OT 8A) is Isaiah 49:14–15; CCC #1942 (The virtue of solidarity is more than material goods).

Do It! Make a prayer journal! Sometimes we get in the habit of worry because we forget to ask God to help us or we don't think about all the times he has helped us. Create a small, blank book that your family can use to record your prayers and leave your worries with God. Don't forget to leave a space to record how God answered those prayers!

Jesus Heals the Official's Son
John 4:46—54

*T*hink of a time when you were sick. What did your parents do to help you feel better? Did they take you to the doctor and get you medicine, or did they bring you chicken soup or ice pops? Parents love their children, and they do everything they can to keep them healthy. In today's story, a rich man with a sick son heard about Jesus and went to see him hoping Jesus could make the boy well.

Then he came again to Cana in Galilee where he had changed the water into wine. Now there was a royal official whose son lay ill in Capernaum. ⁴⁷When he heard that Jesus had come from Judea to Galilee, he went and begged him to come down and heal his son, for he was at the point of death. ⁴⁸Then Jesus said to him, "Unless you see signs and wonders you will not believe." ⁴⁹The official said to him, "Sir, come down before my little boy dies." ⁵⁰Jesus said to him, "Go; your son will live." The man believed the word that Jesus spoke to him and started on his way. ⁵¹As he was going down, his slaves met him and told him that his child was alive. ⁵²So he asked them the hour when he began to recover, and they said to him, "Yesterday at one in the afternoon the fever left him." ⁵³The father realized that this was the hour when Jesus had said to him, "Your son will live." So he himself believed, along with his whole household. ⁵⁴Now this was the second sign that Jesus did after coming from Judea to Galilee.

Let's Pray!

Jesus, while you were here on earth, you gave physical healing to many people as a sign of your ability to heal their souls. When you returned to heaven, you gave us the Sacrament of Anointing to heal us body and soul. Help us to trust in your healing power, just as this father trusted you to heal his son. In the name of the Father, and the Son, and the Holy Spirit, Amen!

Going Deeper:

Read It! CCC #1514–15 (The Sacrament of Anointing of the Sick is for anyone who is ill).

Do It! Have a can drive or bake sale to support St. Jude Children's Hospital.

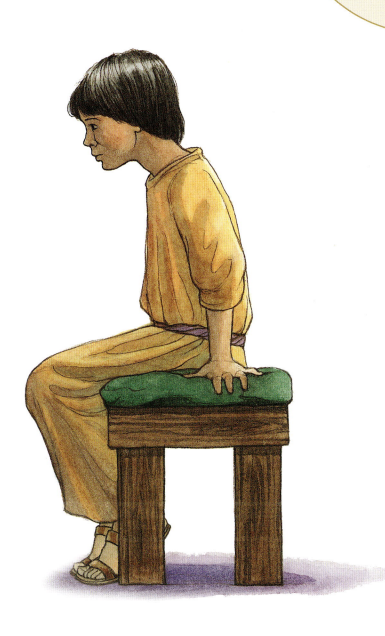

Jesus Heals the Sick

Mark 1:22–34

When God cast Satan and his fallen angels out of heaven, the evil one began to torment the human race. His first great victory was the fall of Adam and Eve, through whom sin and death entered the world. But from that time, evil spirits also bothered the human race, oppressing them with mental illness and other conditions that required the healing touch of God. In today's story, we see that Christ had been given authority over these things as well—an authority he passed to his apostles and those they ordained, ministers of the Sacrament of Anointing.

They were astounded at his [Jesus'] teaching, for he taught them as one having authority, and not as the scribes. ²³Just then there was in their synagogue a man with an unclean spirit, ²⁴and he cried out, "What have you to do with us, Jesus of Nazareth? Have you come to destroy us? I know who you are, the Holy One of God." ²⁵But Jesus rebuked him, saying, "Be silent, and come out of him!" ²⁶And the unclean spirit, convulsing him and crying with a loud voice, came out of him. ²⁷They were all amazed, and they kept on asking one another, "What is this? A new teaching—with authority! He commands even the unclean spirits, and they obey him." ²⁸At once his fame began to spread throughout the surrounding region of Galilee.

29 As soon as they left the synagogue, they entered the house of Simon and Andrew, with James and John. ³⁰Now Simon's mother-in-law was in bed with a fever, and they told him about her at once. ³¹He came and took her by the hand and lifted her up. Then the fever left her, and she began to serve them.

32 That evening, at sundown, they brought to him all who were sick or possessed with demons. ³³And the whole city was gathered around the door. ³⁴And he cured many who were sick with various diseases, and cast out many demons; and he would not permit the demons to speak, because they knew him.

LET'S PRAY!
Prayer for Healing
A Traditonal Catholic Prayer

O God, who are the only source of health and healing, the spirit of calm and the central peace of this universe, grant to me such a consciousness of your indwelling and surrounding presence that I may permit you to give me health and strength and peace, through Jesus Christ our Lord. Amen.

SPECIAL WORDS:
"Unclean spirit" refers to a
demon or fallen angel.

GOING DEEPER:

Read It! The reading today (OT 4B) is Deuteronomy
15:18–20. Other healing stories may be found in
Matthew 8:16–17 and Luke 4:40–41. See also CCC
#1503–05 (Jesus had compassion on those who were
sick).

Do It! What are some ways you can help people with
special needs? Consider volunteering with the
Special Olympics or other local center that helps the
developmentally disabled.

Jesus Feeds 5,000 People
Mark 6:30–44

> *H*ave you ever shared your lunch at school with someone who had forgotten his? The New Testament contains stories of Jesus miraculously feeding large crowds, in this case five thousand men (plus women and children).

The apostles gathered around Jesus, and told him all that they had done and taught. [31]He said to them, "Come away to a deserted place all by yourselves and rest a while." For many were coming and going, and they had no leisure even to eat. [32]And they went away in the boat to a deserted place by themselves. [33]Now many saw them going and recognized them, and they hurried there on foot from all the towns and arrived ahead of them. [34]As he went ashore, he saw a great crowd; and he had compassion for them, because they were like sheep without a shepherd; and he began to teach them many things. [35]When it grew late, his disciples came to him and said, "This is a deserted place, and the hour is now very late; [36]send them away so that they may go . . . and buy something for themselves to eat." [37]But he answered them, "You give them something to eat." They said to him, "Are we to go and buy two hundred denarii worth of bread, and give it to them to eat?" [38]And he said to them, "How many loaves have you? Go and see." When they had found out, they said, "Five, and two fish." [39]Then he ordered them to get all the people to sit down in groups on the green grass. [40]So they sat down in groups of hundreds and of fifties. [41]Taking the five loaves and the two fish, he looked up to heaven, and blessed and broke the loaves, and gave them to his disciples to set before the people; and he divided the two fish among them all. [42]And all ate and were filled; [43]and they took up twelve baskets full of broken pieces and of the fish. [44]Those who had eaten the loaves numbered five thousand men.

LET'S PRAY!

Lord, when the people witnessed this miracle, they immediately wanted to make you their king. But the Father had a different plan, in which you became the Bread of Life. Thank you for the wonderful gift of Eucharist. In the name of the Father, and the Son, and the Holy Spirit, Amen!

GOING DEEPER:

Read It! The reading for today (OT 16B) is Jeremiah 23:1–6; CCC #1335 (The Feeding of the 5,000 anticipates the Eucharist).

Do It! Have fish sandwiches for dinner tonight and talk about your favorite of Jesus' miracles!

SPECIAL WORDS: A denarius was a silver coin worth approximately twenty cents—a full day's wage for a laborer.[34]

Jesus Teaches About the Family

Mark 10:2–9, 13–16

God loves families! He created men and women to get married and love one another for their entire lives. God hates divorce because he knows how much it hurts families. God created children to love and learn from their parents, and to honor and respect them all their lives. When we follow God's order for the family, we help each other to heaven. And that is a good thing!

Some Pharisees came, and to test him they asked, "Is it lawful for a man to divorce his wife?" ³He answered them, "What did Moses command you?" ⁴They said, "Moses allowed a man to write a certificate of dismissal and to divorce her." ⁵But Jesus said to them, "Because of your hardness of heart he wrote this commandment for you. ⁶But from the beginning of creation, 'God made them male and female.' ⁷'For this reason a man shall leave his father and mother and be joined to his wife, ⁸and the two shall become one flesh.' So they are no longer two, but one flesh. ⁹Therefore what God has joined together, let no one separate." . . .

13 People were bringing little children to him in order that he might touch them; and the disciples spoke sternly to them. ¹⁴But when Jesus saw this, he was indignant and said to them, "Let the little children come to me; do not stop them; for it is to such as these that the kingdom of God belongs. ¹⁵Truly I tell you, whoever does not receive the kingdom of God as a little child will never enter it." ¹⁶And he took them up in his arms, laid his hands on them, and blessed them.

LET'S PRAY!

For fathers and mothers, for sisters and brothers,

For all those who love us, and all those we love.

For uncles and aunties and cousins among us,

We thank Thee, dear Father in heaven above!

In the name of the Father, and the Son, and the Holy Spirit, Amen!

GOING DEEPER:

Read It! Today's reading (OT 27B) is Genesis 2:18–24; CCC #2201–06 (God had a plan for the family from the very beginning).

Do It! Movie Night! Watch a good family movie like *Cheaper by the Dozen* or *Life with Father*.

QUOTE OF THE DAY: "We take care of our possessions for our children, but take no care at all for the children themselves. What absurdity! Form the soul of the child aright, and all the rest shall be added."
—St. John Chrysostom

Jesus Walks on Water
Matthew 14:22–36

Do you ever get scared in your bedroom at night? Do strange shadows and noises sometimes make you wish for a brighter night-light? Everyone gets scared sometimes, even the disciples of Jesus, those brave fishermen who were used to being out on the sea alone. In today's story, two water miracles test the faith of the apostles and make them realize that the man they are following has authority even over the wind and waves.

Immediately he [Jesus] made the disciples get into the boat and go on ahead to the other side, while he dismissed the crowds. 23And after he had dismissed the crowds, he went up the mountain by himself to pray. When evening came, . . . 24the boat, battered by the waves, was far from the land, for the wind was against them. 25And early in the morning he came walking toward them on the sea. 26But when the disciples saw him . . . they were terrified, saying, "It is a ghost!" And they cried out in fear. 27But immediately Jesus spoke to them and said, "Take heart, it is I; do not be afraid."

28 Peter answered him, "Lord, if it is you, command me to come to you on the water." 29He said, "Come." So Peter got out of the boat, started walking on the water, and came toward Jesus. 30But when he noticed the strong wind, he became frightened, and beginning to sink, he cried out, "Lord, save me!" 31Jesus immediately reached out his hand and caught him, saying to him, "You of little faith, why did you doubt?" 32When they got into the boat, the wind ceased. 33And those in the boat worshiped him, saying, "Truly you are the Son of God."

34 When they had crossed over, they came to land at Gennesaret. 35After the people of that place recognized him, they sent word throughout the region and brought all who were sick to him, 36and begged him that they might touch even the fringe of his cloak; and all who touched it were healed.

Let's Pray!

"Let [us] hear what God the LORD will speak, for he will speak peace to his people, to his [saints], to those who turn to him in their hearts" (Psalm 85:8). When our hearts are troubled, Lord Jesus, help us to see you in the storm. In the name of the Father, and the Son, and the Holy Spirit, Amen!

Going Deeper:

Read It! The Old Testament reading for today (OT 19A) is 1 Kings 19:9–13.

Do It! Find the Sea of Galilee on a map. Then find Gennesaret! Did you know this body of water was also called by other names? Can you find out what they are?

Special Words: The town of Gennesaret was on the northwest shore of the Sea of Galilee, also called the Sea of Gennesaret.

Simon Becomes Peter

Matthew 16:13–24

The word for rock—Cephas in Aramaic—is petros *(or "Peter") in Greek. In giving Peter the keys to the kingdom of heaven, Jesus was giving him the authority to lead and govern in his absence, including the "binding and loosing" mentioned in verse 22.*[35]

Now when Jesus came into the district of Caesarea Philippi, he asked his disciples, "Who do people say that the Son of Man is?" [14]And they said, "Some say John the Baptist, but others Elijah, and still others Jeremiah or one of the prophets." [15]He said to them, "But who do you say that I am?" [16]Simon Peter answered, "You are the Messiah, the Son of the living God." [17]And Jesus answered him, "Blessed are you, Simon son of Jonah! For flesh and blood has not revealed this to you, but my Father in heaven. [18]And I tell you, you are Peter, and on this rock I will build my church, and the gates of Hades will not prevail against it. [19]I will give you the keys of the kingdom of heaven, and whatever you bind on earth will be bound in heaven, and whatever you loose on earth will be loosed in heaven." [20]Then he sternly ordered the disciples not to tell anyone that he was the Messiah.

21 From that time on, Jesus began to show his disciples that he must go to Jerusalem and undergo great suffering at the hands of the elders and chief priests and scribes, and be killed, and on the third day be raised. [22]And Peter took him aside and began to rebuke him, saying, "God forbid it, Lord! This must never happen to you." [23]But he turned and said to Peter, "Get behind me, Satan! You are a stumbling block to me; for you are setting your mind not on divine things but on human things."

24 Then Jesus told his disciples, "If any want to become my followers, let them deny themselves and take up their cross and follow me."

Let's Pray!

Lord, you said, "If any want to become my followers, let them deny themselves and take up their cross daily and follow me" (Luke 9:23). We don't like to think of suffering for our faith, but we know that when you call us to endure persecution, you give us the strength to endure. Thank you for your faithfulness to us! In the name of the Father, and the Son, and the Holy Spirit, Amen!

Going Deeper:

Read It! The reading today (OT 21A) is Isaiah 22:19–23; CCC #552 (Peter holds first place in the college of Twelve).

Do It! Who is your favorite disciple? Is it Peter, or one of the others? Get out some crayons and paper and draw a picture of your favorite disciple spending time with Jesus.

Jairus's Daughter Raised

Mark 5:21–43

In today's story, we have a miracle within a miracle—a grown woman and a young girl are both healed with the compassionate touch of Jesus. In both stories, Jesus brought healing to people whom doctors could no longer help, an inspiring reminder that when doctors fail, the Great Physician, who created us, knows just what we need!

When Jesus had crossed again in the boat to the other side, a great crowd gathered around him; and he was by the sea. ²²Then one of the leaders of the synagogue named Jairus came and, when he saw him, fell at his feet ²³and begged him repeatedly, "My little daughter is at the point of death. Come and lay your hands on her, so that she may be made well, and live." ²⁴So he went with him.

And a large crowd followed him and pressed in on him. ²⁵Now there was a woman who had been suffering from hemorrhages for twelve years. ²⁶She had endured much under many physicians, and had spent all that she had; and she was no better, but rather grew worse. ²⁷She had heard about Jesus, and came up behind him in the crowd and touched his cloak, ²⁸for she said, "If I but touch his clothes, I will be made well." ²⁹Immediately her hemorrhage stopped; and she felt in her body that she was healed of her disease. ³⁰Immediately aware that power had gone forth from him, Jesus turned about in the crowd and said, "Who touched my clothes?" ³¹And his disciples said to him, "You see the crowd pressing in on you; how can you say, 'Who touched me?'" ³²He looked all around to see who had done it. ³³But the woman, knowing what had happened to her, came in fear and trembling, fell down before him, and told him the whole truth. ³⁴He said to her, "Daughter, your faith has made you well; go in peace, and be healed of your disease."

35 While he was still speaking, some people came from the leader's house to say, "Your daughter is dead. Why trouble the teacher any further?" ³⁶But overhearing what they said, Jesus said to the leader of the synagogue, "Do not fear, only believe." ³⁷He allowed no one to follow him except Peter, James, and John, the brother of James. ³⁸When they came to the house of the leader of the synagogue, he saw a commotion, people weeping and wailing loudly. ³⁹When he had entered, he said to them, "Why do you make a commotion and weep? The child is not dead but sleeping." ⁴⁰And they laughed at him. Then he put them all outside, and took the child's father and mother and those who were with him, and went in where the child was. ⁴¹He took her by the hand and said to her, "Talitha cum," which means, "Little girl, get up!" ⁴²And immediately the girl got up and began to walk about (she was twelve years of age). At this they were overcome with amazement. ⁴³He strictly ordered them that no one should know this, and told them to give her something to eat.

LET'S PRAY!

Young and old, rich and poor . . .
All will one day live no more.
Carry me Jesus, safely o'er.
Have mercy, God, on me! Hail Mary . . .

GOING DEEPER:

Read It! This account, which also appears in Luke
  8:40–56, is one of three times Jesus raised the dead
  (Luke 7:11–17 and John 11:1–44). CCC #1504 (Christ
  continues to heal us through the sacraments).

Do It! Make arrangements to attend a communal healing
  service at your parish. Or show your family the chrism
  (oil) used for anointing of the sick.

The Centurion's Servant

Luke 7:1–10

> *Have you ever prayed for something and been surprised when God answered that prayer with a big yes? In today's story, a powerful man sent friends to ask Jesus to heal his servant, knowing full well that Jesus was a busy man, and a Jewish prophet, who already had many people clamoring for his attention. Would Jesus help him?*

After Jesus had finished all his sayings in the hearing of the people, he entered Capernaum. ²A centurion there had a slave whom he valued highly, and who was ill and close to death. ³When he heard about Jesus, he sent some Jewish elders to him, asking him to come and heal his slave. ⁴When they came to Jesus, they appealed to him earnestly, saying, "He is worthy of having you do this for him, ⁵for he loves our people, and it is he who built our synagogue for us." ⁶And Jesus went with them, but when he was not far from the house, the centurion sent friends to say to him, "Lord, do not trouble yourself, for I am not worthy to have you come under my roof; ⁷therefore I did not presume to come to you. But only speak the word, and let my servant be healed. ⁸For I also am a man set under authority, with soldiers under me; and I say to one, 'Go,' and he goes, and to another, 'Come,' and he comes, and to my slave, 'Do this,' and the slave does it." ⁹When Jesus heard this he was amazed at him, and turning to the crowd that followed him, he said, "I tell you, not even in Israel have I found such faith." ¹⁰When those who had been sent returned to the house, they found the slave in good health.

LET'S PRAY!

Lord, thank you for the gift of our heavenly brothers and sisters, the saints, who pray for us when we need your help the most. As the centurion said, we are not worthy to receive you, but with one word from you, we are healed. Give us faith and courage to ask you for what we need. In the name of the Father, and the Son, and the Holy Spirit, Amen!

SPECIAL WORDS: *A centurion was a Roman officer who led a unit of one hundred soldiers.*

DID YOU KNOW? *The homes of Gentiles were ritually unclean, so by urging Jesus not to come to his house, the centurion showed his respect for Jewish law.*

GOING DEEPER:

Read It! The reading for today (OT 9C) is 1 Kings 8:41–43. This gospel story is also found in Matthew 8:5–13.

Do It! Send a care package to a soldier from your parish or family this week.

THE OUR FATHER

From the Gospel of Matthew

Our Father, who art in heaven,

Hallowed be Thy name.

Thy Kingdom come,

Thy will be done

On earth as it is in heaven.

Give us this day our daily bread.

And forgive us our trespasses,

As we forgive those who trespass against us.

And lead us not into temptation,

But deliver us from evil, Amen.

Forgiven

Luke 7:36–50

*O*ne of the most wonderful things about Jesus was how he made friends with all kinds of people—rich and poor, men and women and children, and especially those who had no other friends. When we show kindness to others, including those who are not very popular or well off, we imitate Jesus! In today's story, a woman repays Jesus' kindness to her in an extraordinary and unexpected way, and teaches some important men about the true meaning of forgiveness.

One of the Pharisees asked Jesus to eat with him, and he went into the Pharisee's house and took his place at the table. [37]And a woman in the city, who was a sinner, having learned that he was eating in the Pharisee's house, brought an alabaster jar of ointment. [38]She stood behind him at his feet, weeping, and began to bathe his feet with her tears and to dry them with her hair. Then she continued kissing his feet and anointing them with the ointment. [39]Now when the Pharisee who had invited him saw it, he said to himself, "If this man were a prophet, he would have known who and what kind of woman this is who is touching him—that she is a sinner." [40]Jesus spoke up and said to him, "Simon, I have something to say to you . . . [41]A certain creditor had two debtors; one owed five hundred denarii, and the other fifty. [42]When they could not pay, he canceled the debts for both of them. Now which of them will love him more?" [43]Simon answered, "I suppose the one for whom he canceled the greater debt." And Jesus said to him, "You have judged rightly." [44]Then turning toward the woman, he said to Simon, "Do you see this woman? I entered your house; you gave me no water for my feet, but she has bathed my feet with her tears and dried them with her hair. [45]You gave me no kiss, but from the time I came in she has not stopped kissing my feet. [46]You did not anoint my head with oil, but she has anointed my feet with ointment. [47]"Therefore, I tell you, her sins, which were many, have been forgiven; hence she has shown great love. But the one to whom little is forgiven, loves little." [48]Then he said to her, "Your sins are forgiven." [49]But those who were at the table with him began to say among themselves, "Who is this who even forgives sins?" [50]And he said to the woman, "Your faith has saved you; go in peace."

LET'S PRAY!

"Blessed are the poor in spirit, for theirs is the kingdom of heaven" (Matthew 5:3). Lord, we admit that though we have many things, we often forget to invest in the spiritual riches that last forever. Teach us to love and care for the poor and lonely. Like blessed Mother Teresa, help us to look at them and see only Jesus. In the name of the Father, and the Son, and the Holy Spirit, Amen!

Read It! The reading for today (OT 11C) is 2 Samuel 12:7–13, in which David is punished for adultery with Bathsheba and the murder of her husband. CCC #2712 (Contemplative prayer is the prayer of a forgiven sinner).

Do It! What can you do to show kindness to the poor this week? Consider donating some clothes and toys to a local shelter.

QUOTE OF THE DAY: "Blessed are those who love you, Lord, and their friends in you. For they are the only ones who will never lose anyone dear to them, since all who are dear to them are in you, our God, who can never be lost."
—St. Augustine

The Man Born Blind

John 9:1–17, 24–25

> *W*hose fault is it?" *When bad things happen, do you look around for someone to blame, or do you look for a solution to the problem? In today's gospel story, some people were very concerned about the underlying cause of a man's blindness, but Jesus saw an opportunity to show the love and care of God. Suddenly a man born blind could see, and the men who should have seen the power of God most clearly in this healing, were suddenly blind!*

As he [Jesus] walked along, he saw a man blind from birth. ²His disciples asked him, "Rabbi, who sinned, this man or his parents, that he was born blind?" ³Jesus answered, "Neither this man nor his parents sinned; he was born blind so that God's works might be revealed in him. ⁴We must work the works of him who sent me while it is day; night is coming when no one can work. ⁵As long as I am in the world, I am the light of the world." ⁶When he had said this, he spat on the ground and made mud with the saliva and spread the mud on the man's eyes, ⁷saying to him, "Go, wash in the pool of Siloam" (which means Sent). Then he went and washed and came back able to see. ⁸The neighbors and those who had seen him before as a beggar began to ask, "Is this not the man who used to sit and beg?" ⁹Some were saying, "It is he." Others were saying, "No, but it is someone like him." He kept saying, "I am the man." ¹⁰But they kept asking him, "Then how were your eyes opened?" ¹¹He answered, "The man called Jesus made mud, spread it on my eyes, and said to me, 'Go to Siloam and wash.' Then I went and washed and received my sight." ¹²They said to him, "Where is he?" He said, "I do not know."

13 They brought to the Pharisees the man who had formerly been blind. ¹⁴Now it was a sabbath day when Jesus made the mud and opened his eyes. ¹⁵Then the Pharisees also began to ask him how he had received his sight. He said to them, "He put mud on my eyes. Then I washed, and now I see." ¹⁶Some of the Pharisees said, "This man is not from God, for he does not observe the sabbath." But others said, "How can a man who is a sinner perform such signs?" And they were divided. ¹⁷So they said again to the blind man, "What do you say about him? It was your eyes he opened." He said, "He is a prophet." . . .

24 . . . The second time they called the man who had been blind, and they said to him, "Give glory to God! We know that this man is a sinner." ²⁵He answered, "I do not know whether he is a sinner. One thing I do know, that though I was blind, now I see."

LET'S PRAY!

Lord, help us to recognize your gifts to us every day. Let us not be blind to your many blessings! In the name of the Father, and the Son, and the Holy Spirit, Amen!

GOING DEEPER:

Read It! The reading for today (LE 4A) is 1 Samuel 16:6–13; CCC #595 (The Jews were divided concerning Jesus).

Do It! Make surprise muffins. Make your favorite muffin batter; then fill the tins only halfway. Place a teaspoon of jelly or a few chocolate chips in the middle, then more batter. Bake as usual.

Lazarus Lives!

John 11:23, 25–29, 32–44

*L*azarus was a dear friend of Jesus; he and his sisters, Mary and Martha, often invited Jesus and his disciples into their home at Bethany. So when Lazarus became sick, Mary and Martha expected Jesus to come quickly and help their sick brother. But Jesus didn't make it in time, and Lazarus died! Now what would Jesus do? The first thing he did was comfort his friends.

Jesus said to her [Martha], "Your brother will rise again . . . 25I am the resurrection and the life. Those who believe in me, even though they die, will live, 26and everyone who lives and believes in me will never die. Do you believe this?" 27She said to him, "Yes, Lord, I believe that you are the Messiah, the Son of God, the one coming into the world."

28 When she had said this, she went back and called her sister Mary, and told her privately, "The Teacher is here and is calling for you." 29And when she heard it, she got up quickly and went to him . . . 32She knelt at his feet and said to him, "Lord, if you had been here, my brother would not have died." 33When Jesus saw her weeping, and the Jews who came with her also weeping, he was greatly disturbed in spirit and deeply moved. 34He said, "Where have you laid him?" They said to him, "Lord, come and see." 35Jesus began to weep. 36So the Jews said, "See how he loved him!" 37But some said, "Could not he who opened the eyes of the blind man have kept this man from dying?"

38 Then Jesus, again greatly disturbed, came to the tomb. It was a cave, and a stone was lying against it. 39Jesus said, "Take away the stone." Martha, the sister of the dead man, said to him, "Lord, already there is a stench because he has been dead four days." 40Jesus said to her, "Did I not tell you that if you believed, you would see the glory of God?" 41So they took away the stone. And Jesus looked upward and said, "Father, I thank you for having heard me. 42I knew that you always hear me, but I have said this for the sake of the crowd standing here, so that they may believe that you sent me." 43When he had said this, he cried with a loud voice, "Lazarus, come out!" 44The dead man came out, his hands and feet bound with strips of cloth, and his face wrapped in a cloth. Jesus said to them, "Unbind him, and let him go."

LET'S PRAY!

Jesus, you weep with us in our grief. We ask that you comfort those who grieve today as you did Martha and Mary. Lord, in your mercy, hear our prayer!

GOING DEEPER:

Read It! Today's reading (LE 5A) is Ezekiel 37:12–14; CCC #2604 (Jesus shows how to ask God for what we want).

Do It! Does everyone in your family have a Bible of their very own? Tonight, get out your craft supplies and make "Jesus gives me new life!" bookmarks for your Bibles!

233

Two Parables of Jesus

Luke 15:1—10

*H*ave you ever lost a mitten or a boot, and searched your room from top to bottom to find it? Remember how happy you were when the lost item turned up, and you could run outside to play? In today's gospel passage, Jesus tells little stories called parables to remind us how much more God tries to help those who wander far away from his love, and how much he rejoices when they are found.

Now all the tax collectors and sinners were coming near to listen to him. ²And the Pharisees and the scribes were grumbling and saying, "This fellow welcomes sinners and eats with them."

3So he told them this parable: ⁴"Which one of you, having a hundred sheep and losing one of them, does not leave the ninety-nine in the wilderness and go after the one that is lost until he finds it? ⁵When he has found it, he lays it on his shoulders and rejoices. ⁶And when he comes home, he calls together his friends and neighbors, saying to them, 'Rejoice with me, for I have found my sheep that was lost.' ⁷Just so, I tell you, there will be more joy in heaven over one sinner who repents than over ninety-nine righteous persons who need no repentance.

8 "Or what woman having ten silver coins, if she loses one of them, does not light a lamp, sweep the house, and search carefully until she finds it? ⁹When she has found it, she calls together her friends and neighbors, saying, 'Rejoice with me, for I have found the coin that I had lost.' ¹⁰Just so, I tell you, there is joy in the presence of the angels of God over one sinner who repents."

LET'S PRAY!

A Prayer to Redeem Lost Time

"O my God! Source of all mercy! I acknowledge Your sovereign power. While recalling the wasted years that are past, I believe that You, Lord, can in an instant turn this loss to gain. Miserable as I am, yet I firmly believe that You can do all things. Please restore to me the time lost, giving me Your grace, both now and in the future, that I may appear before You in wedding garments. Amen."

—St. Teresa of Avila

SPECIAL WORDS:
"Silver coins" were drachmas, Greek coins comparable to a Roman denarius, a day's wage for a soldier.[37]

GOING DEEPER:

Read It! The reading for today (OT 24C) is Exodus 23:7–14; CCC #589 (Jesus' mercy upsets some people).

Do It! Is there a room or closet in your house especially in need of organizing? Go give it a careful clean-up today, and see how many "lost" articles you discover!

The Good Samaritan

Luke 10:25–37

*W*ho is my neighbor?" In response to this question, Jesus tells a story about an unlikely hero, a Samaritan man whose name is not given but whose actions are remembered in one of the most popular of all Jesus' parables. In telling this story, Jesus reminds us of our responsibility to care for all God's children—not only for those in our immediate circle of friends and family.

Just then a lawyer stood up to test Jesus. "Teacher," he said, "what must I do to inherit eternal life?" [26]He said to him, "What is written in the law? What do you read there?" [27]He answered, "You shall love the Lord your God with all your heart, and with all your soul, and with all your strength, and with all your mind; and your neighbor as yourself." [28]And he said to him, "You have given the right answer; do this, and you will live."

29 But wanting to justify himself, he asked Jesus, "And who is my neighbor?" [30]Jesus replied, "A man was going down from Jerusalem to Jericho, and fell into the hands of robbers, who stripped him, beat him, and went away, leaving him half dead. [31]Now by chance a priest was going down that road; and when he saw him, he passed by on the other side. [32]So likewise a Levite, when he came to the place and saw him, passed by on the other side. [33]But a Samaritan while traveling came near him; and when he saw him, he was moved with pity. [34]He went to him and bandaged his wounds, having poured oil and wine on them. Then he put him on his own animal, brought him to an inn, and took care of him. [35]The next day he took out two denarii, gave them to the innkeeper, and said, 'Take care of him; and when I come back, I will repay you whatever more you spend.' [36]"Which of these three, do you think, was a neighbor to the man who fell into the hands of the robbers?" [37]He said, "The one who showed him mercy." Jesus said to him, "Go and do likewise."

LET'S PRAY!

Lord, you are so generous with us! You give us so much out of your abundant blessings. Make us mindful of the needs of those around us, and give us opportunities to serve them out of love for you. In the name of the Father, and the Son, and the Holy Spirit, Amen!

SPECIAL WORDS:
A Levite was a person from the tribe of Levi. Some of the men were priests; other were called to help the priests. The Levite in this story chose to remain ceremonially pure just in case, rather than tend to an immediate, real need.

GOING DEEPER:

Read It! Today's reading (OT 15C) is Deuteronomy 30:10–14; CCC #1825 (Christ died for us while we were still "enemies").

Do It! Learn and say the corporal works of mercy. How many of them have you done?

The Rich Fool
Luke 12:13—21

That's mine!" "No, it's mine!" How often do you squabble over your toys and things, rather than share them with others? In today's gospel story, Jesus warned against the dangers of hoarding, keeping to ourselves things we have been given to be a blessing to other people. Sometimes those blessings are physical things—money, possessions, or food. Other times, the gifts God gives us are less tangible, but no less important—the gift of teaching, of hospitality, of friendship. What happens when we refuse to share? Let's find out what happened to this poor, rich, foolish man!

Someone in the crowd said to him [Jesus], "Teacher, tell my brother to divide the family inheritance with me." ¹⁴But he said to him, "Friend, who set me to be a judge or arbitrator over you?" ¹⁵And he said to them, "Take care! Be on your guard against all kinds of greed; for one's life does not consist in the abundance of possessions." ¹⁶Then he told them a parable: "The land of a rich man produced abundantly. ¹⁷And he thought to himself, 'What should I do, for I have no place to store my crops?' ¹⁸Then he said, 'I will do this: I will pull down my barns and build larger ones, and there I will store all my grain and my goods. ¹⁹And I will say to my soul, 'Soul, you have ample goods laid up for many years; relax, eat, drink, be merry.' ²⁰But God said to him, 'You fool! This very night your life is being demanded of you. And the things you have prepared, whose will they be?' ²¹So it is with those who store up treasures for themselves but are not rich toward God."

LET'S PRAY!

"Let nothing trouble you, let nothing
    frighten you,
      All things pass away, but God never
        changes.
Patience obtains all things,
He who possesses God, has everything,
God alone suffices."

—St. Teresa of Avila

GOING DEEPER:

Read It! The reading today (OT 18C) is Ecclesiastes 1:2, 2:21–23; CCC #549 (Sin keeps us from helping others).

Do It! If you don't already tithe, start today! Malachi 3:10 says when we give one-tenth to God, he will pour down blessings on us out of the windows of heaven!

QUOTE OF THE DAY:
"If you would rise, shun luxury, for luxury lowers and degrades."
—St. John Chrysostom

The Widow and the Judge

Luke 18:1–8

The Pledge of Allegiance that we say at school has this line, "One nation, under God, indivisible, with liberty and justice for all." When people don't put God first, those most in need of justice—the weak and poor—do not receive it. In today's gospel story, Jesus teaches about the connection between faith and real justice.

Then Jesus told them a parable about their need to pray always and not to lose heart. ²He said, "In a certain city there was a judge who neither feared God nor had respect for people. ³In that city there was a widow who kept coming to him and saying, 'Grant me justice against my opponent.' ⁴For a while he refused; but later he said to himself, 'Though I have no fear of God and no respect for anyone, ⁵yet because this widow keeps bothering me, I will grant her justice, so that she may not wear me out by continually coming.'" ⁶And the Lord said, "Listen to what the unjust judge says. ⁷And will not God grant justice to his chosen ones who cry to him day and night? Will he delay long in helping them? ⁸I tell you, he will quickly grant justice to them. And yet, when the Son of Man comes, will he find faith on earth?"

Let's Pray!

I lift my eyes to the hills—
from where will my help come?
²My help comes from the LORD,
who made heaven and earth.
³He will not let your foot be moved;
he who keeps you will not slumber.

—Psalm 121:1–3

GOING DEEPER:

Read It! The reading for today (OT 29C) is Exodus 17:8–13; CCC #2573 (Prayer is the "battle of faith and the triumph of perseverance").

Do It! What does your family need right now? Gather together every day to ask God for those things.

Zacchaeus
Luke 19:1–10

*E*very class seems to have one or two kids who are much smaller—or much bigger!—than the others. Sometimes they use humor or other talents to help them fit in, but other times they wind up feeling left out. In today's gospel story, a rich man who was very short wanted to see Jesus. You'll never guess what happened when Jesus saw him!

He [Jesus] entered Jericho and was passing through it. ²A man was there named Zacchaeus; he was a chief tax collector and was rich. ³He was trying to see who Jesus was, but on account of the crowd he could not, because he was short in stature. ⁴So he ran ahead and climbed a sycamore tree to see him, because he was going to pass that way. ⁵When Jesus came to the place, he looked up and said to him, "Zacchaeus, hurry and come down; for I must stay at your house today." ⁶So he hurried down and was happy to welcome him. ⁷All who saw it began to grumble and said, "He has gone to be the guest of one who is a sinner." ⁸Zacchaeus stood there and said to the Lord, "Look, half of my possessions, Lord, I will give to the poor; and if I have defrauded anyone of anything, I will pay back four times as much." ⁹Then Jesus said to him, "Today salvation has come to this house, because he too is a son of Abraham. ¹⁰For the Son of Man came to seek out and to save the lost."

LET'S PRAY!

Today we pray for those in government—those who make the laws, those who enforce them, and those who represent us around the world. Lord, give each of them wisdom, industry, and integrity to serve you first, the people second, and themselves last. In the name of the Father, and the Son, and the Holy Spirit, Amen!

SPECIAL WORDS:
"Restitution" is the act of giving back something you stole, either the item itself or money to replace it. When Zacchaeus wanted to pay back what he had cheated out of people, he gave them four times what he had taken.

DID YOU KNOW? *At that time, tax collectors were despised because the people's money went to the Roman government. And yet here in Jericho, Jesus chose to stay with one of the most hated men in town!*

GOING DEEPER:

Read It! Today's reading (OT 31C) is from Wisdom 11:22–12:2; CCC #2712 (Humility is a path to grace).

Do It! It takes humility to admit when you've done something wrong! Can you think of a time when you cheated—when you didn't point out an error made in your favor, for example—or didn't pay the full amount you owed on something? What should you have done, and how can you make it right?

A Prodigal Son
Luke 15:11—32

*T*his is the third parable in the "lost" chapter—lost sheep, lost coins, and lost son. God created families to love and care for one another all the way to heaven. So in this story, when the son demands his inheritance and runs away with it, he made his family very sad. In many families, after showing this kind of disrespect for a parent, no child would be welcome home again! But this father was extraordinary in his love, just as our heavenly Father is in his love for us. He is willing to do anything to welcome us back into his kingdom. Listen!

Then Jesus said, "There was a man who had two sons. ¹²The younger of them said to his father, 'Father, give me the share of the property that will belong to me.' So he divided his property between them. ¹³A few days later the younger son gathered all he had and traveled to a distant country, and there he squandered his property in dissolute living. ¹⁴When he had spent everything, a severe famine took place throughout that country, and he began to be in need. ¹⁵So he went and hired himself out to one of the citizens of that country, who sent him to his fields to feed the pigs. ¹⁶He would gladly have filled himself with the pods that the pigs were eating; and no one gave him anything. ¹⁷But when he came to himself he said, 'How many of my father's hired hands have bread enough and to spare, but here I am dying of hunger! ¹⁸I will get up and go to my father, and I will say to him, "Father, I have sinned against heaven and before you; ¹⁹I am no longer worthy to be called your son; treat me like one of your hired hands."' ²⁰So he set off and went to his father. But while he was still far off, his father saw him and was filled with compassion; he ran and put his arms around him and kissed him. ²¹Then

the son said to him, 'Father, I have sinned against heaven and before you; I am no longer worthy to be called your son.' ²²But the father said to his slaves, 'Quickly, bring out a robe—the best one—and put it on him; put a ring on his finger and sandals on his feet. ²³And get the fatted calf and kill it, and let us eat and celebrate; ²⁴for this son of mine was dead and is alive again; he was lost and is found!' And they began to celebrate.

25 "Now his elder son was in the field; and when he came and approached the house, he heard music and dancing. ²⁶He called one of the slaves and asked what was going on. ²⁷He replied, 'Your brother has come, and your father has killed the fatted calf, because he has got him back safe and sound.' ²⁸Then he became angry and refused to go in. His father came out and began to plead with him. ²⁹But he answered his father, 'Listen! For all these years I have been working like a slave for you, and I have never disobeyed your command; yet you have never given me even a young goat so that I might celebrate with my friends. ³⁰But when this son of yours came back, who has devoured your property with prostitutes, you killed the fatted calf for him!'

[31]Then the father said to him, 'Son, you are always with me, and all that is mine is yours. [32]But we had to celebrate and rejoice, because this brother of yours was dead and has come to life; he was lost and has been found.'"

LET'S PRAY!

Act of Contrition

A Traditonal Catholic Prayer

Father, I confess I have sinned against you. In doing evil, and refusing to do good, I have hurt you, whom I ought to love above all things. I firmly resolve, with your help, to do penance, to sin no more, and to avoid every occasion of sin. Your Son, Jesus, suffered and died for me. For his sake, forgive me.

GOING DEEPER:

Read It! The reading today (LE 4C) is Joshua 5:9–12; CCC #1700 (The dignity of the human person comes from being created in the image of God).

Do It! Is there someone in your life you find impossible to love, or to forgive—maybe right in your own family? Take a step toward getting back together today! Light a candle, write a letter, make a phone call, or talk to the person. God is pleased when we take steps, however small, toward unity.

Sheep and Goats
Matthew 25:31–46

The word catholic means "universal"—that is, the gospel message is truly for all the peoples of the world (CCC #849). And so, followers of Jesus have spread all over the world to take this message of hope to nearly every nation on earth. One of the most important ways this message has spread has been through hospitals and schools, built by representatives of Christ and his Church in order to meet the daily needs of the people. In this gospel narrative, Jesus reveals the marks of a true believer, one who shows love in both word and deed.

"When the Son of Man comes in his glory, and all the angels with him, then he will sit on the throne of his glory. [32]All the nations will be gathered before him, and he will separate people one from another as a shepherd separates the sheep from the goats, [33]and he will put the sheep at his right hand and the goats at the left. [34]Then the king will say to those at his right hand, 'Come, you that are blessed by my Father, inherit the kingdom prepared for you from the foundation of the world; [35]for I was hungry and you gave me food, I was thirsty and you gave me something to drink, I was a stranger and you welcomed me, [36]I was naked and you gave me clothing, I was sick and you took care of me, I was in prison and you visited me.' [37]Then the righteous will answer him, 'Lord, when was it that we saw you hungry and gave you food, or thirsty and gave you something to drink? [38]And when was it that we saw you a stranger and welcomed you, or naked and gave you clothing? [39]And when was it that we saw you sick or in prison and visited you?' [40]And the king will answer them, 'Truly I tell you, just as you did it to one of the least of these who are members of my family, you did it to me.' [41]Then he will say to those at his left hand, 'You that are accursed, depart from me into the eternal fire prepared for the devil and his angels; [42]for I was hungry and you gave me no food, I was thirsty and you gave me nothing to drink, [43]I was a stranger and you did not welcome me, naked and you did not give me clothing, sick and in prison and you did not visit me.' [44]Then they also will answer, 'Lord, when was it that we saw you hungry or thirsty or a stranger or naked or sick or in prison, and did not take care of you?' [45]Then he will answer them, 'Truly I tell you, just as you did not do it to one of the least of these, you did not do it to me.' [46]And these will go away into eternal punishment, but the righteous into eternal life."

LET'S PRAY!

Father, there is nothing more important in this life than knowing you and being found in you. Help us to do your will that we may be found as your sheep on the last day. Amen.

GOING DEEPER:

Read It! The reading for this week (OT 34A) is Ezekiel 34:11–17; CCC #2447 (There are spiritual and corporal works of mercy).

Do It! Memorize the spiritual works of mercy as a family. Then as a family look for one practical way to support a foreign missionary or apostolate this week!

The Good Shepherd
John 10:7–16

In the Gospels, Jesus frequently compared himself to people and things to show something true about himself as well as something true about us: "I am the Bread of Life." "I am the Vine." "I am the Great Physician." In today's gospel story, Jesus reveals another way that he shows his love and care for us: as our Good Shepherd, who gives his life for his sheep.

So again Jesus said to them, "Very truly, I tell you, I am the gate for the sheep. ⁸All who came before me are thieves and bandits; but the sheep did not listen to them. ⁹I am the gate. Whoever enters by me will be saved, and will come in and go out and find pasture. ¹⁰The thief comes only to steal and kill and destroy. I came that they may have life, and have it abundantly.

11 "I am the good shepherd. The good shepherd lays down his life for the sheep. ¹²The hired hand, who is not the shepherd and does not own the sheep, sees the wolf coming and leaves the sheep and runs away—and the wolf snatches them and scatters them. ¹³The hired hand runs away because a hired hand does not care for the sheep. ¹⁴I am the good shepherd. I know my own and my own know me, ¹⁵just as the Father knows me and I know the Father. And I lay down my life for the sheep. ¹⁶I have other sheep that do not belong to this fold. I must bring them also, and they will listen to my voice. So there will be one flock, one shepherd."

LET'S PRAY!

The LORD is my shepherd, I shall not want.
² He makes me lie down in green pastures;
he leads me beside still waters;
³he restores my soul.
He leads me in right paths for his name's
   sake.
⁴Even though I walk through the darkest
   valley,
   I fear no evil;
for you are with me;
   your rod and your staff—
   they comfort me.
⁵You prepare a table before me
   in the presence of my enemies;
   you anoint my head with oil;
my cup overflows.
⁶Surely goodness and mercy shall follow me
   all the days of my life,
and I shall dwell in the house of the LORD
         my whole life long.   —Psalm 23

Did You Know? The "other sheep" (vs. 16) may have been a reference to the Gentiles who would later be gathered into the fold of the Church—or to Christians who had separated themselves from the Church in John's time.³⁹

GOING DEEPER:

Read It! The reading for today (EA 4A,B) is Acts 4:8–12; CCC #754 (The Church is the sheepfold).

Do It! Is there a sheep farm or petting zoo in your area? Arrange for a visit this week.

The Transfiguration
Matthew 17:1–13

*T*he following gospel account is known as the "Transfiguration"—the moment when Jesus' divinity came shining through to the disciples, who would later testify to this amazing moment in the life of Christ.

Six days later, Jesus took with him Peter and James and his brother John and led them up a high mountain, by themselves. ²And he was transfigured before them, and his face shone like the sun, and his clothes became dazzling white. ³Suddenly there appeared to them Moses and Elijah, talking with him. ⁴Then Peter said to Jesus, "Lord, it is good for us to be here; if you wish, I will make three dwellings here, one for you, one for Moses, and one for Elijah." ⁵While he was still speaking, suddenly a bright cloud overshadowed them, and from the cloud a voice said, "This is my Son, the Beloved; with him I am well pleased; listen to him!" ⁶When the disciples heard this, they fell to the ground and were overcome by fear. ⁷But Jesus came and touched them, saying, "Get up and do not be afraid." ⁸And when they looked up, they saw no one except Jesus himself alone.

9 As they were coming down the mountain, Jesus ordered them, "Tell no one about the vision until after the Son of Man has been raised from the dead." ¹⁰And the disciples asked him, "Why, then, do the scribes say that Elijah must come first?" ¹¹He replied, "Elijah is indeed coming and will restore all things; ¹²but I tell you that Elijah has already come, and they did not recognize him, but they did to him whatever they pleased. So also the Son of Man is about to suffer at their hands." ¹³Then the disciples understood that he was speaking to them about John the Baptist.

LET'S PRAY!
Anima Christi
A Traditonal Catholic Prayer

Soul of Christ, sanctify me.
Body of Christ, save me.
Blood of Christ, inebriate me.
Water from Christ's side, wash me.
Passion of Christ, strengthen me,
O good Jesus, hear me.
Within Thy wounds hide me.
    suffer me not to be separated from Thee.
From the malicious enemy defend me.
In the hour of my death call me
And bid me come unto Thee,
That I may praise Thee with Thy saints,
    and with Thy angels,
    forever and ever, Amen.

GOING DEEPER:

Read It! Today's reading (LE 2A) is Genesis 12:1–4. The story is told in all three Synoptic Gospels (Mark 9:2–13; Luke 9:28–36); CCC #554–55 (The Transfiguration is a foretaste of the kingdom of God).

Do It! Make fun decorative signs together for your home or garden. Get some scrap wood (Mom or Dad may want to sand the edges for little ones), and cover the signs with craft paint. Write sayings that remind you that God loves you!

APOSTLES' CREED

I believe in God the Father, Almighty,

Maker of heaven and earth. I believe in Jesus Christ,

his only begotten Son, our Lord: who was conceived

by the Holy Ghost, born of the Virgin Mary,

suffered under Pontius Pilate; was crucified,

dead and buried: He descended into hell: The third day

he rose again from the dead: He ascended into heaven,

and sits at the right hand of God the Father Almighty:

From thence he shall come to judge the quick and

the dead: I believe in the Holy Ghost,

the holy Catholic Church, the communion of saints,

the forgiveness of sins, the resurrection of the body,

and the life everlasting. Amen.

Who Is the Greatest?
Matthew 18:1–6

*T*hink a moment about all the people who are important to you. Your parents and grandparents, teachers and coaches, pastor and dentist and babysitter all work together for your good. In today's gospel story, we discover an important truth: you are important to God, too! In fact, Jesus said that the kingdom of God belongs to those who become just like you! Listen!

At that time the disciples came to Jesus and asked, "Who is the greatest in the kingdom of heaven?" ²He called a child, whom he put among them, ³and said, "Truly I tell you, unless you change and become like children, you will never enter the kingdom of heaven. ⁴Whoever becomes humble like this child is the greatest in the kingdom of heaven. ⁵Whoever welcomes one such child in my name welcomes me.

6 "If any of you put a stumbling block before one of these little ones who believe in me, it would be better for you if a great millstone were fastened around your neck and you were drowned in the depth of the sea."

LET'S PRAY!

Thank you, God, for all the people in our lives who help us to grow as a family. Thank you for our teachers and pastors and friends. And thank you for loving each of us right now, just as we are at this moment. Even if we were the only ones in the world, you would have died for us! Help us to live in a way that pleases you always. In the name of the Father, and the Son, and the Holy Spirit, Amen!

GOING DEEPER:

Read It! CCC #2785 (The kingdom belongs to "little children").

Do It! Did you know there are 500,000 children in the United States in need of permanent or temporary homes, with more than 125,000 of them available for adoption? Please pray for their "forever families" to find them.

QUOTE OF THE DAY:
"To become a child in relation to God is the condition for entering the kingdom."
—CCC #526

Jesus Rides into Jerusalem

Matthew 21:1–14

As they approached Jerusalem for the Passover, Jesus instructed his followers to go into the village and get a colt, and bring it. You see, the prophet Zechariah had promised that the Messiah would come into the city riding on a donkey (Zechariah 9:9). Just as King Solomon had ridden to his coronation on the colt that had belonged to his father, David (1 Kings 1:33–44), so Jesus entered the City of David, ready to do the will of his Father.

When they had come near Jerusalem and had reached Bethphage, at the Mount of Olives, Jesus sent two disciples, ²saying to them, "Go into the village ahead of you, and immediately you will find a donkey tied, and a colt with her; untie them and bring them to me. ³If anyone says anything to you, just say this, 'The Lord needs them.' And he will send them immediately." ⁴This took place to fulfill what had been spoken through the prophet, saying,

5 "Tell the daughter of Zion,
Look, your king is coming to you,
humble, and mounted on a donkey,
and on a colt, the foal of a donkey."

⁶The disciples went and did as Jesus had directed them; ⁷they brought the donkey and the colt, and put their cloaks on them, and he sat on them. ⁸A very large crowd spread their cloaks on the road, and others cut branches from the trees and spread them on the road. ⁹The crowds that went ahead of him and that followed were shouting,

"Hosanna to the Son of David!
Blessed is the one who comes in the name of the Lord!
Hosanna in the highest heaven!"

¹⁰When he entered Jerusalem, the whole city was in turmoil, asking, "Who is this?" ¹¹The crowds were saying, "This is the prophet Jesus from Nazareth in Galilee."

12 Then Jesus entered the temple and drove out all who were selling and buying in the temple, and he overturned the tables of the money changers and the seats of those who sold doves. ¹³He said to them, "It is written,

'My house shall be called a house of prayer';
but you are making it a den of robbers."

14 The blind and the lame came to him in the temple, and he cured them.

LET'S PRAY!

Palm Sunday Prayer of Adoration

A Traditonal Catholic Prayer

"Hosanna, Hosanna,
Hosanna to the Son of David!
Blessed is he who comes in the name of the Lord!
Hosanna in the highest!"

SPECIAL WORDS: *The Hebrew word* Hosanna *means "Save us!" It is also a cry of praise.*

Read It! This is the processional reading for Palm
   Sunday (A). The other readings are Isaiah 50:4–7
   and Matthew 26:14–27, 66. CCC #559 (The people
   shouted, "Hosanna!" when Jesus rode into the city,
   and we do it today during the Liturgy of the Eucharist).
Do It! Do you have palm fronds around the house, or can you
   obtain some from a local florist? Make palm crosses!

*Did You Know? By riding into
Jerusalem, Jesus also imitated
King Jehu, who rode into
Samaria to tear down the false
temple to Baal, just as Jesus had
purified the temple in Jerusalem
by driving out the money
changers and merchants!*
(2 Kings 9:11–10:28)

Jesus Washes the Disciples' Feet
John 13:1–17

The excitement of Palm Sunday did not last for long. Within a few days, the people turned against Jesus and called for his death! During Holy Week, just before Easter, we remember this last week in the earthly life of Christ. This gospel story is about Holy Thursday, when Jesus took up the job usually reserved for the lowliest household servant. He washed the feet of the guests as they arrived for dinner. He wanted to show his disciples, who often argued who was greatest among them, what it meant to love not just with words but with actions, too.

Now before the festival of the Passover, Jesus knew that his hour had come to depart from this world and go to the Father. Having loved his own who were in the world, he loved them to the end. ²The devil had already put it into the heart of Judas son of Simon Iscariot to betray him. And during supper ³Jesus, knowing that the Father had given all things into his hands, and that he had come from God and was going to God, ⁴got up from the table, took off his outer robe, and tied a towel around himself. ⁵Then he poured water into a basin and began to wash the disciples' feet and to wipe them with the towel that was tied around him. ⁶He came to Simon Peter, who said to him, "Lord, are you going to wash my feet?" ⁷Jesus answered, "You do not know now what I am doing, but later you will understand." ⁸Peter said to him, "You will never wash my feet." Jesus answered, "Unless I wash you, you have no share with me." ⁹Simon Peter said to him, "Lord, not my feet only but also my hands and my head!" ¹⁰Jesus said to him, "One who has bathed does not need to wash, except for the feet, but is entirely clean. And you are clean, though not all of you." ¹¹For he knew who was to betray him; for this reason he said, "Not all of you are clean."

12 After he had washed their feet, had put on his robe, and had returned to the table, he said to them, "Do you know what I have done to you? ¹³You call me Teacher and Lord—and you are right, for that is what I am. ¹⁴So if I, your Lord and Teacher, have washed your feet, you also ought to wash one another's feet. ¹⁵For I have set you an example, that you also should do as I have done to you. ¹⁶Very truly, I tell you, servants are not greater than their master, nor are messengers greater than the one who sent them. ¹⁷If you know these things, you are blessed if you do them."

LET'S PRAY!

"Take my life and let it be consecrated, Lord, to Thee.

Take my hands and let them move at the impulse of Thy love.

Take my feet and let them be swift and beautiful for Thee!"—Frances Havergal

QUOTE OF THE DAY: *Jesus said,*
"I am the living bread that
came down from heaven.
Whoever eats of this bread will
live forever; and the bread that
I will give for the life of the
world is my flesh."
—John 6:51

GOING DEEPER:

Read It! The first reading for today's passage, read on Holy Thursday (A, B, C), is Exodus 12:1–14; CCC #1337 (The apostles were made priests).

Do It! What is the worst chore in your house, the one everyone hates the most? Very likely it's something different for everyone. This week, imitate Jesus and do that chore out of love for someone in your family.

Jesus Gives Us the Eucharist

Mark 14:17–26

*A*s they all gathered together for their final Passover meal together, the Lord knew that his time on earth was almost over. For three years he had shared his life with the Twelve who had been chosen to bring the gospel message to the world. Jesus knew that they were going to need his strength to carry on the work they had been called to do. And so, the bread and wine of that Passover feast were transformed into the extraordinary gift of the Eucharist!

When it was evening, he [Jesus] came with the twelve. [18]And when they had taken their places and were eating, Jesus said, "Truly I tell you, one of you will betray me, one who is eating with me." [19]They began to be distressed and to say to him one after another, "Surely, not I?" [20]He said to them, "It is one of the twelve, one who is dipping bread into the bowl with me. [21]For the Son of Man goes as it is written of him, but woe to that one by whom the Son of Man is betrayed! It would have been better for that one not to have been born."

22 While they were eating, he took a loaf of bread, and after blessing it he broke it, gave it to them, and said, "Take; this is my body." [23]Then he took a cup, and after giving thanks he gave it to them, and all of them drank from it. [24]He said to them, "This is my blood of the covenant, which is poured out for many. [25]Truly I tell you, I will never again drink of the fruit of the vine until that day when I drink it new in the kingdom of God."

26 When they had sung the hymn, they went out to the Mount of Olives.

LET'S PRAY!

Glory Be

A Traditonal Catholic Prayer

Glory be to the Father and to the Son and to the Holy Spirit!

As it was in the beginning, is now and ever shall be, world without end, Amen.

GOING DEEPER:

Read It! Today's reading (Palm Sunday B) is Isaiah 50:4–7; CCC #1328 (What is the Eucharist?).

Do It! Celebrate a seder meal! Check online for directions.

SPECIAL WORDS: The Eucharist is a sacrament in which we receive Jesus—Body and Blood, soul and divinity—under the appearances of bread and wine. The word itself means "thanksgiving."

261

Jesus Our High Priest

John 17:1, 6–8, 11–16, 20–23

After supper was over, Jesus and his disciples made their way to Gethsemane to pray. Along the way, Jesus spoke to them about what was ahead, and what they must do: keep the commandments, love one another, and wait for the Holy Spirit to come. Although Jesus dreaded the pain and suffering that were in store for him, he was most concerned about his disciples. So in his final hours before his death, he prayed for his disciples, that they would be strong, and they would be one, just as he and the Father were one.

After Jesus had spoken these words, he looked up to heaven and said, "Father . . .

6 "I have made your name known to those whom you gave me from the world. They were yours, and you gave them to me, and they have kept your word. ⁷Now they know that everything you have given me is from you; ⁸for the words that you gave to me I have given to them, and they have received them and know in truth that I came from you; and they have believed that you sent me. . . . ¹¹And now I am no longer in the world, but they are in the world, and I am coming to you. Holy Father, protect them in your name that you have given me, so that they may be one, as we are one. ¹²While I was with them, I protected them in your name that you have given me. I guarded them, and not one of them was lost except the one destined to be lost, so that the scripture might be fulfilled. ¹³But now I am coming to you, and I speak these things in the world so that they may have my joy made complete in themselves. ¹⁴I have given them your word, and the world has hated them because they do not belong to the world, just as I do not belong to the world. ¹⁵I am not asking you to take them out of the world, but I ask you to protect them from the evil one. ¹⁶They do not belong to the world, just as I do not belong to the world. . . .

20 "I ask not only on behalf of these, but also on behalf of those who will believe in me through their word, ²¹that they may all be one. As you, Father, are in me and I am in you, may they also be in us, so that the world may believe that you have sent me. ²²The glory that you have given me I have given them, so that they may be one, as we are one, ²³I in them and you in me, that they may become completely one, so that the world may know that you have sent me and have loved them even as you have loved me."

Let's Pray!

Lord, while you were on earth you prayed for unity among your followers, and yet there is so much division in the Church! Help us, Lord, to bridge the barriers between believers, that your name would be glorified. In the name of the Father, and the Son, and the Holy Spirit, Amen.

SPECIAL WORDS: *To sanctify something is to make it holy or set apart.*

DID YOU KNOW? In his High Priestly prayer, Jesus prayed both for the original apostles (17:6–19) and for future ones (17:20–21).

GOING DEEPER:

Read It! This gospel account is read each year (EA 7A, B, C). The first reading is taken from Acts 1 (A, B) or Acts 7:55–60 (C). See also CCC #2602 (Jesus often prayed alone).

Do It! Since Jesus was God, why did he have to pray? (Read the Catechism to find the answer!) Write down your answers and share and compare as family members.

Judas Betrays Christ
Luke 22:39–53

Have you ever heard of a "fair-weather friend"? Someone who likes to have fun with you and play with you until you need help or are in trouble, and that friend is nowhere to be found? Sadly, one of the Twelve was such a "friend." Judas Iscariot was happy to be with Jesus when times were good, but when the people turned against Jesus, Judas did too!

He [Jesus] came out and went, as was his custom, to the Mount of Olives; and the disciples followed him. 40When he reached the place, he said to them, "Pray that you may not come into the time of trial." 41Then he withdrew from them about a stone's throw, knelt down, and prayed, 42"Father, if you are willing, remove this cup from me; yet, not my will but yours be done." 43Then an angel from heaven appeared to him and gave him strength. 44In his anguish he prayed more earnestly, and his sweat became like great drops of blood falling down on the ground. 45When he got up from prayer, he came to the disciples and found them sleeping because of grief, 46and he said to them, "Why are you sleeping? Get up and pray that you may not come into the time of trial."

47 While he was still speaking, suddenly a crowd came, and the one called Judas, one of the twelve, was leading them. He approached Jesus to kiss him; 48but Jesus said to him, "Judas, is it with a kiss that you are betraying the Son of Man?" 49When those who were around him saw what was coming, they asked, "Lord, should we strike with the sword?" 50Then one of them struck the slave of the high priest and cut off his right ear. 51But Jesus said, "No more of this!" And he touched his ear and healed him. 52Then Jesus said to the chief priests, the officers of the temple police, and the elders who had come for him, "Have you come out with swords and clubs as if I were a bandit? 53When I was with you day after day in the temple, you did not lay hands on me. But this is your hour, and the power of darkness!"

LET'S PRAY!
Lord, hear the prayers of those who call,
Forgive the sins of those who fall,
As Thee we confess,
And humbly profess
That Thou art our all in all!

GOING DEEPER:
Read It! The reading today (OT 34C) is 2 Samuel 5:1–3; CCC #599 (Jesus died not by coincidence, but according to God's mysterious plan).

Do It! Make crosses together to remind yourselves of Jesus' sacrificial love for you! Try paper, sticks from the yard, or other materials. Get creative! And put them somewhere you can see them every day.

Peter Denies Jesus
Matthew 26:57–59, 69–75

When the soldiers had arrested Jesus, the frightened and confused disciples ran away. But Peter quickly came to his senses and began to follow the soldiers from a safe distance. Jesus had predicted that Peter would deny being a follower of Jesus, not just once but three times (Mark 14:30)! This was something Peter could not imagine! Let's see what happens.

Those who had arrested Jesus took him to Caiaphas the high priest, in whose house the scribes and the elders had gathered. 58But Peter was following him at a distance, as far as the courtyard of the high priest; and going inside, he sat with the guards in order to see how this would end. 59Now the chief priests and the whole council were looking for false testimony against Jesus so that they might put him to death. . . .

69Now Peter was sitting outside in the courtyard. A servant-girl came to him and said, "You also were with Jesus the Galilean." 70But he denied it before all of them, saying, "I do not know what you are talking about." 71When he went out to the porch, another servant-girl saw him, and she said to the bystanders, "This man was with Jesus of Nazareth." 72Again he denied it with an oath, "I do not know the man."

73After a little while the bystanders came up and said to Peter, "Certainly you are also one of them, for your accent betrays you." 74Then he began to curse, and he swore an oath, "I do not know the man!" At that moment the cock crowed. 75Then Peter remembered what Jesus had said: "Before the cock crows, you will deny me three times." And he went out and wept bitterly.

LET'S PRAY!

Father, we thank you that even though there are times we are not faithful to you, you forgive us and accept us. We love you! Amen.

QUOTE OF THE DAY:
"Our friends are all those who unjustly afflict us with trials and ordeals, shame and injustice, sorrows and torments, martyrdom and death; we must love them greatly for we all possess eternal life because of them."—St. Francis of Assisi

DID YOU KNOW? John's gospel
says that "another disciple"
(most likely John himself) was
also present, and was able to
get the two of them into the
courtyard of the high priest
Caiaphas (John 18:15).

GOING DEEPER:

Read It! Peter's denials appear in all four gospels
(Matthew 26:69–75; Mark 14:66–72; Luke 22:54–62;
and John 18:15–18, 25–27). See also CCC #1428–29
(Peter had a second conversion).

Do It! When we sin, and confess our mistake, God causes
good things to happen as a result (Romans 8:28).
Discuss what good came out of Peter's mistake.

Jesus Goes Before Pilate
Matthew 27:15–26

*H*ave you ever had to choose up sides to be on a team? Standing there, waiting for your name to be called as first one then the other team captain chooses one kid, then the next, and the next. It feels great if your name is called right away, but not so good if you have to wait. In today's gospel story, Jesus went before Pilate, who let the people decide between Jesus and another prisoner named Barabbas. Which one would be punished, and which one released?

Now at the festival the governor was accustomed to release a prisoner for the crowd, anyone whom they wanted. ¹⁶At that time they had a notorious prisoner, called Jesus Barabbas. ¹⁷So after they had gathered, Pilate said to them, "Whom do you want me to release for you, Jesus Barabbas or Jesus who is called the Messiah?" ¹⁸For he realized that it was out of jealousy that they had handed him over. ¹⁹While he was sitting on the judgment seat, his wife sent word to him, "Have nothing to do with that innocent man, for today I have suffered a great deal because of a dream about him." ²⁰Now the chief priests and the elders persuaded the crowds to ask for Barabbas and to have Jesus killed. ²¹The governor again said to them, "Which of the two do you want me to release for you?" And they said, "Barabbas." ²²Pilate said to them, "Then what should I do with Jesus who is called the Messiah?" All of them said, "Let him be crucified!" ²³Then he asked, "Why, what evil has he done?" But they shouted all the more, "Let him be crucified!"

24 So when Pilate saw that he could do nothing, but rather that a riot was beginning, he took some water and washed his hands before the crowd, saying, "I am innocent of this man's blood; see to it yourselves." ²⁵Then the people as a whole answered, "His blood be on us and on our children!" ²⁶So he released Barabbas for them; and after flogging Jesus, he handed him over to be crucified.

LET'S PRAY!

The LORD is king, he is robed in majesty;
the LORD is robed, he is girded with strength.
He has established the world; it shall never be moved;
²your throne is established from of old;
you are from everlasting.

—Psalm 93:1–2

GOING DEEPER:

Read It! CCC #597 (Who killed Jesus?).

Do It! Movie Night! Watch the *Story of Jesus for Children* film together as a family.

DID YOU KNOW? Pedro Sarubbi, the actor who played Barabbas *in* The Passion of the Christ, said this part had a profound effect in his search for God. In the scene where Pilate releases him, Sarubbi recalls looking up and seeing not an actor, but Jesus himself.[40]

Jesus Carries His Cross

Mark 15:16–27

The Via Dolorosa—Way of Suffering—walked by Jesus on his way to be crucified is the basis for a special set of prayers called the Stations of the Cross. We often pray these prayers during Fridays in Lent to remind us of all the ways our Lord suffered for us. In today's gospel reading, we remember again just how much God loves us, how much he was willing to sacrifice just so we could be with him in the kingdom of heaven!

Then the soldiers led him into the courtyard of the palace (that is, the governor's headquarters); and they called together the whole cohort. [17]And they clothed him in a purple cloak; and after twisting some thorns into a crown, they put it on him. [18]And they began saluting him, "Hail, King of the Jews!" [19]They struck his head with a reed, spat upon him, and knelt down in homage to him. [20]After mocking him, they stripped him of the purple cloak and put his own clothes on him. Then they led him out to crucify him.

21 They compelled a passer-by, who was coming in from the country, to carry his cross; it was Simon of Cyrene, the father of Alexander and Rufus. [22]Then they brought Jesus to the place called Golgotha (which means the place of a skull). [23]And they offered him wine mixed with myrrh; but he did not take it. [24]And they crucified him, and divided his clothes among them, casting lots to decide what each should take.

25 It was nine o'clock in the morning when they crucified him. [26]The inscription of the charge against him read, "The King of the Jews." [27]And with him they crucified two bandits, one on his right and one on his left.

Let's Pray!
Stations of the Cross Prayer

Lord Jesus Christ, take me along that holy
    way you once took to your death,
Take my mind, my memory, above all my
    reluctant heart,
and let me see what once you did for love
    of me and all the world.

Special Words:
Myrrh, one of the three gifts of the Magi, was used to treat battle wounds, certain infections, and skin inflammations. Here, it was used as a painkiller, like morphine.[41]

Going Deeper:

Read It! CCC #1615 ("It is by following Christ, renouncing themselves, and taking up their crosses that spouses . . . 'receive' the original meaning of marriage and live it with the help of Christ").

Do It! This week, pray the Stations of the Cross with your family—either at church or at home.

Jesus Is Crucified

John 19:16–25

*D*o you have a crucifix, a statue of Jesus on the cross, in your church? Crucifixes remind us of how much Jesus suffered out of love for us. The body (or "corpus") on the crucifix reminds us that when we suffer—and everyone suffers sometimes—we have a Savior who understands our pain. We can trust him, no matter what.

So they took Jesus; [17]and carrying the cross by himself, he went out to what is called The Place of the Skull, which in Hebrew is called Golgotha. [18] There they crucified him, and with him two others, one on either side, with Jesus between them. [19]Pilate also had an inscription written and put on the cross. It read, "Jesus of Nazareth, the King of the Jews." [20]Many of the Jews read this inscription, because the place where Jesus was crucified was near the city; and it was written in Hebrew, in Latin, and in Greek. [21]Then the chief priests of the Jews said to Pilate, "Do not write, 'The King of the Jews,' but, 'This man said, I am King of the Jews.'" [22]Pilate answered, "What I have written I have written." [23]When the soldiers had crucified Jesus, they took his clothes and divided them into four parts, one for each soldier. They also took his tunic; now the tunic was seamless, woven in one piece from the top. [24]So they said to one another, "Let us not tear it, but cast lots for it to see who will get it." This was to fulfill what the scripture says,

"They divided my clothes among
themselves,
and for my clothing they cast lots."

[25]And that is what the soldiers did. Meanwhile, standing near the cross of Jesus were his mother, and his mother's sister, Mary the wife of Clopas, and Mary Magdalene.

LET'S PRAY!

Jesus Prayer
A Traditonal Catholic Prayer

Lord Jesus Christ, Son of God, have mercy on me, a sinner!

GOING DEEPER:

Read It! This is read on Good Friday (A, B, C) with Isaiah 52:13–53:12. See also CCC #766 (The Church was born of Jesus' total self-giving).

Do It! Write a prayer or poem to Jesus, telling him how you feel when you look at the crucifix.

QUOTE OF THE DAY: "As Eve was formed by the sleeping Adam's side, so the Church was born from the pierced heart of Christ hanging dead upon the cross."
—*St. Ambrose, CCC #766*

Behold Your Mother
John 19:25–30

For six long hours Jesus hung on the cross, suspended between heaven and earth. During that time, the Blessed Mother and a small group of Jesus' followers stood nearby, unwilling to leave Jesus no matter how much it hurt to look. Even then, Jesus thought not of himself, but of his beloved mother. And so, from the cross, Jesus entrusted Mary to "the disciple whom he loved" (John) and in so doing, gave her to all of us, his Church! Because of Jesus, his Father became our heavenly Father, and his mother, our spiritual mother as well.

Meanwhile, standing near the cross of Jesus were his mother, and his mother's sister, Mary the wife of Clopas, and Mary Magdalene. ²⁶When Jesus saw his mother and the disciple whom he loved standing beside her, he said to his mother, "Woman, here is your son." ²⁷Then he said to the disciple, "Here is your mother." And from that hour the disciple took her into his own home.

28 After this, when Jesus knew that all was now finished, he said (in order to fulfill the scripture), "I am thirsty." ²⁹A jar full of sour wine was standing there. So they put a sponge full of the wine on a branch of hyssop and held it to his mouth. ³⁰When Jesus had received the wine, he said, "It is finished." Then he bowed his head and gave up his spirit.

LET'S PRAY!

As we contemplate Your death, Lord Jesus, we understand how much You must have loved us. Help us to draw close to You as we offer the Sorrowful Mysteries of the Rosary now. (Pray the Rosary).

Read It! CCC #964 (Why did Jesus say, "Woman, behold your son"?).

Do It! Mothers are such a special blessing from God. Give your mom a great big hug, and thank God for her!

QUOTE OF THE DAY: *"The rosary is the book of the blind, where souls see and there enact the greatest drama of love the world has ever known; . . . The power of the rosary is beyond description."—Archbishop Fulton Sheen*

Jesus Is Buried

John 19:38–42

Have you ever lost a pet or a family member you love very much? It's one of the hardest things in the world. Death leaves a big hole in your heart; for a long time you may think that hole will never fill again. That's how it felt when Jesus died too. His friends and family didn't understand why Jesus had died or that three days later, they would be happy again when he came back to life! At that moment, all they could do was bury Jesus with great tenderness and love.

After these things, Joseph of Arimathea, who was a disciple of Jesus, though a secret one because of his fear of the Jews, asked Pilate to let him take away the body of Jesus. Pilate gave him permission; so he came and removed his body. ³⁹Nicodemus, who had at first come to Jesus by night, also came, bringing a mixture of myrrh and aloes, weighing about a hundred pounds. ⁴⁰They took the body of Jesus and wrapped it with the spices in linen cloths, according to the burial custom of the Jews. ⁴¹Now there was a garden in the place where he was crucified, and in the garden there was a new tomb in which no one had ever been laid. ⁴²And so, because it was the Jewish day of Preparation, and the tomb was nearby, they laid Jesus there.

LET'S PRAY!
Rosary Prayer for Someone Who Has Died
A Traditonal Catholic Prayer

When someone dies, it can be a great comfort to offer a Rosary. On each large bead of the Rosary, after the Glory Be, say: "Eternal rest grant unto [him, her], O Lord. And let perpetual light shine upon [him, her]. May [his, her] soul, and the souls of all the faithful departed, through the mercy of God, rest in peace. Amen."

SPECIAL WORDS: The "Rosary" is a traditional Catholic prayer, which is attributed to St. Dominic. Prayed on special prayer beads (made of five large and fifty-three small beads), we use it to meditate on the Joyful, Sorrowful, Luminous, and Glorious Mysteries in the story of Jesus and the Blessed Mother. The repetitive prayers help to clear our minds of distractions, so we can better lift our thoughts toward God. The Rosary can be a tremendous gift during times of great stress or sorrow, when our minds can't think of what to say. Turn the page for instructions.

Read It! CCC #628 (Baptism is a symbol of death).

Do It! Tonight before bed, pray the rosary together as a family.

DID YOU KNOW? Joseph of Arimathea may have been the uncle of the Virgin Mary. Some people think he became a missionary to Gaul and Briton.[43]

HOW TO PRAY THE ROSARY

1. Make the Sign of the Cross, and say the "Apostles' Creed."
2. Say the "Our Father."
3. Say three "Hail Marys," one on each small bead above cross.
4. Say the "Glory be to the Father."
5. Announce the First Mystery; then say the "Our Father."
6. Say ten "Hail Marys," while meditating on the Mystery.
7. Say the "Glory be to the Father."
8. Announce the Second Mystery; then say the "Our Father."
9. Repeat 6 and 7 and continue with the Third, Fourth, and Fifth Mysteries in the same manner.
10. Say "Hail, Holy Queen."
11. Make the sign of the Cross.

JOYFUL MYSTERIES

The Annunciation: The Angel appears to Mary (Luke 1:26–38).

The Visitation: Mary goes to see Elizabeth (Luke 1:39–49).

The Nativity: Jesus is born (Luke 2:6–12).

The Presentation: Simeon and Anna Meet Jesus in the Temple (Luke 2:22–35).

The Reunion: Joseph and Mary find Jesus in the Temple (Luke 2:41–51).

LUMINOUS MYSTERIES

The Baptism: Jesus is baptized by John the Baptist (Matthew 3:13–17).

The Wedding: Jesus' first miracle, turning water to wine (John 2:1–12).

The Proclamation: Jesus proclaims the Kingdom of God (Mark 1:15).

The Transfiguration: Jesus reveals his divine nature to the disciples (Luke 9:28–35).

The Eucharist: Jesus institutes the Blessed Sacrament (Mark 14:22–25).

SORROWFUL MYSTERIES

The Garden: Jesus in Gethsemane (Matthew 26:36–39).

The Pillar: Jesus is scourged (Mark 15:15).

The Crown: Jesus is crowned with thorns (Matthew 27:27–31).

The Struggle: Jesus carries his cross (Luke 23:26–32).

The Crucifixion: Jesus is crucified and dies (John 19:25–27).

GLORIOUS MYSTERIES

The Resurrection: The women find the empty tomb (Matthew 28:1–6).

The Ascension: Jesus returns to heaven (Luke 24:36–51).

The Paraclete: The Holy Spirit descends at Pentecost (Acts 2:1–4).

The Assumption: Mary is taken into heaven (Judith 13:18-20; 15:10).

The Coronation: Mary is crowned queen of heaven (Revelation 12:1).

Jesus Is Alive!

John 20:1–10

Imagine you were a Roman soldier, put in charge of guarding the tomb of Jesus the Nazarene. In the marketplace and on the street, everyone was talking about the trial and execution of this man, so beloved by some and so hated by others. Some say he had predicted that he would rise from the dead after three days, and you were sent to make sure it didn't happen. Then suddenly, in a flash of blinding light, the tomb was empty! What now?

Early on the first day of the week, while it was still dark, Mary Magdalene came to the tomb and saw that the stone had been removed from the tomb. ²So she ran and went to Simon Peter and the other disciple, the one whom Jesus loved, and said to them, "They have taken the Lord out of the tomb, and we do not know where they have laid him." ³Then Peter and the other disciple set out and went toward the tomb. ⁴The two were running together, but the other disciple outran Peter and reached the tomb first. ⁵He bent down to look in and saw the linen wrappings lying there, but he did not go in. ⁶Then Simon Peter came, following him, and went into the tomb. He saw the linen wrappings lying there, ⁷and the cloth that had been on Jesus' head, not lying with the linen wrappings but rolled up in a place by itself. ⁸Then the other disciple, who reached the tomb first, also went in, and he saw and believed; ⁹for as yet they did not understand the scripture, that he must rise from the dead. ¹⁰Then the disciples returned to their homes.

LET'S PRAY!

Dear Jesus, your disciples must have been so thrilled to find you had risen from the dead. Help us to remember you and your resurrection with the same enthusiasm every day! Amen.

GOING DEEPER:

Read It! CCC #640 (How is Jesus' resurrection different from that of Lazarus or Jairus's daughter?).

Do It! Using the letters of the word *resurrection*, make an acrostic that tells what Jesus' resurrection means to you.

DID YOU KNOW? Although this account mentions only Mary Magdalene at the tomb, the use of "we" (vs. 2) suggests she may not have been alone, which is consistent with other accounts.

Mary Sees Jesus
John 20:11–18

*S*everal women followed Jesus and the Twelve, tending to their needs. One was Mary Magdalene, from whom Jesus had driven away seven evil spirits (Luke 8:2). How she loved Jesus for freeing her from such bondage! When Jesus was arrested and crucified, she stayed nearby. Early Sunday morning, she and a few others returned to the tomb to tend to his body and discovered that the heavy stone over the tomb was rolled away and the tomb was empty! She ran to get Peter and the others, but after they returned home, all Mary could do was stand by the tomb and weep. What had they done with Jesus?

Mary stood weeping outside the tomb. As she wept, she bent over to look into the tomb; [12]and she saw two angels in white, sitting where the body of Jesus had been lying, one at the head and the other at the feet. [13]They said to her, "Woman, why are you weeping?" She said to them, "They have taken away my Lord, and I do not know where they have laid him." [14]When she had said this, she turned around and saw Jesus standing there, but she did not know that it was Jesus. [15]Jesus said to her, "Woman, why are you weeping? Whom are you looking for?" Supposing him to be the gardener, she said to him, "Sir, if you have carried him away, tell me where you have laid him, and I will take him away." [16]Jesus said to her, "Mary!" She turned and said to him in Hebrew, "Rabbouni!" (which means Teacher). [17]Jesus said to her, "Do not hold on to me, because I have not yet ascended to the Father. But go to my brothers and say to them, 'I am ascending to my Father and your Father, to my God and your God.'" [18]Mary Magdalene went and announced to the disciples, "I have seen the Lord"; and she told them that he had said these things to her.

Let's Pray!

All over the world, people are sad and feeling far away from you, God. Help them to know your presence. In the name of the Father, and the Son, and the Holy Spirit, Amen!

Going Deeper:

Read It! The reading today (EA 1A, B, C) is Acts 10:34, 37–43; CCC #641 (Mary Magdalene was the first to see Jesus after he rose from death).

Do It! When Jesus rose from the dead, a giant stone had been rolled away. Find some interesting stones or rocks, and decorate them with craft paint to be paper weights!

Did You Know?
The Jews counted time differently than we do. Jesus died on Friday about 3:00 p.m. (Day 1), Sabbath was from sundown Friday to sundown Saturday (Day 2); Saturday evening would have started the third day.

Doubting Thomas
John 20:19–28

*P*rove it!" It's what you might say if someone tells you something amazing has just happened—something you find hard to believe. In today's gospel story, St. Thomas, or "doubting Thomas," as he is sometimes called, has a hard time believing the news that Jesus had appeared to the disciples (verse 24). He said that he was not going to believe it unless he could see him too. And what do you think happened?

When it was evening on that day, the first day of the week, and the doors of the house where the disciples had met were locked for fear of the Jews, Jesus came and stood among them and said, "Peace be with you." ²⁰After he said this, he showed them his hands and his side. Then the disciples rejoiced when they saw the Lord. ²¹Jesus said to them again, "Peace be with you. As the Father has sent me, so I send you." ²²When he had said this, he breathed on them and said to them, "Receive the Holy Spirit. ²³If you forgive the sins of any, they are forgiven them; if you retain the sins of any, they are retained."

24 But Thomas (who was called the Twin), one of the twelve, was not with them when Jesus came. ²⁵So the other disciples told him, "We have seen the Lord." But he said to them, "Unless I see the mark of the nails in his hands, and put my finger in the mark of the nails and my hand in his side, I will not believe."

26 A week later his disciples were again in the house, and Thomas was with them. Although the doors were shut, Jesus came and stood among them and said, "Peace be with you." ²⁷Then he said to Thomas, "Put your finger here and see my hands. Reach out your hand and put it in my side. Do not doubt but believe." ²⁸Thomas answered him, "My Lord and my God!"

Let's Pray!
Lord, send us your Spirit so that though we have never seen Jesus, our faith in him might never waiver. In the name of the Father, and the Son, and the Holy Spirit, Amen!

GOING DEEPER:

Read It! CCC #644 (Other disciples doubted).

Do It! Do you ever doubt God's love for you? Check out CCC #1806 (The virtue of prudence, right reason in action, helps us overcome doubt).

Jesus Forgives Peter

John 21:1–19

*B*efore the cock crows you will deny me three times," Jesus had warned Peter, who strongly said he would not (Mark 14:30–31). But sure enough, on the night Jesus was arrested, Simon Peter said three times that he did not know his dear Friend. Now that Jesus was alive, Peter wondered, how could Jesus ever forgive him for saying such things? Peter was so ashamed and so afraid of what Jesus would say to him when they met again.

After these things Jesus showed himself again to the disciples by the Sea of Tiberias; and he showed himself in this way. ²Gathered there together were Simon Peter, Thomas called the Twin, Nathanael of Cana in Galilee, the sons of Zebedee, and two others of his disciples. ³Simon Peter said to them, "I am going fishing." They said to him, "We will go with you." They went out and got into the boat, but that night they caught nothing.

4 Just after daybreak, Jesus stood on the beach; but the disciples did not know that it was Jesus. ⁵Jesus said to them, "Children, you have no fish, have you?" They answered him, "No." ⁶He said to them, "Cast the net to the right side of the boat, and you will find some." So they cast it, and now they were not able to haul it in because there were so many fish. ⁷That disciple whom Jesus loved said to Peter, "It is the Lord!" When Simon Peter heard that it was the Lord, he put on some clothes, for he was naked, and jumped into the sea. ⁸But the other disciples came in the boat, dragging the net full of fish, for they were not far from the land, only about a hundred yards off.

9 When they had gone ashore, they saw a charcoal fire there, with fish on it, and bread. ¹⁰Jesus said to them, "Bring some of the fish that you have just caught." ¹¹So Simon Peter went aboard and hauled the net ashore, full of large fish, a hundred fifty-three of them; and though there were so many, the net was not torn. ¹²Jesus said to them, "Come and have breakfast." Now none of the disciples dared to ask him, "Who are you?" because they knew it was the Lord. ¹³Jesus came and took the bread and gave it to them, and did the same with the fish. ¹⁴This was now the third time that Jesus appeared to the disciples after he was raised from the dead.

15 When they had finished breakfast, Jesus said to Simon Peter, "Simon son of John, do you love me more than these?" He said to him, "Yes, Lord; you know that I love you." Jesus said to him, "Feed my lambs." ¹⁶A second time he said to him, "Simon son of John, do you love me?" He said to him, "Yes, Lord; you know that I love you." Jesus said to him, "Tend my sheep." ¹⁷He said to him the third time, "Simon son of John, do you love me?" Peter felt hurt because he said to him the third time, "Do you love me?" And he said to him, "Lord, you know everything; you know that I love you." Jesus said to him, "Feed my sheep. ¹⁸Very truly, I tell you, when you were younger, you used to fasten your own belt and to go wherever you wished. But when you grow old, you will

stretch out your hands, and someone else will fasten a belt around you and take you where you do not wish to go." [19](He said this to indicate the kind of death by which he would glorify God.) After this he said to him, "Follow me."

LET'S PRAY!

Father, we thank you for your blessed forgiveness. We thank you for providing us grace, even when we deny you. In the name of the Father, and the Son, and the Holy Spirit, Amen.

GOING DEEPER:

Read It! CCC #1851 (The Passion reveals the murderous nature of sin).

Do It! Can you think of a time when you were embarrassed to talk about God, and God forgave you and gave you a second chance? Talk about these times together and what you can do to not be afraid to talk about Jesus.

Travelers to Emmaus
Luke 24:13–20, 25–31

The same day that the disciples discovered the empty tomb, believers several miles away were also catching a glimpse of the risen Christ. Like Mary Magdalene, they did not immediately recognize him, and they spoke quite some time before their eyes were opened.

Now on that same day two of them were going to a village called Emmaus, about seven miles from Jerusalem, ¹⁴and talking with each other about all these things that had happened. ¹⁵While they were talking and discussing, Jesus himself came near and went with them, ¹⁶but their eyes were kept from recognizing him. ¹⁷And he said to them, "What are you discussing with each other while you walk along?" They stood still, looking sad. ¹⁸Then one of them, whose name was Cleopas, answered him, "Are you the only stranger in Jerusalem who does not know the things that have taken place there in these days?" ¹⁹He asked them, "What things?" They replied, "The things about Jesus of Nazareth, who was a prophet mighty in deed and word before God and all the people, ²⁰and how our chief priests and leaders handed him over to be condemned to death and crucified him. . . ." ²⁵Then he said to them, "Oh, how foolish you are, and how slow of heart to believe all that the prophets have declared! ²⁶Was it not necessary that the Messiah should suffer these things and then enter into his glory?" ²⁷Then beginning with Moses and all the prophets, he interpreted to them the things about himself in all the scriptures.

28 As they came near the village . . . 29 they urged him strongly, "Stay with us, because it is almost evening. . . ." ³⁰When he was at the table with them, he took bread, blessed and broke it, and gave it to them. ³¹Then their eyes were opened, and they recognized him; and he vanished from their sight.

LET'S PRAY!
Emmaus Prayer for Priests
A Traditonal Catholic Prayer

Lord Jesus, hear our prayer
For the spiritual renewal of priests.
We praise you for giving their ministry to
   the Church.
In these days renew them with the gifts
   of your Spirit.
Give priests enthusiasm for the Gospel,
Zeal for the salvation of all,
Courage in leadership, humility in service,
Fellowship with one another and with all
   their brothers and sisters in You.
For You love them, Lord Jesus,
And we love and pray for them in Your
   name. Amen.

GOING DEEPER:
Read It! Today's reading (EA 3A) is Acts 2:22–33; CCC #1094 (The Old
   Testament showed things that would come in the New Testament).
Do It! Light a candle and offer the "Emmaus Prayer for Priests" for your pastor!

The Ascension
Luke 24:36–51

Right away the disciples at Emmaus got up and went right back to Jerusalem, to tell Peter and the others what had happened. They had known it was Jesus in the "breaking of the bread"—when he offered himself to them in the Eucharist.

While they were talking about this, Jesus himself stood among them and said to them, "Peace be with you." [37]They were startled and terrified, and thought that they were seeing a ghost. [38]He said to them, "Why are you frightened, and why do doubts arise in your hearts? [39]Look at my hands and my feet; see that it is I myself. Touch me and see; for a ghost does not have flesh and bones as you see that I have." [40]And when he had said this, he showed them his hands and his feet. [41]While in their joy they were disbelieving and still wondering, he said to them, "Have you anything here to eat?" [42]They gave him a piece of broiled fish, [43]and he took it and ate in their presence.

44 Then he said to them, "These are my words that I spoke to you while I was still with you—that everything written about me in the law of Moses, the prophets, and the psalms must be fulfilled."

[45]Then he opened their minds to understand the scriptures, [46]and he said to them, "Thus it is written, that the Messiah is to suffer and to rise from the dead on the third day, [47]and that repentance and forgiveness of sins is to be proclaimed in his name to all nations, beginning from Jerusalem. [48]You are witnesses of these things. [49]And see, I am sending upon you what my Father promised; so stay here in the city until you have been clothed with power from on high."

50 Then he led them out as far as Bethany, and, lifting up his hands, he blessed them. [51]While he was blessing them, he withdrew from them and was carried up into heaven.

Let's Pray!

Maranatha . . . Come, Lord Jesus, come!
Our Father . . .

Going Deeper:

Read It! The reading today (EA 3B) is Acts 3:13–19; CCC
  #665–67 (Christ intercedes for us in heaven).
Do It! Learn the "Our Father" in a language other than
  English.

Did You Know? The "Convent of the Pater Noster," built on the Mount of Olives, has a collection of one-hundred and forty tiles with the "Our Father" written in different languages.

Other Apostles
Acts 1:13–17, 21–26

When Judas died (Matthew 27:5) the apostles gathered to name his successor. Very little is known about Matthias, the man who took Judas's place. Soon the Apostle Paul also emerged and began to take the gospel message to the Gentiles. These fourteen men, who had met Jesus himself, had special authority to teach and defend the teachings of the Lord. They passed this authority onto other men, as Jesus instructed, and soon the Church began to grow all over the world!

When they had entered the city, they went to the room upstairs where they were staying, Peter, and John, and James, and Andrew, Philip and Thomas, Bartholomew and Matthew, James son of Alphaeus, and Simon the Zealot, and Judas son of James. [14]All these were constantly devoting themselves to prayer, together with certain women, including Mary the mother of Jesus, as well as his brothers.

[15] In those days Peter stood up among the believers (together the crowd numbered about one hundred twenty persons) and said, [16]"Friends, the scripture had to be fulfilled, which the Holy Spirit through David foretold concerning Judas, who became a guide for those who arrested Jesus—[17]for he was numbered among us and was allotted his share in this ministry. . . . [21]So one of the men who have accompanied us during all the time that the Lord Jesus went in and out among us, [22]beginning from the baptism of John until the day when he was taken up from us—one of these must become a witness with us to his resurrection."

[23]So they proposed two, Joseph called Barsabbas, who was also known as Justus, and Matthias. [24]Then they prayed and said, "Lord, you know everyone's heart. Show us which one of these two you have chosen [25]to take the place in this ministry and apostleship from which Judas turned aside to go to his own place." [26]And they cast lots for them, and the lot fell on Matthias; and he was added to the eleven apostles.

LET'S PRAY!
Prayer of Our Lady of Fatima

O my Jesus, forgive us our sins, save us from the fires of Hell, lead all souls to Heaven, especially those most in need of your mercy.

DID YOU KNOW? *Among
the seventy closest followers
of Jesus, Matthias was with
Jesus from his baptism
to his ascension
(Acts 1:21–22).*

GOING DEEPER:

Read It! The reading today (EA 7B) is John 17:1–11;
CCC #642 (Apostles are the primary witnesses to the
Resurrection).

Do It! Learn more about what happened to the apostles
and early Christians.

Pentecost
Acts 2:1–11

Fifty days after the Resurrection—just ten days after Jesus ascended into heaven—the Holy Spirit came upon the apostles, causing them to proclaim the gospel with great power to men from nations around the world (verses 9–11). Can you imagine what it must have been like, to hear that great rush of wind and to see what looked like tongues of fire leap around the room?

When the day of Pentecost had come, they were all together in one place. ²And suddenly from heaven there came a sound like the rush of a violent wind, and it filled the entire house where they were sitting. ³Divided tongues, as of fire, appeared among them, and a tongue rested on each of them. ⁴All of them were filled with the Holy Spirit and began to speak in other languages, as the Spirit gave them ability.

5 Now there were devout Jews from every nation under heaven living in Jerusalem. ⁶And at this sound the crowd gathered and was bewildered, because each one heard them speaking in the native language of each. ⁷Amazed and astonished, they asked, "Are not all these who are speaking Galileans? ⁸And how is it that we hear, each of us, in our own native language? ⁹Parthians, Medes, Elamites, and residents of Mesopotamia, Judea and Cappadocia, Pontus and Asia, ¹⁰Phrygia and Pamphylia, Egypt and the parts of Libya belonging to Cyrene, and visitors from Rome, both Jews and proselytes, ¹¹Cretans and Arabs—in our own languages we hear them speaking about God's deeds of power."

Let's Pray!

Lord, we thank you for sending us your Holy Spirit to be with us at all times. Help us to be aware of your presence everyday, and speak through us so all we come in contact with can hear from you. Amen.

Going Deeper:

Read It! The gospel reading today (Pentecost A) is John 20:19–23; CCC #2623 (The Spirit came on the apostles on the day of Pentecost).

Do It! Create a Pentecost votive candle with an empty soup can.

Did You Know?
Pentecost was also called the "Feast of Firstfruits" and the "Feast of Harvest."

Peter Heals the Lame Man

Acts 3:1–10

The Beautiful Gate was a favorite entrance to the temple. Since many people passed by it every day, it was a good place for a beggar to sit and ask for money. So when Peter and John healed a man there, many people soon knew what had happened.

One day Peter and John were going up to the temple at the hour of prayer, at three o'clock in the afternoon. ²And a man lame from birth was being carried in. People would lay him daily at the gate of the temple called the Beautiful Gate so that he could ask for alms from those entering the temple. ³When he saw Peter and John about to go into the temple, he asked them for alms. ⁴Peter looked intently at him, as did John, and said, "Look at us." ⁵And he fixed his attention on them, expecting to receive something from them. ⁶But Peter said, "I have no silver or gold, but what I have I give you; in the name of Jesus Christ of Nazareth, stand up and walk." ⁷And he took him by the right hand and raised him up; and immediately his feet and ankles were made strong.

⁸Jumping up, he stood and began to walk, and he entered the temple with them, walking and leaping and praising God. ⁹All the people saw him walking and praising God, ¹⁰and they recognized him as the one who used to sit and ask for alms at the Beautiful Gate of the temple; and they were filled with wonder and amazement at what had happened to him.

LET'S PRAY!

"Give us, Lord, a humble, quiet, peaceable, patient, tender, and charitable mind, and in all our thoughts, words and deeds a taste of the Holy Spirit. Give us, Lord, a lively faith, a firm hope, a fervent charity, a love of you."
—St. Thomas More

SPECIAL WORDS:
The "Beautiful Gate" (or
"Golden Gate") is on the east
side of the temple. Some think
it was in the temple court
between the court of Gentiles
and the court of women.

GOING DEEPER:

Read It! This is the first reading of the Feast of Saints
   Peter and Paul (B). The gospel is John 21:15–20; CCC
   #2640 (The prayer of praise).

Do It! Thank God for your physical abilities today! As
   a family, go outside and play a game of tag, kickball,
   baseball, or another active game.

Peter and John Arrested

Acts 4:1–14, 21–22

*A*s the early Church quickly grew from a handful to 5,000 members, the Jewish religious leaders became very nervous about the power that the apostles had. Early Christians were Jews who continued to observe the Jewish sabbath and were watched with suspicion because of their gatherings on Sunday (the day of Resurrection) to "break bread." This was a special worry for the Sadducees, a Jewish group who did not believe in the Resurrection.

While Peter and John were speaking to the people, the priests, the captain of the temple, and the Sadducees came to them, ²much annoyed because they were teaching the people and proclaiming that in Jesus there is the resurrection of the dead. ³So they arrested them and put them in custody until the next day, for it was already evening. ⁴But many of those who heard the word believed; and they numbered about five thousand.

5 The next day their rulers, elders, and scribes assembled in Jerusalem, ⁶with Annas the high priest, Caiaphas, John, and Alexander, and all who were of the high-priestly family. ⁷When they had made the prisoners stand in their midst, they inquired, "By what power or by what name did you do this?" ⁸Then Peter, filled with the Holy Spirit, said to them, "Rulers of the people and elders, ⁹if we are questioned today because of a good deed done to someone who was sick and are asked how this man has been healed, ¹⁰let it be known to all of you, and to all the people of Israel, that this man [the lame man healed in Acts 3] is standing before you in good health by the name of Jesus Christ of Nazareth, whom you crucified, whom God raised from the dead. ¹¹This Jesus is

'the stone that was rejected by you, the builders;

it has become the cornerstone.'

¹²There is salvation in no one else, for there is no other name under heaven given among mortals by which we must be saved."

13 Now when they saw the boldness of Peter and John and realized that they were uneducated and ordinary men, they were amazed and recognized them as companions of Jesus. ¹⁴When they saw the man who had been cured standing beside them, they had nothing to say in opposition. . . . ²¹After threatening them again, they let them go, finding no way to punish them because of the people, for all of them praised God for what had happened. ²²For the man on whom this sign of healing had been performed was more than forty years old.

LET'S PRAY!

"Thank you, Lord, for the sacraments of healing, especially the anointing of the sick. Thank you for godly priests who through the sacraments offer your healing touch to the world. In the name of the Father, and the Son, and the Holy Spirit, Amen!"

QUOTE OF THE DAY:
*"Prayer in private results
in boldness in public."*
—Edwin Louis Cole

GOING DEEPER:

Read It! The gospel reading today (EA 4 B) is John 10:11–18; See also CCC #1918–23 (overview of social justice).

Do It! Take a walk together as a family and pray for those in your neighborhood who might need God's healing touch.

Ananias and Sapphira

Acts 4:33–35; 5:1–11

In the early Christian community, believers often pooled their resources and lived all together so that those with greater wealth could tend to the needs of those who had less, treating one another as true brothers and sisters in Christ. This was especially important because some new believers lost everything, including family ties, to worship Christ and be followers of "the Way." No one was forced to give up their wealth, but those who chose to make this sacrifice were greatly admired within the community. Sadly, one couple made a very bad choice!

With great power the apostles gave their testimony to the resurrection of the Lord Jesus, and great grace was upon them all. [34]There was not a needy person among them, for as many as owned lands or houses sold them and brought the proceeds of what was sold. [35]They laid it at the apostles' feet, and it was distributed to each as any had need. . . .

5 But a man named Ananias, with the consent of his wife Sapphira, sold a piece of property; [2]with his wife's knowledge, he kept back some of the proceeds, and brought only a part and laid it at the apostles' feet. [3]"Ananias," Peter asked, "why has Satan filled your heart to lie to the Holy Spirit and to keep back part of the proceeds of the land? [4]While it remained unsold, did it not remain your own? And after it was sold, were not the proceeds at your disposal? How is it that you have contrived this deed in your heart? You did not lie to us but to God!" [5]Now when Ananias heard these words, he fell down and died. And great fear seized all who heard of it. [6]The young men came and wrapped up his body, then carried him out and buried him.

[7] After an interval of about three hours his wife came in, not knowing what had happened. [8]Peter said to her, "Tell me whether you and your husband sold the land for such and such a price." And she said, "Yes, that was the price." [9]Then Peter said to her, "How is it that you have agreed together to put the Spirit of the Lord to the test? Look, the feet of those who have buried your husband are at the door, and they will carry you out." [10]Immediately she fell down at his feet and died. When the young men came in they found her dead, so they carried her out and buried her beside her husband. [11]And great fear seized the whole church and all who heard of these things.

LET'S PRAY!

Lord, we thank you and we bless you for your many gifts to us. Make us mindful of the needs of others, so that we become good stewards of all you have entrusted to us. In the name of the Father, and the Son, and the Holy Spirit, Amen!

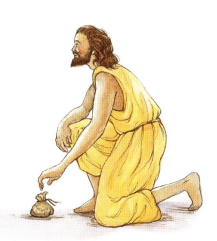

GOING DEEPER:

Read It! The reading for today (EA 2B) is John 10:19–31; CCC #1886–88 (People should share their spiritual knowledge with people in the society).

Do It! What does this Catechism passage reveal about why Ananias and Sapphira were judged so harshly?

BLESSED ARE YOU, LOVING FATHER, RULER OF THE UNIVERSE

A Traditonal Catholic Prayer

You have given us your Son,

And have made us temples of your Holy Spirit.

Fill our family with your light and peace.

Have mercy on all who suffer,

And bring us to everlasting joy with you, Father,

We bless your name forever and ever. Amen.

The Great Escape
Acts 5:12–26

*A*s the apostles experienced greater and greater resistance from the Jewish leaders, and more and more admiration from the people, they had to make a choice. If they continued to preach and teach as Jesus had instructed them, their lives might be in danger. Should they move on and find a safer place to preach the gospel, or stay right where they were, regardless of the consequences?

Now many signs and wonders were done among the people through the apostles. And they were all together in Solomon's Portico. [13]None of the rest dared to join them, but the people held them in high esteem. [14]Yet more than ever believers were added to the Lord, great numbers of both men and women, [15]so that they even carried out the sick into the streets, and laid them on cots and mats, in order that Peter's shadow might fall on some of them as he came by. [16]A great number of people would also gather from the towns around Jerusalem, bringing the sick and those tormented by unclean spirits, and they were all cured.

[17] Then the high priest took action; he and all who were with him (that is, the sect of the Sadducees), being filled with jealousy, [18]arrested the apostles and put them in the public prison. [19]But during the night an angel of the Lord opened the prison doors, brought them out, and said, [20]"Go, stand in the temple and tell the people the whole message about this life." [21]When they heard this, they entered the temple at daybreak and went on with their teaching.

When the high priest and those with him arrived, they called together the council and the whole body of the elders of Israel, and sent to the prison to have them brought. [22]But when the temple police went there, they did not find them in the prison; so they returned and reported, [23]"We found the prison securely locked and the guards standing at the doors, but when we opened them, we found no one inside." [24]Now when the captain of the temple and the chief priests heard these words, they were perplexed about them, wondering what might be going on. [25]Then someone arrived and announced, "Look, the men whom you put in prison are standing in the temple and teaching the people!" [26]Then the captain went with the temple police and brought them, but without violence, for they were afraid of being stoned by the people.

LET'S PRAY!
Father, thank you for your miraculous protection of your disciples! And thank you for your miraculous protection of us! Amen.

GOING DEEPER:

Read It! The gospel reading for today (EA 6C) is John 14:23–29; CCC #334 ("The whole life of the Church benefits from the mysterious and powerful help of angels").

Do It! In many parts of the world, Christians are still harmed, and sometimes even killed, for their faith! Take time today to pray for those believers who are suffering for Jesus.

Wise Gamaliel
Acts 5:27–29, 33–42

In today's New Testament story, a wise Jewish rabbi, who may have been a secret follower of Christ, influences the Sanhedrin in order to help the apostles.

When they [the temple police] had brought them [Peter and the apostles], they had them stand before the council. The high priest questioned them, [28]saying, "We gave you strict orders not to teach in this name, yet here you have filled Jerusalem with your teaching and you are determined to bring this man's blood on us." [29]But Peter and the apostles answered, "We must obey God rather than any human authority. . . ."

33 When they heard this, they were enraged and wanted to kill them. [34]But a Pharisee in the council named Gamaliel, a teacher of the law, respected by all the people, stood up and ordered the men to be put outside for a short time. [35]Then he said to them, "Fellow Israelites, consider carefully what you propose to do to these men. [36]For some time ago Theudas rose up, claiming to be somebody, and a number of men, about four hundred, joined him; but he was killed, and all who followed him were dispersed and disappeared. [37]After him Judas the Galilean rose up at the time of the census and got people to follow him; he also perished, and all who followed him were scattered. [38]So in the present case, I tell you, keep away from these men and let them alone; because if this plan or this undertaking is of human origin, it will fail; [39]but if it is of God, you will not be able to overthrow them—in that case you may even be found fighting against God!"

They were convinced by him, [40]and when they had called in the apostles, they had them flogged. Then they ordered them not to speak in the name of Jesus, and let them go. [41]As they left the council, they rejoiced that they were considered worthy to suffer dishonor for the sake of the name. [42]And every day in the temple and at home they did not cease to teach and proclaim Jesus as the Messiah.

LET'S PRAY!

Lord, help us to seek your will in every aspect of our lives, so we are always in harmony with the movement of your Spirit. In the name of the Father, and the Son, and the Holy Spirit, Amen!

GOING DEEPER:

Read It! CCC #2242 (What should we do when faced with an unjust law?).

Do It! Read the Catechism to help you answer this question: Is it ever okay to disobey the law?

The First Deacons
Acts 6:2–5, 8–15

Have you ever thought about how busy a priest's life must be—saying Mass, attending to the needs of families, running the parish, and everything else a priest must do—all without the support of family? The apostles also felt pulled in many different directions, especially with attending to the needs of the poor widows in their communities. They needed some helpers!

The twelve called together the whole community of the disciples and said, "It is not right that we should neglect the word of God in order to wait on tables. ³Therefore, friends, select from among yourselves seven men of good standing, full of the Spirit and of wisdom, whom we may appoint to this task, ⁴while we, for our part, will devote ourselves to prayer and to serving the word." ⁵What they said pleased the whole community, and they chose Stephen, a man full of faith and the Holy Spirit, together with Philip, Prochorus, Nicanor, Timon, Parmenas, and Nicolaus, a proselyte of Antioch. . . .

8 Stephen, full of grace and power, did great wonders and signs among the people. ⁹Then some of those who belonged to the synagogue of the Freedmen (as it was called), Cyrenians, Alexandrians, and others of those from Cilicia and Asia, stood up and argued with Stephen. ¹⁰But they could not withstand the wisdom and the Spirit with which he spoke. ¹¹Then they secretly instigated some men to say, "We have heard him speak blasphemous words against Moses and God." ¹²They stirred up the people as well as the elders and the scribes; then they suddenly confronted

him, seized him, and brought him before the council. ¹³They set up false witnesses who said, "This man never stops saying things against this holy place and the law; ¹⁴for we have heard him say that this Jesus of Nazareth will destroy this place and will change the customs that Moses handed on to us." ¹⁵And all who sat in the council looked intently at him, and they saw that his face was like the face of an angel.

Let's Pray!

God our Father, hear our prayer for your faithful people. In our vocation and ministry, may each of us be instruments of your love. Give to your servants the gifts of grace we need to fulfill our calling; through our Lord and Savior Jesus Christ, who reigns with you, in the unity of the Holy Spirit, one God, now and forever. Amen!

Special Words: A "proselyte" is someone who converts from another faith. The "synagogue of Freedmen" may have been for released Roman slaves who had converted to the faith, or for Jews from the northern African community of Libertum.⁴⁶

GOING DEEPER:

Read It! The reading today (EA 5A) is John 14:1–12; CCC #1570 (What is a deacon?).

Do It! Deacons are still actively used in the Church today. Send a thank-you note to the deacons in your parish for all the good work they do.

Stephen Dies a Martyr
Acts 7:54–8:1

*S*t. Stephen is considered the first Christian martyr for holding on to his faith in Jesus even when he faced death. The Church Father Tertullian said, "The blood of the martyrs is the seed of the Church," and here we see that the sacrifice of Stephen did indeed bear rich fruit. Saul of Tarsus, the young Pharisee who witnessed his death, was to become one of the most powerful teachers of the truth of the gospel the world has ever known!

When they heard these things, they became enraged and ground their teeth at Stephen. 55But filled with the Holy Spirit, he gazed into heaven and saw the glory of God and Jesus standing at the right hand of God. 56"Look," he said, "I see the heavens opened and the Son of Man standing at the right hand of God!" 57But they covered their ears, and with a loud shout all rushed together against him. 58Then they dragged him out of the city and began to stone him; and the witnesses laid their coats at the feet of a young man named Saul. 59While they were stoning Stephen, he prayed, "Lord Jesus, receive my spirit." 60Then he knelt down and cried out in a loud voice, "Lord, do not hold this sin against them." When he had said this, he died.

8 And Saul approved of their killing him. That day a severe persecution began against the church in Jerusalem, and all except the apostles were scattered throughout the countryside of Judea and Samaria.

Let's Pray!

Lord, you taught that "blessed are those who are persecuted for righteousness' sake" (Matthew 5:10). Send out your special blessing today for those who are suffering for the faith. In the name of the Father, and the Son, and the Holy Spirit, Amen!

GOING DEEPER:

Read It Read John 15:13. How does this apply to martyrs, or people who die for Jesus?

Do It! Through your church or other organization, such as Missionaries of Charity (founded by Mother Teresa), find missionaries or other church workers in another part of the world. Write letters together as a family to let them know you are praying for them, and include happy drawings or pictures.

Saul Persecutes the Christians

Acts 8:1–8

*B*orn to the tribe of Benjamin and raised a Roman citizen in one of the three most important centers of learning in the ancient world, Saul of Tarsus was a man with a bright future ahead of him. As a Pharisee, he was familiar with both Greek and Roman culture, and he was very committed to following the law of Moses. Sadly, he was part of the first great persecution of the Church and did his best to stamp out all traces of Christianity in Jerusalem and the surrounding country! And yet this, too, was part of God's plan. Thanks to Paul, the apostles scattered from Jerusalem, beginning the first missionary journeys of the apostles.

Saul approved of their killing him [Stephen].

That day a severe persecution began against the church in Jerusalem, and all except the apostles were scattered throughout the countryside of Judea and Samaria. [2]Devout men buried Stephen and made loud lamentation over him. [3]But Saul was ravaging the church by entering house after house; dragging off both men and women, he committed them to prison.

[4] Now those who were scattered went from place to place, proclaiming the word. [5]Philip went down to the city of Samaria and proclaimed the Messiah to them. [6]The crowds with one accord listened eagerly to what was said by Philip, hearing and seeing the signs that he did, [7]for unclean spirits, crying with loud shrieks, came out of many who were possessed; and many others who were paralyzed or lame were cured. [8]So there was great joy in that city.

LET'S PRAY!

Lord Jesus, those who loved you best often endured great hardships out of love for you. When I encounter suffering, help me to see it as an opportunity to trust you more. In the name of the Father, and the Son, and the Holy Spirit, Amen!

GOING DEEPER:

Read It! Today's gospel reading (EA 6A) is John 14:15–21.

Do It! Talk about a time in your life when something bad happened, but God brought good out of it anyway.

Simon the Magician

Acts 8:9, 14—22, 24

Magic tricks are often nothing more than practiced illusions, but that isn't always true—not now or in the time of the apostles! Sorcerers and magicians were well-known in the ancient world. Today's story reminds us that the power of God and the miracle working of the apostles are incompatible with the power of darkness. In this story, Simon the magician turned from his wicked ways and followed Christ!

Now a certain man named Simon had previously practiced magic in the city and amazed the people of Samaria, saying that he was someone great. . . .

14 Now when the apostles at Jerusalem heard that Samaria had accepted the word of God, they sent Peter and John to them. ¹⁵The two went down and prayed for them that they might receive the Holy Spirit ¹⁶(for as yet the Spirit had not come upon any of them; they had only been baptized in the name of the Lord Jesus). ¹⁷Then Peter and John laid their hands on them, and they received the Holy Spirit. ¹⁸Now when Simon saw that the Spirit was given through the laying on of the apostles' hands, he offered them money, ¹⁹saying, "Give me also this power so that anyone on whom I lay my hands may receive the Holy Spirit." ²⁰But Peter said to him, "May your silver perish with you, because you thought you could obtain God's gift with money! ²¹You have no part or share in this, for your heart is not right before God. ²²Repent therefore of this wickedness of yours, and pray to the Lord that, if possible, the intent of your heart may be forgiven you." . . . ²⁴Simon answered, "Pray for me to the Lord, that nothing of what you have said may happen to me."

LET'S PRAY!

Act of Contrition

A Traditonal Catholic Prayer

O my God, I am heartily sorry for having offended Thee, and I detest all my sins because I dread the loss of Heaven and the pains of Hell; but most of all because they offend Thee, my God, Who art all-good and deserving of all my love. I firmly resolve, with the help of Thy grace, to confess my sins, to do penance, and to amend my life. Amen.

GOING DEEPER:

Read It! CCC #2115–17 (God's people are not to practice
divination and magic).

Do It! Do you have any supernatural "games," like tarot
cards, Ouija boards, or other devices, used to contact
the spiritual world? Time to do a little housecleaning—
these things are not for Christians!

Philip and the Ethiopian
Acts 8:26–35

*P*hilip traveled and preached among the Samaritan people of Judea, baptizing them in the name of the Lord. Very early on, baptism was a public profession of faith, sometimes dramatic, such as when 3,000 people were baptized on the day of Pentecost, other times less so, such as when the Lord sent Philip to this Ethiopian court official.

An angel of the Lord said to Philip, "Get up and go toward the south to the road that goes down from Jerusalem to Gaza." (This is a wilderness road.) 27So he got up and went. Now there was an Ethiopian eunuch, a court official of the Candace, queen of the Ethiopians, in charge of her entire treasury. He had come to Jerusalem to worship 28and was returning home; seated in his chariot, he was reading the prophet Isaiah.

29Then the Spirit said to Philip, "Go over to this chariot and join it." 30So Philip ran up to it and heard him reading the prophet Isaiah. He asked, "Do you understand what you are reading?" 31He replied, "How can I, unless someone guides me?" And he invited Philip to get in and sit beside him. 32Now the passage of the scripture that he was reading was this:

"Like a sheep he was led to the slaughter,
and like a lamb silent before its shearer,
so he does not open his mouth.
33 In his humiliation justice was denied him.
Who can describe his generation?
For his life is taken away from the earth."

34The eunuch asked Philip, "About whom, may I ask you, does the prophet say this, about himself or about someone else?" 35Then Philip began to speak, and starting with this scripture, he proclaimed to him the good news about Jesus.

LET'S PRAY!

From the cowardice that dare not face new truth,
From the laziness that is contented with half truth,
From the arrogance that thinks it knows all truth,
Good Lord, deliver me.48

"Come and hear, all you who fear God,
and I will tell you what he has done for me.
17 I cried aloud to him,
and he was extolled with my tongue.
18 If I had cherished iniquity in my heart,
the Lord would not have listened.
19 But truly God has listened;
he has given heed to the words of my prayer." —Psalm 66:16–19

GOING DEEPER:

Read It! CCC #849 (The missionary mandate of the church is Matthew 28:19–20).

Do It! Is God showing you something from the Bible that you didn't know before? What is it?

Damascus Road
Acts 9:1–9

*S*aul of Tarsus was a brilliant man, but when it came to Jesus, it took a real miracle for him to see the light of truth! Let's listen to the story.

Meanwhile Saul, still breathing threats and murder against the disciples of the Lord, went to the high priest ²and asked him for letters to the synagogues at Damascus, so that if he found any who belonged to the Way, men or women, he might bring them bound to Jerusalem. ³Now as he was going along and approaching Damascus, suddenly a light from heaven flashed around him. ⁴He fell to the ground and heard a voice saying to him, "Saul, Saul, why do you persecute me?" ⁵He asked, "Who are you, Lord?" The reply came, "I am Jesus, whom you are persecuting. ⁶But get up and enter the city, and you will be told what you are to do." ⁷The men who were traveling with him stood speechless because they heard the voice but saw no one. ⁸Saul got up from the ground, and though his eyes were open, he could see nothing; so they led him by the hand and brought him into Damascus. ⁹For three days he was without sight, and neither ate nor drank.

LET'S PRAY!

Open our eyes, Lord. We want to see Jesus!

Give us the grace to see you in everyone we meet,

And especially in the Holy Eucharist.

In the name of the Father, and the Son, and the Holy Spirit, Amen!

GOING DEEPER:

Read It! CCC #639 (Paul testified to the Resurrection of Christ).

Do It! By Saul being struck blind, the future apostle was placed in a position of great humility and dependence on those he had formerly persecuted, forcing him to become "like a little child." To see what this was like, go into the backyard, divide into teams, blindfold the adults, and see how long it takes the children to lead the grown-ups from one end of the yard to the other.

DID YOU KNOW? Like Abraham and Simon Peter, Saul's name change reflects a change of heart or conversion. Unlike the first two men, however, he is still called "Saul" during his first missionary journey.[49]

Ananias Heals Saul
Acts 9:10–22

*I*magine someone at school or in your neighborhood was a bully, saying mean things to you or one of your brothers or sisters. How easy would it be for you to show love to this person, to offer to help if he were in trouble? In today's story, that is exactly what happened to the Christians at Damascus. God sent Ananias on an incredible journey, to help a man who had done so much to hurt other Christians in that city! What will he do? Laugh or forgive?

Now there was a disciple in Damascus named Ananias. The Lord said to him in a vision, "Ananias." He answered, "Here I am, Lord." 11The Lord said to him, "Get up and go to the street called Straight, and at the house of Judas look for a man of Tarsus named Saul. At this moment he is praying, 12and he has seen in a vision a man named Ananias come in and lay his hands on him so that he might regain his sight." 13But Ananias answered, "Lord, I have heard from many about this man, how much evil he has done to your saints in Jerusalem; 14and here he has authority from the chief priests to bind all who invoke your name." 15But the Lord said to him, "Go, for he is an instrument whom I have chosen to bring my name before Gentiles and kings and before the people of Israel; 16I myself will show him how much he must suffer for the sake of my name." 17So Ananias went and entered the house. He laid his hands on Saul and said, "Brother Saul, the Lord Jesus, who appeared to you on your way here, has sent me so that you may regain your sight and be filled with the Holy Spirit." 18And immediately something like scales fell from his eyes, and his sight was restored. Then he got up and was baptized, 19and after taking some food, he regained his strength.

For several days he was with the disciples in Damascus, 20and immediately he began to proclaim Jesus in the synagogues, saying, "He is the Son of God." 21All who heard him were amazed and said, "Is not this the man who made havoc in Jerusalem among those who invoked this name? And has he not come here for the purpose of bringing them bound before the chief priests?" 22Saul became increasingly more powerful and confounded the Jews who lived in Damascus by proving that Jesus was the Messiah.

LET'S PRAY!

Thank you, Lord, for giving us the power to forgive even those who hurt those we love. In the name of the Father, and the Son, and the Holy Spirit, Amen!

GOING DEEPER:

Read It! CCC #442 (Paul taught the Jews and Gentiles that Jesus is the Son of God).

Do It! "Forgive us our trespasses as we forgive those who trespass against us." When you say these words, who comes to mind? Someone you need to forgive, or at least ask God for the willingness to forgive?

Saul Escapes Damascus
Acts 9:23—31

*S*t. Paul had not been preaching in Damascus long before the Jews decided to kill him. He sneaked out of the city and went to Arabia, where he spent three years (Galatians 1:18). He then returned to Jerusalem, where he spent two weeks before the Jews again tried to kill the newest apostle. And yet, nothing stopped St. Paul. He was determined to tell the world the good news!

After some time had passed, the Jews plotted to kill him, ²⁴but their plot became known to Saul. They were watching the gates day and night so that they might kill him; ²⁵but his disciples took him by night and let him down through an opening in the wall, lowering him in a basket.

26 When he had come to Jerusalem, he attempted to join the disciples; and they were all afraid of him, for they did not believe that he was a disciple. ²⁷But Barnabas took him, brought him to the apostles, and described for them how on the road he had seen the Lord, who had spoken to him, and how in Damascus he had spoken boldly in the name of Jesus. ²⁸So he went in and out among them in Jerusalem, speaking boldly in the name of the Lord. ²⁹He spoke and argued with the Hellenists; but they were attempting to kill him. ³⁰When the believers learned of it, they brought him down to Caesarea and sent him off to Tarsus.

31 Meanwhile the church throughout Judea, Galilee, and Samaria had peace and was built up. Living in the fear of the Lord and in the comfort of the Holy Spirit, it increased in numbers.

LET'S PRAY!
Prayer to Redeem Lost Time
A Traditonal Catholic Prayer

O my God, source of all mercy! You are the sovereign Lord. And though as I look over my life, I see that I have wasted so much time in idleness, I believe that you, O Lord, can with a word turn this loss to gain. You can do all things.

Restore unto me the time that has been lost, by your grace, both in time past and in time yet to come, that when I stand before you in heaven I shall hear you say to me, "Well done, good and faithful servant!" In the name of the Father, and the Son, and the Holy Spirit, Amen!

GOING DEEPER:

Read It! CCC # 1422 (Penance atones and reconciles with the Church for past offenses).

Do It! Pick a closet or drawer that the family can clean out together. Play some music and make it a fun activity.

DID YOU KNOW? The believers at Damascus did not at first believe Paul's conversion was real, and the Jews hated him for leaving their side! It must have been a lonely time for Paul, a time when he had to depend on God alone.

DIVINE MERCY CHAPLET

This prayer, given to St. Faustina Kowalska, is prayed on Rosary beads.

1. Begin with the Sign of the Cross, one Our Father, one Hail Mary and The Apostles' Creed.

2. Then, on the Our Father beads, say the following: "Eternal Father, I offer You the Body and Blood, Soul and Divinity of Your dearly beloved Son, Our Lord Jesus Christ, in atonement for our sins and those of the whole world."

3. On the ten Hail Mary beads, say the following: "For the sake of His sorrowful Passion, have mercy on us and on the whole world." (Repeat for all five decades.)

4. Conclude with: "Holy God, holy Mighty One, holy Immortal One, have mercy on us and on the whole world." (Repeat three times.)

Dorcas Raised

Acts 9:32-43

In the early Church, the wealthier members often tended to the needs of those who had less, and the whole community loved them for their generosity. In today's story, one kind soul named Dorcas (Tabitha in Aramaic), who had died, became a living testimony of the Spirit's power when Peter raised her back to life!

Now as Peter went here and there among all the believers, he came down also to the saints living in Lydda. ³³There he found a man named Aeneas, who had been bed-ridden for eight years, for he was paralyzed. ³⁴Peter said to him, "Aeneas, Jesus Christ heals you; get up and make your bed!" And immediately he got up. ³⁵And all the residents of Lydda and Sharon saw him and turned to the Lord.

36 Now in Joppa there was a disciple whose name was Tabitha, which in Greek is Dorcas. She was devoted to good works and acts of charity. ³⁷At that time she became ill and died. When they had washed her, they laid her in a room upstairs. ³⁸Since Lydda was near Joppa, the disciples, who heard that Peter was there, sent two men to him with the request, "Please come to us without delay." ³⁹So Peter got up and went with them; and when he arrived, they took him to the room upstairs. All the widows stood beside him, weeping and showing tunics and other clothing that Dorcas had made while she was with them. ⁴⁰Peter put all of them outside, and then he knelt down and prayed. He turned to the body and said, "Tabitha, get up." Then she opened her eyes, and seeing Peter, she sat up. ⁴¹He gave her his hand and helped her up. Then calling the saints and widows, he showed her to be alive. ⁴²This became known throughout Joppa, and many believed in the Lord. ⁴³Meanwhile he stayed in Joppa for some time with a certain Simon, a tanner.

LET'S PRAY!
De Profundis
A Traditonal Catholic Prayer

Out of the depths I cry to You, O Lord; Lord, hear my voice.

Let Your ears be attentive to my voice in supplication.

If You, O Lord, mark iniquities, Lord, who can stand?

But with You is forgiveness, that You may be revered.

I trust in the Lord; my soul trusts in His word.

My soul waits for the Lord more than sentinels wait for the dawn.

More than sentinels wait for the dawn, let Israel wait for the Lord,

For with the Lord is kindness and with Him is plenteous redemption;

And He will redeem Israel from all their iniquities.

SPECIAL WORDS: "The saints"
in verse 41 are also referred
to as "the holy ones."

GOING DEEPER:

Read It! CCC #1507 (The healing power of the apostles
came from invoking the name of Christ).

Do It! Read the Catechism to find the answer to this
question; Since Dorcas's miraculous healing was only
temporary—sooner or later, she would die again—what
was the sign's significance?

Angels to the Rescue

Acts 12:1–11

*O*ur guardian angels watch out for us every day of our lives—as we go to school, ride on the bus, or chat with friends. Although they cannot entirely shield us from the consequences of our actions, these angels work hard to shield us from true spiritual dangers, urging us toward virtue and keeping us on the pathway toward God. In today's Bible story, St. James is martyred, and Peter is delivered from mortal danger by God's special messenger.

About that time King Herod laid violent hands upon some who belonged to the church. ²He had James, the brother of John, killed with the sword. ³After he saw that it pleased the Jews, he proceeded to arrest Peter also. (This was during the festival of Unleavened Bread.) ⁴When he had seized him, he put him in prison and handed him over to four squads of soldiers to guard him, intending to bring him out to the people after the Passover. ⁵While Peter was kept in prison, the church prayed fervently to God for him.

6 The very night before Herod was going to bring him out, Peter, bound with two chains, was sleeping between two soldiers, while guards in front of the door were keeping watch over the prison. ⁷Suddenly an angel of the Lord appeared and a light shone in the cell. He tapped Peter on the side and woke him, saying, "Get up quickly." And the chains fell off his wrists. ⁸The angel said to him, "Fasten your belt and put on your sandals." He did so. Then he said to him, "Wrap your cloak around you and follow me." ⁹Peter went out and followed him; he did not realize that what was happening with the angel's help was real; he thought he was seeing a vision. ¹⁰After they had passed the first and the second guard, they came before the iron gate leading into the city. It opened for them of its own accord, and they went outside and walked along a lane, when suddenly the angel left him. ¹¹Then Peter came to himself and said, "Now I am sure that the Lord has sent his angel and rescued me from the hands of Herod and from all that the Jewish people were expecting."

LET'S PRAY!

Thank you, God, for angels—your messengers of light and truth! In the name of the Father, and the Son, and the Holy Spirit, Amen!

GOING DEEPER:

Read It! The gospel reading for today (the Feasts of Saints Peter and Paul, B) is Matthew 16:13–19.

Do It! Get out the angels from your Christmas decorations and set them in your prayer corner this week to remind your family of their guardian angels, whose presence helps us in so many ways!

"Peter, Come In!"
Acts 12:12—19

*H*ello! Come on in!" It's the first thing you say to guests, isn't it? You invite them in, give them a comfortable seat, and offer them something to drink. You would never think of leaving your visitors on the front step! But that is exactly what happened in today's Bible story. When Peter emerged from prison after the angel miraculously released him, he made his way to safety only to be left on the street by a surprised servant girl!

As soon as he realized this [that he was free], he went to the house of Mary, the mother of John whose other name was Mark, where many had gathered and were praying. [13]When he knocked at the outer gate, a maid named Rhoda came to answer. [14]On recognizing Peter's voice, she was so overjoyed that, instead of opening the gate, she ran in and announced that Peter was standing at the gate. [15]They said to her, "You are out of your mind!" But she insisted that it was so. They said, "It is his angel." [16]Meanwhile Peter continued knocking; and when they opened the gate, they saw him and were amazed. [17]He motioned to them with his hand to be silent, and described for them how the Lord had brought him out of the prison. And he added, "Tell this to James and to the believers." Then he left and went to another place.

18 When morning came, there was no small commotion among the soldiers over what had become of Peter. [19]When Herod had searched for him and could not find him, he examined the guards and ordered them to be put to death. Then Peter went down from Judea to Caesarea and stayed there.

LET'S PRAY!
Hail, Holy Queen
A Traditonal Catholic Prayer

Hail, holy Queen, Mother of mercy; our life, our sweetness, and our hope. To thee we cry, poor banished children of Eve. To thee we send up our sighs, mourning and weeping in this valley of tears. Turn then, most gracious advocate, thine eyes of mercy toward us. And after this, our exile, show unto us the blessed fruit of thy womb, Jesus. O clement, O loving, O sweet Virgin Mary; pray for us, O holy Mother of God, that we may be made worthy of the promises of Christ.

GOING DEEPER:

Read It! CCC #1884 (God has respect for personal
freedom).

Do It! Talk about a time you were (or someone you know
was) in a dangerous situation and unexpectedly
delivered from harm.

Paul and Barnabas Preach
Acts 13:42–49

*T*he church at Antioch, of which St. Paul was a leader, was among the most influen-
tial of Gentile Christian communities, and served as the missionary's "home base."
The journey to Galatia was a 300-mile trek by way of Cyprus. When Paul and Barnabas
reached the church in Pisidian Antioch, they began to preach, and many Jews and Gentiles
were converted. But those who did not believe ran the two men out of town!⁵⁰

As Paul and Barnabas were going out, the people urged them to speak about these things again the next sabbath. ⁴³When the meeting of the synagogue broke up, many Jews and devout converts to Judaism followed Paul and Barnabas, who spoke to them and urged them to continue in the grace of God.

44 The next sabbath almost the whole city gathered to hear the word of the Lord. ⁴⁵But when the Jews saw the crowds, they were filled with jealousy; and blaspheming, they contradicted what was spoken by Paul. ⁴⁶Then both Paul and Barnabas spoke out boldly, saying, "It was necessary that the word of God should be spoken first to you. Since you reject it and judge yourselves to be unworthy of eternal life, we are now turning to the Gentiles. ⁴⁷For so the Lord has commanded us, saying,

'I have set you to be a light for the
      Gentiles,
so that you may bring salvation to the
      ends of the earth.'"

48 When the Gentiles heard this, they were glad and praised the word of the Lord; and as many as had been destined for eternal life became believers. ⁴⁹Thus the word of the Lord spread throughout the region.

Let's Pray!
Dear Lord, thank you for your followers who boldly proclaim you message. Help us to do the same. Amen.

Going Deeper:
Read It! This is the second reading for the Feast of John the Baptist (B); CCC #2850 (Jesus prayed that his followers would be one).
Do It! Pretend two friends start fighting. What should you do—take sides or make peace?

Special Words:
Barnabas means "son of encouragement." He helped Paul get started in ministry. They went separate ways after a dispute over his cousin, John Mark (Acts 15:2). They later reconciled, and John Mark wrote the gospel of Mark.

Paul Is Stoned

Acts 14:8—21

To show the Gentile audience the truth of his message, Paul healed a lame man—a miracle similar to the one Peter performed in Acts 3:2—10. However, the response was very different: this time instead of believing in Jesus, the people proclaimed Paul and Barnabas to be gods! Of course the two men did not allow this to continue, and soon the crowd got ugly!

In Lystra there was a man sitting who could not use his feet and had never walked, for he had been crippled from birth. 9He listened to Paul as he was speaking. And Paul, looking at him intently and seeing that he had faith to be healed, 10said in a loud voice, "Stand upright on your feet." And the man sprang up and began to walk. 11When the crowds saw what Paul had done, they shouted in the Lycaonian language, "The gods have come down to us in human form!" 12Barnabas they called Zeus, and Paul they called Hermes, because he was the chief speaker. 13The priest of Zeus, whose temple was just outside the city, brought oxen and garlands to the gates; he and the crowds wanted to offer sacrifice. 14When the apostles Barnabas and Paul heard of it, they tore their clothes and rushed out into the crowd, shouting, 15"Friends, why are you doing this? We are mortals just like you, and we bring you good news, that you should turn from these worthless things to the living God, who made the heaven and the earth and the sea and all that is in them. 16In past generations he allowed all the nations to follow their own ways; 17yet he has not left himself without a witness in doing good—giving you rains from heaven and fruitful seasons, and filling you with food and your hearts with joy." 18Even with these words, they scarcely restrained the crowds from offering sacrifice to them.

19But Jews came there from Antioch and Iconium and won over the crowds. Then they stoned Paul and dragged him out of the city, supposing that he was dead. 20But when the disciples surrounded him, he got up and went into the city. The next day he went on with Barnabas to Derbe.

21 After they had proclaimed the good news to that city and had made many disciples, they returned to Lystra, then on to Iconium and Antioch.

LET'S PRAY!

Dear God, we know that there are people who are suffering for your name. Please bless them and use us to bless them. In the name of the Father, and the Son, and the Holy Spirit, Amen!

GOING DEEPER:

Read It! Read CCC #2097 (To adore God is to acknowledge the "nothingness of the creature").

Do It! What little things can you do today to show love to God?

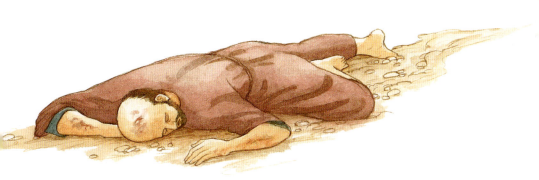

Peter Decides What's Best

Acts 15:1–12

The Council of Jerusalem (AD 50) was the first great church council, where the apostles and elders of the churches gathered to make decisions that affected the Christian community. Here, the leaders of the church needed to decide what Gentile converts needed to do in order to become part of the Christian community and full members of the body of Christ.

Then certain individuals came down from Judea and were teaching the brothers, "Unless you are circumcised according to the custom of Moses, you cannot be saved." ²And after Paul and Barnabas had no small dissension and debate with them, Paul and Barnabas and some of the others were appointed to go up to Jerusalem to discuss this question with the apostles and the elders. ³So they were sent on their way by the church, and as they passed through both Phoenicia and Samaria, they reported the conversion of the Gentiles, and brought great joy to all the believers. ⁴When they came to Jerusalem, they were welcomed by the church and the apostles and the elders, and they reported all that God had done with them. ⁵But some believers who belonged to the sect of the Pharisees stood up and said, "It is necessary for them to be circumcised and ordered to keep the law of Moses."

6 The apostles and the elders met together to consider this matter. ⁷After there had been much debate, Peter stood up and said to them, "My brothers, you know that in the early days God made a choice among you, that I should be the one through whom the Gentiles would hear the message of the good news and become believers. ⁸And God, who knows the human heart, testified to them by giving them the Holy Spirit, just as he did to us; ⁹and in cleansing their hearts by faith he has made no distinction between them and us. ¹⁰Now therefore why are you putting God to the test by placing on the neck of the disciples a yoke that neither our ancestors nor we have been able to bear? ¹¹On the contrary, we believe that we will be saved through the grace of the Lord Jesus, just as they will."

12 The whole assembly kept silence, and listened to Barnabas and Paul as they told of all the signs and wonders that God had done through them among the Gentiles.

Let's Pray!

Lord, help us to live according to the wisdom of St. Francis, who explained how we Christians are to live: "In essentials, unity; in non-essentials, liberty; in all things, charity." In the name of the Father, and the Son, and the Holy Spirit, Amen!

GOING DEEPER

Read It! The gospel reading today (EA 6C) is John 14:23–29; CCC #2036 (The Magisterium extends also to natural law).

Do It! Discuss: What does today's story teach us about how we are to regard the teaching authority of the Magisterium (the bishops in union with the pope)? See above.

Paul and Timothy

Acts 16:1—10

*P*aul and Barnabas had a disagreement over a young man named John Mark, whom Paul judged harshly and Barnabas wanted to give a second chance. The two apostles parted ways, and in a short time, Paul set out again, this time with Silas. Before many miles passed, Paul encountered another young man, Timothy, who became like a son to St. Paul, and gave the older man ample opportunity to become an "encourager" (like Barnabas)!

Paul went on also to Derbe and to Lystra, where there was a disciple named Timothy, the son of a Jewish woman who was a believer; but his father was a Greek. ²He was well spoken of by the believers in Lystra and Iconium. ³Paul wanted Timothy to accompany him; and he took him and had him circumcised because of the Jews who were in those places, for they all knew that his father was a Greek. ⁴As they went from town to town, they delivered to them for observance the decisions that had been reached by the apostles and elders who were in Jerusalem. ⁵So the churches were strengthened in the faith and increased in numbers daily.

6 They went through the region of Phrygia and Galatia, having been forbidden by the Holy Spirit to speak the word in Asia. ⁷When they had come opposite Mysia, they attempted to go into Bithynia, but the Spirit of Jesus did not allow them; ⁸so, passing by Mysia, they went down to Troas. ⁹During the night Paul had a vision: there stood a man of Macedonia pleading with him and saying, "Come over to Macedonia and help us." ¹⁰When he had seen the vision, we immediately tried to cross over to Macedonia, being convinced that God had called us to proclaim the good news to them.

Let's Pray!

Thank you, God, for the opportunity to help others grow in faith, hope, and love. So often, every opportunity to teach presents an opportunity to learn! Today, please bless all the religious education teachers in the world, that they would do their task diligently and well, and with great faith. In the name of the Father, and the Son, and the Holy Spirit, Amen!

Lydia Believes
Acts 16:11—15

In Philippi, St. Paul met a wealthy woman from the seaside town of Thyatira, who listened intently to the words of Paul and asked to be baptized, with her entire household, regardless of what that decision might cost her in terms of her own social standing.

We set sail from Troas and took a straight course to Samothrace, the following day to Neapolis, ¹²and from there to Philippi, which is a leading city of the district of Macedonia and a Roman colony. We remained in this city for some days. ¹³On the sabbath day we went outside the gate by the river, where we supposed there was a place of prayer; and we sat down and spoke to the women who had gathered there. ¹⁴A certain woman named Lydia, a worshiper of God, was listening to us; she was from the city of Thyatira and a dealer in purple cloth. The Lord opened her heart to listen eagerly to what was said by Paul. ¹⁵When she and her household were baptized, she urged us, saying, "If you have judged me to be faithful to the Lord, come and stay at my home." And she prevailed upon us.

Let's Pray!
Lord, thank you for your faithful followers. Help us to show hospitality and grace to others so your kingdom may be furthered. Amen.

GOING DEEPER:

Read It! CCC #1928–32 (We show respect for all people because they are children of God).

Do It! Start using your money God's way, right away! When you get your allowance, have your mom and dad help you to set money aside to give (to God), save, and spend.

Paul's Good News
Acts 16:22—34

*P*aul and Silas never wasted an opportunity to preach the gospel. Even when they were in prison, they trusted that God allowed it for a reason. In the following story, that reason soon became clear: God wanted them to tell the jailer and his entire family about God's love!

The crowd joined in attacking [Paul and Silas], and the magistrates had them stripped of their clothing and ordered them to be beaten with rods. ²³After they had given them a severe flogging, they threw them into prison and ordered the jailer to keep them securely. ²⁴Following these instructions, he put them in the innermost cell and fastened their feet in the stocks.

25 About midnight Paul and Silas were praying and singing hymns to God, and the prisoners were listening to them. ²⁶Suddenly there was an earthquake, so violent that the foundations of the prison were shaken; and immediately all the doors were opened and everyone's chains were unfastened. ²⁷When the jailer woke up and saw the prison doors wide open, he drew his sword and was about to kill himself, since he supposed that the prisoners had escaped. ²⁸But Paul shouted in a loud voice, "Do not harm yourself, for we are all here." ²⁹The jailer called for lights, and rushing in, he fell down trembling before Paul and Silas. ³⁰Then he brought them

outside and said, "Sirs, what must I do to be saved?" ³¹They answered, "Believe on the Lord Jesus, and you will be saved, you and your household." ³²They spoke the word of the Lord to him and to all who were in his house. ³³At the same hour of the night he took them and washed their wounds; then he and his entire family were baptized without delay. ³⁴He brought them up into the house and set food before them; and he and his entire household rejoiced that he had become a believer in God.

LET'S PRAY!

Thank you, Lord, that even when life doesn't go according to *our* plans, nothing takes you by surprise. Help us to use each moment as an opportunity to praise you, and share your goodness with the world. In the name of the Father, and the Son, and the Holy Spirit, Amen!

GOING DEEPER:

Read It! CCC #1231–32 (Infant baptism is initiation into lifelong Christian formation and growth).
Do It! Angel Tree Ministries provides Christmas gifts and other support for children of inmates. Consider getting your parish involved!

DID YOU KNOW?
Although most new Christians were baptized as adults, this story makes it clear that children also received the sacrament: the "household" of the jailer would have included small children.

Paul Speaks in Athens

Acts 17:16–25, 34

Inside every heart is a longing for God—a longing our Creator places there, so that we want to be in relationship with him. In some parts of the world, where the gospel has not yet reached, God reveals himself through his creation and other means. In today's story, the apostle Paul enlightens the minds of some Greeks, who had raised an altar in worship of the God whose name they did not know.

While Paul was waiting for them in Athens, he was deeply distressed to see that the city was full of idols. [17]So he argued in the synagogue with the Jews and the devout persons, and also in the marketplace every day with those who happened to be there. [18]Also some Epicurean and Stoic philosophers debated with him. Some said, "What does this babbler want to say?" Others said, "He seems to be a proclaimer of foreign divinities." (This was because he was telling the good news about Jesus and the resurrection.) [19]So they took him and brought him to the Areopagus and asked him, "May we know what this new teaching is that you are presenting? [20]It sounds rather strange to us, so we would like to know what it means." [21]Now all the Athenians and the foreigners living there would spend their time in nothing but telling or hearing something new.

22 Then Paul stood in front of the Areopagus and said, "Athenians, I see how extremely religious you are in every way.

[23]For as I went through the city and looked carefully at the objects of your worship, I found among them an altar with the inscription, 'To an unknown god.' What therefore you worship as unknown, this I proclaim to you. [24]The God who made the world and everything in it, he who is Lord of heaven and earth, does not live in shrines made by human hands, [25]nor is he served by human hands, as though he needed anything, since he himself gives to all mortals life and breath and all things." . . . [34] Some of them joined him and became believers.

Let's Pray!

Heavenly Father, thank you for creating us to be part of your great family. Thank you for the men and women who are serving you in distant lands, to bring your truth to those who have never heard it. Be especially close to them today. In the name of the Father, and the Son, and the Holy Spirit, Amen!

Going Deeper:

Read It! CCC #27–28 (The desire for God is written on the human heart).

Do It! Practice role-playing with your family about what you would say to someone you met who had never heard of Jesus

DOXOLOGY

by Thomas Ken

Praise God from whom all blessings flow,

Praise him all creatures here below,

Praise him above, ye heavenly hosts,

Praise Father, Son and Holy Ghost!

Amen.

Jesus Comes to Paul

Acts 18:9–15, 18

Jesus, I Trust in You!" These are the words found underneath the image of Divine Mercy, which shows white and red rays streaming from the heart of Jesus. This image was given to St. Faustina Kowalska, to whom Jesus gave a special task: to tell the world of the great mercy of God. In today's story, Jesus appeared to St. Paul to encourage him to carry out an important task as well: to preach the gospel to people who were desperate to hear the life-saving message.

One night the Lord said to Paul in a vision, "Do not be afraid, but speak and do not be silent; [10]for I am with you, and no one will lay a hand on you to harm you, for there are many in this city who are my people." [11]He stayed there a year and six months, teaching the word of God among them.

[12] But when Gallio was proconsul of Achaia, the Jews made a united attack on Paul and brought him before the tribunal. [13]They said, "This man is persuading people to worship God in ways that are contrary to the law." [14]Just as Paul was about to speak, Gallio said to the Jews, "If it were a matter of crime or serious villainy, I would be justified in accepting the complaint of you Jews; [15]but since it is a matter of questions about words and names and your own law, see to it yourselves; I do not wish to be a judge of these matters." . . .

[18] After staying there for a considerable time, Paul said farewell to the believers and sailed for Syria, accompanied by Priscilla and Aquila.

LET'S PRAY!

Holy Spirit, give us courage when we suffer from the bad choices of other people. In the name of the Father, and the Son, and the Holy Spirit, Amen!"

GOING DEEPER:

Read It! CCC #1806 (Prudence is a virtue).
Do It! Is there a copy of the Divine Mercy image in your church, or nearby? Go and see it this Sunday!

QUOTE OF THE DAY: "I have learned that the greatest power is hidden in patience."
—St. Faustina Diary #1514

Priscilla, Aquila, and Apollos

Acts 18:24–28; 19:1–5

Just as Mary, Martha, and Lazarus were good friends of Jesus and provided a place of welcome and retreat for him, so Paul had a pair of special friends called Priscilla and Aquila.

Now there came to Ephesus a Jew named Apollos, a native of Alexandria. He was an eloquent man, well-versed in the scriptures. 25He had been instructed in the Way of the Lord; and he spoke with burning enthusiasm and taught accurately the things concerning Jesus, though he knew only the baptism of John. 26He began to speak boldly in the synagogue; but when Priscilla and Aquila heard him, they took him aside and explained the Way of God to him more accurately. 27And when he wished to cross over to Achaia, the believers encouraged him and wrote to the disciples to welcome him. On his arrival he greatly helped those who through grace had become believers, 28for he powerfully refuted the Jews in public, showing by the scriptures that the Messiah is Jesus.

19While Apollos was in Corinth, Paul passed through the interior regions and came to Ephesus, where he found some disciples. 2He said to them, "Did you receive the Holy Spirit when you became believers?" They replied, "No, we have not even heard that there is a Holy Spirit." 3Then he said, "Into what then were you baptized?" They answered, "Into John's baptism." 4Paul said, "John baptized with the baptism of repentance, telling the people to believe in the one who was to come after him, that is, in Jesus." 5On hearing this, they were baptized in the name of the Lord Jesus.

LET'S PRAY!

Holy Spirit, make us hungry for truth! Our Father . . .

GOING DEEPER:

Read It! The Scriptures refer to church meetings
in Priscilla and Aquila's homes in Ephesus (1
Corinthians 16:19; 2 Timothy 4:19) and Rome
(Romans 16:3–5).

Do It! Research tent making and make a small one the way
Priscilla and Aquila and Paul made large ones.

Demetrius the Silversmith

Acts 19:23–41

*B*lessed are the peacemakers," Jesus proclaimed in his Sermon on the Mount. In today's story, a greedy and fearful group of Ephesians started a riot, hoping to rid the city of Christ and Christians. Afraid the people would no longer buy their little idols, Demetrius and the artisans accused the outsiders of dishonoring their god, Artemis. Let's see what happened!

About that time no little disturbance broke out concerning the Way. [24]A man named Demetrius, a silversmith who made silver shrines of Artemis, brought no little business to the artisans. [25]These he gathered together, with the workers of the same trade, and said, "Men, you know that we get our wealth from this business. [26]You also see and hear that not only in Ephesus but in almost the whole of Asia this Paul has persuaded and drawn away a considerable number of people by saying that gods made with hands are not gods. [27]And there is danger not only that this trade of ours may come into disrepute but also that the temple of the great goddess Artemis will be scorned, and she will be deprived of her majesty that brought all Asia and the world to worship her."

28 When they heard this, they were enraged and shouted, "Great is Artemis of the Ephesians!" [29]The city was filled with the confusion; and people rushed together to the theater, dragging with them Gaius and Aristarchus, Macedonians who were Paul's travel companions. [30]Paul wished to go into the crowd, but the disciples would not let him; [31]even some officials of the province of Asia, who were friendly to him, sent him a message urging him not to venture into the theater. [32]Meanwhile, some were shouting one thing, some another; for the assembly was in confusion, and most of them did not know why they had come together. [33]Some of the crowd gave instructions to Alexander, whom the Jews had pushed forward. And Alexander motioned for silence and tried to make a defense before the people. [34]But when they recognized that he was a Jew, for about two hours all of them shouted in unison, "Great is Artemis of the Ephesians!" [35]But when the town clerk had quieted the crowd, he said, "Citizens of Ephesus, who is there that does not know that the city of the Ephesians is the temple keeper of the great Artemis and of the statue that fell from heaven? [36]Since these things cannot be denied, you ought to be quiet and do nothing rash. [37]You have brought these men here who are neither temple robbers nor blasphemers of our goddess. [38]If therefore Demetrius and the artisans with him have a complaint against anyone, the courts are open, and there are proconsuls; let them bring charges there against one another. [39]If there is anything further you want to know, it must be settled in the regular assembly. [40]For we are in danger of being charged with rioting today, since there is no cause that we can give to justify this commotion." [41]When he had said this, he dismissed the assembly.

SPECIAL WORDS: *Artemis was one of the most widely adored of the Greek deities. Apollo's twin, she was considered goddess of fertility and childbirth.*

DID YOU KNOW? *The temple of Artemis at Ephesus was one of the seven wonders of the ancient world.*

LET'S PRAY!

Father, we thank you that you are the one true God. Help us to never have any idols in our lives; help us to always put you first. In the name of the Father, and the Son, and the Holy Spirt, Amen!

GOING DEEPER:

Read It! CCC #2237 (Political authorities have an obligation to respect the rights of the human person).

Do It! God gives us all talents, but it is up to us to choose to use them for good. What are your talents as individuals and as a family? Write them down and make a point to use them for God this week!

Don't Sleep in Church!
Acts 20:7–16

Have you ever seen someone fall asleep in a strange place? Does your dad sometimes fall asleep in his chair after dinner; do your friends doze off in class or in church? The best way to prevent this is to take good care of our bodies by getting enough good food, rest, and exercise. In today's story, a young man fell asleep while St. Paul was speaking and learned this lesson the hard way!

On the first day of the week, when we met to break bread, Paul was holding a discussion with them; since he intended to leave the next day, he continued speaking until midnight. [8]There were many lamps in the room upstairs where we were meeting. [9]A young man named Eutychus, who was sitting in the window, began to sink off into a deep sleep while Paul talked still longer. Overcome by sleep, he fell to the ground three floors below and was picked up dead. [10]But Paul went down, and bending over him took him in his arms, and said, "Do not be alarmed, for his life is in him." [11]Then Paul went upstairs, and after he had broken bread and eaten, he continued to converse with them until dawn; then he left. [12]Meanwhile they had taken the boy away alive and were not a little comforted.

13 We went ahead to the ship and set sail for Assos, intending to take Paul on board there; for he had made this arrangement, intending to go by land himself. [14]When he met us in Assos, we took him on board and went to Mitylene. [15]We sailed from there, and on the following day we arrived opposite Chios. The next day we touched at Samos, and the day after that we came to Miletus. [16]For Paul had decided to sail past Ephesus, so that he might not have to spend time in Asia; he was eager to be in Jerusalem, if possible, on the day of Pentecost.

Let's Pray!

Lord, I don't want to miss a single word of what you want to tell me today. Give me ears to hear what you want to say! In the name of the Father, and the Son, and the Holy Spirit, Amen!

GOING DEEPER:

Read It! In Galatians 5, St. Paul talks about the "fruit of the Spirit." Read that passage at dinner this week!

Do It! Create a special fruit bowl labeled with all the "fruit of the Spirit." Then make a fruit salad, and see how many "fruits" you can name with each bite!

Paul Says Good-bye

Acts 20:17–38

*S*t. Paul had spent about twelve years on his three missionary journeys (AD 45–57), traveling to all the places where Christianity had begun to grow throughout Asia and Greece. The work was hard and at times dangerous, and in this story St. Paul said good-bye to his friends at Ephesus with a full heart. He was unsure whether he would see his friends again until they were all in heaven, and he wanted to be sure that they would remain strong in their faith after he was gone.

From Miletus he [Paul] sent a message to Ephesus, asking the elders of the church to meet him. [18]When they came to him, he said to them: "You yourselves know how I lived among you the entire time from the first day that I set foot in Asia, [19]serving the Lord with all humility and with tears, enduring the trials that came to me through the plots of the Jews. [20]I did not shrink from doing anything helpful, proclaiming the message to you and teaching you publicly and from house to house, [21]as I testified to both Jews and Greeks about repentance toward God and faith toward our Lord Jesus. [22]"And now, as a captive to the Spirit, I am on my way to Jerusalem, not knowing what will happen to me there, [23]except that the Holy Spirit testifies to me in every city that imprisonment and persecutions are waiting for me. [24]But I do not count my life of any value to myself, if only I may finish my course and the ministry that I received from the Lord Jesus, to testify to the good news of God's grace.

[25] "And now I know that none of you, among whom I have gone about proclaiming the kingdom, will ever see my face again. [26]"Therefore I declare to you this day that I am not responsible for the blood of any of you, [27]for I did not shrink from declaring to you the whole purpose of God. [28]Keep watch over yourselves and over all the flock, of which the Holy Spirit has made you overseers, to shepherd the church of God that he obtained with the blood of his own Son. [29]I know that after I have gone, savage wolves will come in among you, not sparing the flock. [30]Some even from your own group will come distorting the truth in order to entice the disciples to follow them. [31]"Therefore be alert, remembering that for three years I did not cease night or day to warn everyone with tears. [32]And now I commend you to God and to the message of his grace, a message that is able to build you up and to give you the inheritance among all who are sanctified. [33]I coveted no one's silver or gold or clothing. [34]You know for yourselves that I worked with my own hands to support myself and my companions. [35]In all this I have given you an example that by such work we must support the weak, remembering the words of the Lord Jesus, for he himself said, 'It is more blessed to give than to receive.'"

[36] When he had finished speaking, he knelt down with them all and prayed. [37]There was much weeping among them all; they embraced Paul and kissed him,

[38]grieving especially because of what he had said, that they would not see him again. Then they brought him to the ship.

LET'S PRAY!

"Only one life, yes only one, Now let me say, 'Thy will be done';
   And when at last I'll hear the call, I know I'll say 'twas worth it all;
   Only one life, 'twill soon be past, Only what's done for Christ will last."
—C. T. Studd

GOING DEEPER:

Read It! CCC #957 (The communion of saints helps us to draw closer to God).

Do It! Just as it is natural to feel especially close to certain people here on earth, we may be able to identify in a particular way with certain saints. Share with your family who your favorites are and why.

Paul Is Warned

Acts 21:7–14

*S*t. Paul first encountered the prophet Agabus in Antioch. The prophet had predicted worldwide famine and appealed to the church at Antioch to assist the church in Jerusalem (Acts 11:27–28). In today's story, the old prophet meets with Paul again, this time to warn Paul not to return to Jerusalem because the Jews there would hand him over to the Gentiles.

When we had finished the voyage from Tyre, we arrived at Ptolemais; and we greeted the believers and stayed with them for one day. [8]The next day we left and came to Caesarea; and we went into the house of Philip the evangelist, one of the seven, and stayed with him. [9]He had four unmarried daughters who had the gift of prophecy. [10]While we were staying there for several days, a prophet named Agabus came down from Judea. [11]He came to us and took Paul's belt, bound his own feet and hands with it, and said, "Thus says the Holy Spirit, 'This is the way the Jews in Jerusalem will bind the man who owns this belt and will hand him over to the Gentiles.'" [12]When we heard this, we and the people there urged him not to go up to Jerusalem. [13]Then Paul answered, "What are you doing, weeping and breaking my heart? For I am ready not only to be bound but even to die in Jerusalem for the name of the Lord Jesus." [14]Since he would not be persuaded, we remained silent except to say, "The Lord's will be done."

LET'S PRAY!

God, thank you for your apostles who fearlessly spread your message, even in the face of death. Help us to be always mindful of Christians who are suffering for you. Amen.

GOING DEEPER:

Read It! CCC #51–52 (What is "God's will"?).

Do It! Based on this Catechism reading, what do you think God's will is for you today?

SPECIAL WORDS: "One of the seven" refers to the appointment of deacons (Acts 6:2–3). However, it appears that Philip was primarily a preacher among the Greeks, not a caretaker of widows.[55]

The Plot Against Paul

Acts 23:12–18, 20–22

*W*hen Paul's nephew overheard that the Jews were conspiring to kill Paul, he quickly informed his uncle of the plot. His brave actions may have very well saved Paul's life—it took seventy horsemen and four-hundred armed soldiers to get the apostle out of Jerusalem under cover of darkness![56]

In the morning the Jews joined in a conspiracy and bound themselves by an oath neither to eat nor drink until they had killed Paul. [13]There were more than forty who joined in this conspiracy. [14]They went to the chief priests and elders and said, "We have strictly bound ourselves by an oath to taste no food until we have killed Paul. [15]Now then, you and the council must notify the tribune to bring him down to you, on the pretext that you want to make a more thorough examination of his case. And we are ready to do away with him before he arrives."

16 Now the son of Paul's sister heard about the ambush; so he went and gained entrance to the barracks and told Paul. [17]Paul called one of the centurions and said, "Take this young man to the tribune, for he has something to report to him." [18]So he took him, brought him to the tribune, and said, "The prisoner Paul called me and asked me to bring this young man to you; he has something to tell you." [20]He answered, "The Jews have agreed to ask you to bring Paul down to the council tomorrow, as though they were going to inquire more thoroughly into his case. [21]But do not be persuaded by them, for more than forty of their men are lying in ambush for him. They have bound themselves by an oath neither to eat nor drink until they kill him. They are ready now and are waiting for your consent." [22]So the tribune dismissed the young man, ordering him, "Tell no one that you have informed me of this."

LET'S PRAY!

When I feel angry, God, help me not to act in vengeance or spite. In the name of the Father, and the Son, and the Holy Spirit, Amen!

QUOTE OF THE DAY: "Be not angry that you cannot make others as you wish them to be since you cannot make yourself as you wish to be."
—Thomas à Kempis

GOING DEEPER:

Read It! CCC #2302–03 (Anger breaks the fifth
commandment: "Thou shalt not kill").

Do It! In today's story, Paul's enemies promised not to eat
until he was dead. Have you ever said something rash
(If you ___, I'll ___.), and regretted it? Talk about what
happened.

Paul Speaks to Agrippa and Bernice

Acts 25:23–25; 26:1–3, 29

Because St. Paul was a Roman citizen, he was entitled to special treatment in the Roman courts. When brought before Felix at Caesarea, Paul's words made the Roman governor of Judea so uncomfortable that the governor dismissed the apostle and held him there for two years (Acts 24:27). Finally, Paul appealed to the emperor as a way to break the deadlock. He was then brought before King Agrippa and his sister Bernice; Agrippa had been given the title "king" by the Roman emperor Claudius.[57]

So on the next day Agrippa and Bernice came with great pomp, and they entered the audience hall with the military tribunes and the prominent men of the city. Then Festus gave the order and Paul was brought in. [24]And Festus said, "King Agrippa and all here present with us, you see this man about whom the whole Jewish community petitioned me, both in Jerusalem and here, shouting that he ought not to live any longer. [25]But I found that he had done nothing deserving death; and when he appealed to his Imperial Majesty, I decided to send him. . . .

26 Agrippa said to Paul, "You have permission to speak for yourself." Then Paul stretched out his hand and began to defend himself:

[2] "I consider myself fortunate that it is before you, King Agrippa, I am to make my defense today against all the accusations of the Jews, [3]because you are especially familiar with all the customs and controversies of the Jews; therefore I beg of you to listen to me patiently. [29]. . . I pray to God that not only you but also all who are listening to me today might become such as I am—except for these chains."

LET'S PRAY!

O Word of God, enlighten my mind, be on my lips, and transform my heart, so that everyone who meets me will see only Jesus. In the name of the Father, and the Son, and the Holy Spirit, Amen!

QUOTE OF THE DAY: "Cheerfulness
prepares a glorious mind for
all the noblest acts of religion—
love, adoration, praise, and
every union with our God . . .
—St. Elizabeth Seton[58]

GOING DEEPER:

Read It! The full text of St. Paul's speech to King Agrippa,
and the king's response, are recorded in Acts 26.

Do It! It's very important to vote for, pray for, and
communicate with our government leaders. This
week as a family, research who all of your elected
representatives are. Write them letters about
important issues or just to let them know you are
praying for them.

Shipwrecked!

Acts 27:33–44; 28:1

It was too late in the year to sail to Rome from Judea. The weather gets stormy, and the seas get too rough. Paul warned the crew about this. However, the centurion, the pilot, and the owner of the ship Paul was on were determined to try anyway (Acts 27:10–12). They wound up nearly losing their lives. For two weeks, they battled to keep the ship together, and Paul did his best to encourage the crew and solders (Acts 27:33–37).

Just before daybreak, Paul urged all of them to take some food, saying, "Today is the fourteenth day that you have been in suspense and remaining without food, having eaten nothing. ³⁴Therefore I urge you to take some food, for it will help you survive; for none of you will lose a hair from your heads." ³⁵After he had said this, he took bread; and giving thanks to God in the presence of all, he broke it and began to eat. ³⁶Then all of them were encouraged and took food for themselves. ³⁷(We were in all two hundred seventy-six persons in the ship.) ³⁸After they had satisfied their hunger, they lightened the ship by throwing the wheat into the sea.

39 In the morning they did not recognize the land, but they noticed a bay with a beach, on which they planned to run the ship ashore, if they could. ⁴⁰So they cast off the anchors and left them in the sea. At the same time they loosened the ropes that tied the steering-oars; then hoisting the foresail to the wind, they made for the beach. ⁴¹But striking a reef, they ran the ship aground; the bow stuck and remained immovable, but the stern was being broken up by the force of the waves. ⁴²The soldiers' plan was to kill the prisoners, so that none might swim away and escape; ⁴³but the centurion, wishing to save Paul, kept them from carrying out their plan. He ordered those who could swim to jump overboard first and make for the land, ⁴⁴and the rest to follow, some on planks and others on pieces of the ship. And so it was that all were brought safely to land.

28 After we had reached safety, we then learned that the island was called Malta.

LET'S PRAY!

Give me a cheerful heart, O God. Glory be . . .

GOING DEEPER:

Read It! CCC #1750–54 (How to know right from wrong).

Do It! Does your family have a plan in case of emergency—fire, storm, or other disaster? This week, talk about ways to stay safe and even put together an emergency kit! Research online what items you would need in your kit according to your region of the country.

Snakebite!

Acts 28:2–6, 11–14

It was impossible to sail across the Mediterranean Sea in winter, so the survivors of the shipwreck had to spend the winter on the island of Malta. Although Paul's life was once again threatened (the first time in the shipwreck, the second time by a snakebite) the apostle used these situations as opportunities to bring others closer to Christ.

The natives showed us unusual kindness. Since it had begun to rain and was cold, they kindled a fire and welcomed all of us around it. ³Paul had gathered a bundle of brushwood and was putting it on the fire, when a viper, driven out by the heat, fastened itself on his hand. ⁴When the natives saw the creature hanging from his hand, they said to one another, "This man must be a murderer; though he has escaped from the sea, justice has not allowed him to live." ⁵He, however, shook off the creature into the fire and suffered no harm. ⁶They were expecting him to swell up or drop dead, but after they had waited a long time and saw that nothing unusual had happened to him, they changed their minds and began to say that he was a god. . . .

11 Three months later we set sail on a ship that had wintered at the island, an Alexandrian ship with the Twin Brothers as its figurehead. ¹²We put in at Syracuse and stayed there for three days; ¹³then we weighed anchor and came to Rhegium. After one day there a south wind sprang up, and on the second day we came to Puteoli. ¹⁴There we found believers and were invited to stay with them for seven days. And so we came to Rome.

LET'S PRAY!

Some went down to the sea in ships,
 doing business on the great waters;
²⁴they saw the deeds of the LORD,
his wondrous works in the deep.
²⁵For he commanded, and raised the
  stormy wind,
which lifted up the waves of the sea.
²⁶They mounted up to heaven, they went
  down to the depths;
  their courage melted away in their evil
  plight;
²⁷they reeled and staggered like drunken
  men,
  and were at their wits' end.
²⁸Then they cried to the LORD in their
  trouble,
  and he delivered them from their
  distress;
²⁹he made the storm be still,
  and the waves of the sea were hushed.
³⁰Then they were glad because they had
  quiet,
  and he brought them to their desired
  haven."
  —Psalm 107:23–30 RSV

Read It! CCC #2288–91 (Why we must show respect for the
   body by not taking chances with our health).

Do It! When was the last time you went to the doctor or
   dentist, or did something to take care of your body? Is it
   time to make an appointment for someone in your family?

ST. PATRICK'S PRAYER

Christ, be with me, Christ before me, Christ behind me.

Christ in me, Christ beneath me, Christ above me.

Christ on my right, Christ on my left, Christ where I lie,

Christ where I sit. Christ where I arise,

Christ in the heart of every man who thinks of me.

Christ in the mouth of every man who speaks of me.

Christ in every eye that sees me, Christ in every

ear that hears me. Salvation is of the Christ.

May your salvation, O Lord, be ever with us.

Paul in Rome
Acts 28:16–23, 30–31

Go and say to this people: 'Keep listening, but do not comprehend; keep looking, but do not understand.'" (Isaiah 6:9). These words of the prophet Isaiah described the attitude of the men who for so long had been trying to kill Paul. Even though Paul was a highly educated Jew, he seldom received a fair hearing among his own people. In today's story, Paul continued to try to reach the Jews of Rome, where he would spend the next two years of his life, trying to persuade them to believe in Jesus.

When we came into Rome, Paul was allowed to live by himself, with the soldier who was guarding him.

17 Three days later he called together the local leaders of the Jews. When they had assembled, he said to them, "Brothers, though I had done nothing against our people or the customs of our ancestors, yet I was arrested in Jerusalem and handed over to the Romans. ¹⁸"When they had examined me, the Romans wanted to release me, because there was no reason for the death penalty in my case. ¹⁹But when the Jews objected, I was compelled to appeal to the emperor—even though I had no charge to bring against my nation. ²⁰For this reason therefore I have asked to see you and speak with you, since it is for the sake of the hope of Israel that I am bound with this chain." ²¹They replied, "We have received no letters from Judea about you, and none of the brothers coming here has reported or spoken anything evil about you. ²²But we would like to hear from you what you think, for with regard to this sect we know that everywhere it is spoken against."

23 After they had set a day to meet with him, they came to him at his lodgings in great numbers. From morning until evening he explained the matter to them, testifying to the kingdom of God and trying to convince them about Jesus both from the law of Moses and from the prophets. . . .

30 He lived there two whole years at his own expense and welcomed all who came to him, ³¹proclaiming the kingdom of God and teaching about the Lord Jesus Christ with all boldness and without hindrance.

LET'S PRAY!

Every hidden and thankless task, done willingly for love of God, is a song of love in the ears of our heavenly Father. Thank you, Lord, to serve you even in these things!

GOING DEEPER:

Read It! CCC #531–33 (Hidden in prison, St. Paul
    continued to work to share the love of Christ . . . a
    model of hidden virtue.).

Do It! Think of something you can do this week to bless
    someone—anonymously!

This Is My Body
1 Corinthians 11:23–28, 33–34

*D*o you remember making your first Holy Communion, dressed in your best and standing before the priest to receive Jesus for the very first time? In the Eucharist, we receive Jesus himself under the forms of bread and wine. This spiritual food heals and strengthens us, and keeps us close to the heart of Christ who promised he would never leave us or forsake us! Today's reading is from the first epistle of St. Paul to the church at Corinth, to help them understand just how important it is to receive the Eucharist reverently and with thanks.

For I received from the Lord what I also handed on to you, that the Lord Jesus on the night when he was betrayed took a loaf of bread, 24and when he had given thanks, he broke it and said, "This is my body that is for you. Do this in remembrance of me." 25In the same way he took the cup also, after supper, saying, "This cup is the new covenant in my blood. Do this, as often as you drink it, in remembrance of me." 26For as often as you eat this bread and drink the cup, you proclaim the Lord's death until he comes.

27 Whoever, therefore, eats the bread or drinks the cup of the Lord in an unworthy manner will be answerable for the body and blood of the Lord. 28Examine yourselves, and only then eat of the bread and drink of the cup. . . .

33 So then, my brothers and sisters, when you come together to eat, wait for one another. 34If you are hungry, eat at home, so that when you come together, it will not be for your condemnation.

LET'S PRAY!
Traditional Catholic Hymn

O Jesus, we adore Thee, Our Victim and our Priest,

Whose precious Blood and Body become our sacred Feast.

O Sacrament most holy, O Sacrament divine!

All praise and all thanksgiving be every moment Thine.

GOING DEEPER:

Read It! CCC #1334 (The Eucharist is the source and meaning of the Christian life); 1322–1419 (A systematic teaching of the Eucharist).

Do It! Try to read CCC #1322–1419 to have a fresh appreciation for what a gift Jesus has given us!

We Are the Body of Christ
Ephesians 1:1–6, 13–23

Did you know the Bible tells us that we are God's adopted sons and daughters? In the book of Galatians, we read, "But when the time had fully come, God sent forth his Son, born of woman, born under the law, to redeem those who were under the law, so that we might receive adoption as sons. And because you are sons, God has sent the Spirit of his Son into our hearts, crying, 'Abba! Father!'" (4:4–6 RSV). And so, we approach God as part of a family—with the angels and saints in heaven, our friends and family here on earth, and all those people through the ages and around the world that God counts as his children too!

Paul, an apostle of Christ Jesus by the will of God,

To the saints who are in Ephesus and are faithful in Christ Jesus:

2 Grace to you and peace from God our Father and the Lord Jesus Christ.

3 Blessed be the God and Father of our Lord Jesus Christ, who has blessed us in Christ with every spiritual blessing in the heavenly places, 4just as he chose us in Christ before the foundation of the world to be holy and blameless before him in love. 5He destined us for adoption as his children through Jesus Christ, according to the good pleasure of his will, 6to the praise of his glorious grace that he freely bestowed on us in the Beloved. . . . 13In him you also, when you had heard the word of truth, the gospel of your salvation, and had believed in him, were marked with the seal of the promised Holy Spirit; 14this is the pledge of our inheritance toward redemption as God's own people, to the praise of his glory.

15 I have heard of your faith in the Lord Jesus and your love toward all the saints, and for this reason 16I do not cease to give thanks for you as I remember you in my prayers. 17I pray that the God of our Lord Jesus Christ, the Father of glory, may give you a spirit of wisdom and revelation as you come to know him, 18so that, with the eyes of your heart enlightened, you may know what is the hope to which he has called you, what are the riches of his glorious inheritance among the saints, 19and what is the immeasurable greatness of his power for us who believe, according to the working of his great power. 20God put this power to work in Christ when he raised him from the dead and seated him at his right hand in the heavenly places, 21far above all rule and authority and power and dominion, and above every name that is named, not only in this age but also in the age to come. 22And he has put all things under his feet and has made him the head over all things for the church, 23which is his body, the fullness of him who fills all in all.

Prayer of Abandonment

Father,

I abandon myself into your hands; do with me what you will.

Whatever you may do, I thank you:

I am ready for all, I accept all.

Let only your will be done in me, and in all your creatures.

I wish no more than this, O Lord.

Into your hands I commend my soul;

I offer it to you

with all the love of my heart,

for I love you, Lord,

and so need to give myself,

to surrender myself into your hands,

without reserve,

and with boundless confidence,

for you are my Father.

—Blessed Charles de Foucauld

GOING DEEPER:

Read It! CCC #2626–28 (We must bless and adore God
    our Father).

Do It! After Mass this week, spend another hour
    as a family expressing your love for God.
    Go on a nature walk, and thank God
    for what you see. Write a special prayer
    of thanksgiving, or spend some time
    playing or listening to sacred music.

The Armor of God

Ephesians 6:10–24

*C*an you imagine being a police officer or a soldier and going off to work in your pajamas? That's silly, isn't it? You'd be more comfortable that way, but you wouldn't have the protection or the tools you needed to do the job well and safely. In the same way, God gives each of us tools, which are called the "armor of God." Let's listen!

Finally, be strong in the Lord and in the strength of his power. [11]Put on the whole armor of God, so that you may be able to stand against the wiles of the devil. [12]For our struggle is not against enemies of blood and flesh, but against the rulers, against the authorities, against the cosmic powers of this present darkness, against the spiritual forces of evil in the heavenly places. [13]Therefore take up the whole armor of God, so that you may be able to withstand on that evil day, and having done everything, to stand firm. [14]Stand therefore, and fasten the belt of truth around your waist, and put on the breastplate of righteousness. [15]As shoes for your feet put on whatever will make you ready to proclaim the gospel of peace. [16]With all of these, take the shield of faith, with which you will be able to quench all the flaming arrows of the evil one. [17]Take the helmet of salvation, and the sword of the Spirit, which is the word of God.

18 Pray in the Spirit at all times in every prayer and supplication. To that end keep alert and always persevere in supplication for all the saints.

[19]Pray also for me, so that when I speak, a message may be given to me to make known with boldness the mystery of the gospel, [20]for which I am an ambassador in chains. Pray that I may declare it boldly, as I must speak.

21 So that you also may know how I am and what I am doing, Tychicus will tell you everything. He is a dear brother and a faithful minister in the Lord. [22]I am sending him to you for this very purpose, to let you know how we are, and to encourage your hearts.

23 Peace be to the whole community, and love with faith, from God the Father and the Lord Jesus Christ. [24]Grace be with all who have an undying love for our Lord Jesus Christ.

LET'S PRAY:

Lord, help me to be like St. Michael, your angel warrior, who fights evil with goodness and truth. Help me always to remember to use the tools you have given me to do Your will. In the name of the Father, and the Son, and the Holy Spirit, Amen!

Read It! CCC #2629 (In prayer of petition we show we understand our
   relationship with God).

Do It! Draw a picture of you with your "holy armor," and tape it to your bathroom
   mirror to remind you to "suit up" every morning before you leave home!

Live as Children of Light

Philippians 2:12–27

The church at Philippi was the first church Paul established in Europe, early in his second missionary journey (Acts 16). Luke, who wrote both the gospel of Luke and the book of the Acts of the Apostles, was its pastor for the first six years. Yet it was not without its problems, as we read in today's Scripture passage.

Therefore, my beloved, just as you have always obeyed me, not only in my presence, but much more now in my absence, work out your own salvation with fear and trembling; ¹³for it is God who is at work in you, enabling you both to will and to work for his good pleasure.

14 Do all things without murmuring and arguing, ¹⁵so that you may be blameless and innocent, children of God without blemish in the midst of a crooked and perverse generation, in which you shine like stars in the world. ¹⁶It is by your holding fast to the word of life that I can boast on the day of Christ that I did not run in vain or labor in vain. ¹⁷But even if I am being poured out as a libation over the sacrifice and the offering of your faith, I am glad and rejoice with all of you—¹⁸and in the same way you also must be glad and rejoice with me.

19 I hope in the Lord Jesus to send Timothy to you soon, so that I may be cheered by news of you. ²⁰I have no one like him who will be genuinely concerned for your welfare. ²¹All of them are seeking their own interests, not those of Jesus Christ. ²²But Timothy's worth you know, how like a son with a father he has served with me in the work of the gospel. ²³I hope therefore to send him as soon as I see how things go with me; ²⁴and I trust in the Lord that I will also come soon.

25 Still, I think it necessary to send to you Epaphroditus—my brother and co-worker and fellow soldier, your messenger and minister to my need; ²⁶for he has been longing for all of you, and has been distressed because you heard that he was ill. ²⁷He was indeed so ill that he nearly died. But God had mercy on him, and not only on him but on me also, so that I would not have one sorrow after another.

LET'S PRAY!

Prayer of St. Therese of the Little Flower

May today there be peace within.

May you trust God that you are exactly where you are meant to be.

May you not forget the infinite possibilities that are born of faith.

May you use those gifts that you have received, and pass on the love that has been given to you.

May you be confident knowing you are a child of God. Let this presence settle into your bones, and allow your soul the freedom to sing, dance, praise and love.

It is there for each and every one of us.

GOING DEEPER:

Read It! CCC #2204–06 (What is a Christian family?).

Do It! Is there someone in your life who finds it hard to balance work and the rest of life? Plan a special meal or other fun activity to enjoy together.

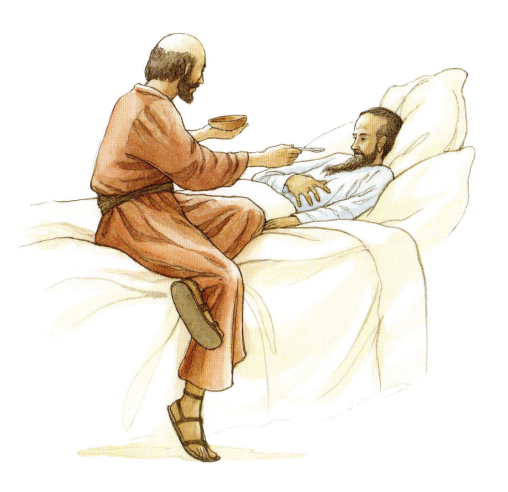

Run to Win the Prize

Philippians 3:8–17

*O*n your mark . . . Get set . . . Go!" And with the sound of the starting pistol, the runners' shoes kick up dust as they circle the track, their legs pumping faster and faster as the crowds scream their encouragement! This is the image St. Paul called to mind when he wrote, "forgetting what lies behind and straining toward what lies ahead." Are you running for the prize too?

I regard everything as loss because of the surpassing value of knowing Christ Jesus my Lord. For his sake I have suffered the loss of all things, and I regard them as rubbish, in order that I may gain Christ [9]and be found in him, not having a righteousness of my own that comes from the law, but one that comes through faith in Christ, the righteousness from God based on faith. [10]I want to know Christ and the power of his resurrection and the sharing of his sufferings by becoming like him in his death, [11]if somehow I may attain the resurrection from the dead.

12 Not that I have already obtained this or have already reached the goal; but I press on to make it my own, because Christ Jesus has made me his own. [13]Beloved, I do not consider that I have made it my own; but this one thing I do: forgetting what lies behind and straining forward to what lies ahead, [14]I press on toward the goal for the prize of the heavenly call of God in Christ Jesus. [15]Let those of us then who are mature be of the same mind; and if you think differently about anything, this too God will reveal to you. [16]Only let us hold fast to what we have attained.

17 Brothers and sisters, join in imitating me, and observe those who live according to the example you have in us.

LET'S PRAY!

Our Lady of Fatima Prayer

O my Jesus, forgive us our sins, save us from the fires of hell, lead all souls to Heaven, especially those who have most need of your mercy.

GOING DEEPER:

Read It! CCC #1434–49 (Why we need to "clean up" after sin trips us up!).

Do It! Run for the prize! Participate in a local walk or run benefit as a family (you can find one through charitymile.com).

Think About This!

Philippians 4:4–9

The great joy of St. Paul rings out in this letter. No matter what had happened to him—the beatings, stonings, shipwreck, and even the unjust imprisonments—Paul was a man who was truly free. He had discovered an unshakable source of true happiness: the Lord himself!

Rejoice in the Lord always; again I will say, Rejoice. 5Let your gentleness be known to everyone. The Lord is near. 6Do not worry about anything, but in everything by prayer and supplication with thanksgiving let your requests be made known to God. 7And the peace of God, which surpasses all understanding, will guard your hearts and your minds in Christ Jesus.

8 Finally, beloved, whatever is true, whatever is honorable, whatever is just, whatever is pure, whatever is pleasing, whatever is commendable, if there is any excellence and if there is anything worthy of praise, think about these things. 9Keep on doing the things that you have learned and received and heard and seen in me, and the God of peace will be with you.

LET'S PRAY!

Dear God, Please be in control of what I say and help me to speak only words that bring joy to the lives of other people. In the name of the Father, and the Son, and the Holy Spirit, Amen!

Read It! CCC #2488 ("Should I say something?" Read this and decide!).

Do It! Play the "Telephone" game with your friends or as a family. Sit in a circle, and one person whispers a secret joke or little story to the next person, who then whispers the same thing to the next person, and so on. The last person in the circle repeats what he heard to the whole group. How close was it to the original? What does this experiment tell us about gossip and whether we should always believe everything we hear?

QUOTE OF THE DAY: *"Don't worry when you are not recognized, but strive to be worthy of recognition."*
—Abraham Lincoln

The Lord Will Return

1 Thessalonians 4:13—5:2

Do you ever wonder what heaven will be like? Will there be high, puffy clouds with big mansions perched on top? A giant zoo with every animal that has ever lived roaming in its natural habitat? There is much about heaven that we don't know and won't know until we get there. But there is also a lot about heaven that we can know for sure, the most important being that we will get to see Jesus face-to-face!

But we do not want you to be uninformed, brothers and sisters, about those who have died, so that you may not grieve as others do who have no hope. ¹⁴For since we believe that Jesus died and rose again, even so, through Jesus, God will bring with him those who have died. ¹⁵For this we declare to you by the word of the Lord, that we who are alive, who are left until the coming of the Lord, will by no means precede those who have died. ¹⁶For the Lord himself, with a cry of command, with the archangel's call and with the sound of God's trumpet, will descend from heaven, and the dead in Christ will rise first. ¹⁷Then we who are alive, who are left, will be caught up in the clouds together with them to meet the Lord in the air; and so we will be with the Lord forever. ¹⁸Therefore encourage one another with these words.

5 Now concerning the times and the seasons, brothers and sisters, you do not need to have anything written to you. ²For you yourselves know very well that the day of the Lord will come like a thief in the night.

LET'S PRAY!
"Come, Lord Jesus, come!"

GOING DEEPER:
Read It! CCC #668—70 ("He will come again in glory . . .").

Do It! Let each family member share the answer to this question: If you knew Jesus was coming back tomorrow, what would you do today?

DID YOU KNOW?
Like most believers back then, St. Paul believed that Christ would return to earth within his own lifetime (1 Thessalonians 5:1—2).

Handing on the Faith
1 Timothy 4:6–5:2

*B*ecause most early Christians believed that Jesus would return to earth in a short time, the temptation was strong to quit doing the normal, daily things of life in order to take care of what they saw as more pressing, spiritual matters. In his letter to Timothy, St. Paul urged his young friend to "avoid profane myths" and to "let no one despise your youth." Instead, Timothy was to guide the community in their relationships with one another, helping each other to grow in virtue and refrain from sin. In that way, whether Christ returned right away or not, they would all be on the right track for heaven!

If you put these instructions before the brothers and sisters, you will be a good servant of Christ Jesus, nourished on the words of the faith and of the sound teaching that you have followed. ⁷Have nothing to do with profane myths and old wives' tales. Train yourself in godliness, ⁸for, while physical training is of some value, godliness is valuable in every way, holding promise for both the present life and the life to come. ⁹The saying is sure and worthy of full acceptance. ¹⁰For to this end we toil and struggle, because we have our hope set on the living God, who is the Savior of all people, especially of those who believe.

11 These are the things you must insist on and teach. ¹²Let no one despise your youth, but set the believers an example in speech and conduct, in love, in faith, in purity. ¹³Until I arrive, give attention to the public reading of scripture, to exhorting, to teaching. ¹⁴Do not neglect the gift that is in you, which was given to you through prophecy with the laying on of hands by the council of elders. ¹⁵Put these things into practice, devote yourself to them, so that all may see your progress. ¹⁶Pay close attention to yourself and to your teaching; continue in these things, for in doing this you will save both yourself and your hearers.

5 Do not speak harshly to an older man, but speak to him as to a father, to younger men as brothers, ²to older women as mothers, to younger women as sisters— with absolute purity.

LET'S PRAY!
A Morning Offering

God, please come to my assistance. Lord, make haste to help me.

Glory be to the Father, and to the Son, and to the Holy Spirit:

As it was in the beginning, is now and ever shall be, world without end, Amen!

As morning breaks I look to you, O Lord, to be my strength this day.⁵⁹

GOING DEEPER:

Read It! CCC #2089 (Heresy is denying or doubting biblical truth).

Do It! Suppose a friend said to you, "I don't believe Jesus is really God." What would you say?

Onesimus the Runaway

Philemon 10–19

*T*his little book of the Bible was Paul's attempt to reconcile a runaway slave and new Christian, Onesimus, with his former master, Philemon, who was also a Christian. Onesimus may have stolen money from his master. Paul taught Onesimus the gospel and wrote this letter to Philemon about how Christians are to forgive and accept one another. It's a good example for all relationships—bosses/workers, husbands/wives, parents/children, and friends/friends.

I am appealing to you for my child, Onesimus, whose father I have become during my imprisonment. [11]Formerly he was useless to you, but now he is indeed useful both to you and to me. [12]I am sending him, that is, my own heart, back to you. [13]I wanted to keep him with me, so that he might be of service to me in your place during my imprisonment for the gospel; [14]but I preferred to do nothing without your consent, in order that your good deed might be voluntary and not something forced. [15]Perhaps this is the reason he was separated from you for a while, so that you might have him back forever, [16]no longer as a slave but more than a slave, a beloved brother—especially to me but how much more to you, both in the flesh and in the Lord.

17 So if you consider me your partner, welcome him as you would welcome me. [18]If he has wronged you in any way, or owes you anything, charge that to my account. [19]I, Paul, am writing this with my own hand: I will repay it. I say nothing about your owing me even your own self.

LET'S PRAY!

Lord, every day is a gift from you. And so today we give our day back to you, every moment, every hour, with the hope that you would be pleased with what we have done, what we have said, and where we have gone. We want to do your will, O God!

DID YOU KNOW? This runaway
slave went on to be a coworker
with St. Paul in spreading the
gospel and was martyred
in Rome in AD 90.

GOING DEEPER:

Read It! Colossians 4:9, where Onesimus is also
    mentioned; CCC #2414 (Slavery of human beings is
    forbidden).

Do It! The name Onesimus means "profitable or useful."
    Research the meaning of your name, and see how you
    can use that meaning as you serve God.

What Is Faith?
Hebrews 11:5–10, 13–16; 12:1–4

*W*hat is faith?" Chapter 11 in the book of Hebrews attempts to answer this question. One after the other, the great "heroes of the faith" are brought out and introduced to the reader. These great examples remind us of how God's faithfulness to us has been lived out from one generation to the next, all the way up to the present!

By faith Enoch was taken so that he did not experience death; and "he was not found, because God had taken him." For it was attested before he was taken away that "he had pleased God." ⁶And without faith it is impossible to please God, for whoever would approach him must believe that he exists and that he rewards those who seek him. ₇By faith Noah, warned by God about events as yet unseen, respected the warning and built an ark to save his household; by this he condemned the world and became an heir to the righteousness that is in accordance with faith.

8 By faith Abraham obeyed when he was called to set out for a place that he was to receive as an inheritance; and he set out, not knowing where he was going. ⁹By faith he stayed for a time in the land he had been promised, as in a foreign land, living in tents, as did Isaac and Jacob, who were heirs with him of the same promise. ¹⁰For he looked forward to the city that has foundations, whose architect and builder is God. . . .

13 All of these died in faith without having received the promises, but from a distance they saw and greeted them. They confessed that they were strangers and foreigners on the earth, ¹⁴for people who speak in this way make it clear that they are seeking a homeland. ¹⁵If they had been thinking of the land that they had left behind, they would have had opportunity to return. ¹⁶But as it is, they desire a better country, that is, a heavenly one. Therefore God is not ashamed to be called their God; indeed, he has prepared a city for them. . . .

12 Therefore, since we are surrounded by so great a cloud of witnesses, let us also lay aside every weight and the sin that clings so closely, and let us run with perseverance the race that is set before us, ²looking to Jesus the pioneer and perfecter of our faith, who for the sake of the joy that was set before him endured the cross, disregarding its shame, and has taken his seat at the right hand of the throne of God.

3 Consider him who endured such hostility against himself from sinners, so that you may not grow weary or lose heart. ⁴In your struggle against sin you have not yet resisted to the point of shedding your blood.

Faith of Our Fathers

   "Faith of our fathers, living still
   in spite of dungeon, fire and sword;
   O, how our hearts beat high with joy
   Whene'er we hear that glorious word!
   Faith of our fathers, holy faith!
   We will be true to Thee till death!"
—Frederick W. Faber

DID YOU KNOW? St. Teresa of Avila once said that, in addition to love, the two virtues most necessary to the Christian life are humility and detachment. . . .

GOING DEEPER:

Read It! CCC #2087 ("Our moral life has its source in
   faith in God who reveals his love to us").
Do It! What things do you do just because you love God?
   Talk about it!

STATIONS OF THE CROSS PRAYER

Lord Jesus Christ, take me along that holy way you once took to
   your death,
Take my mind, my memory, above all, my reluctant heart,
and let me see what once you did for love of me and all the world.

How to Please God

James 1:22–27

The first chapter of James was written for the Christian who is "of two minds"—wanting to live with one foot planted firmly in the world and the other heading toward heaven. What a disaster—it's enough to split a person in two! And so, in this chapter, James reminds us of the basic teachings of Christian living, holding in front of our faces a spiritual mirror by which we can see a reflection of who we are . . . and who God wants us to be.

But be doers of the word, and not merely hearers who deceive themselves. ²³For if any are hearers of the word and not doers, they are like those who look at themselves in a mirror; ²⁴for they look at themselves and, on going away, immediately forget what they were like. ²⁵But those who look into the perfect law, the law of liberty, and persevere, being not hearers who forget but doers who act—they will be blessed in their doing.

26If any think they are religious, and do not bridle their tongues but deceive their hearts, their religion is worthless. ²⁷Religion that is pure and undefiled before God, the Father, is this: to care for orphans and widows in their distress, and to keep oneself unstained by the world.

LET'S PRAY!

Prayer of St. Francis

Make me a channel of your peace.
Where there is hatred let me bring your
    love.
Where there is injury, your pardon, Lord
And where there's doubt, true faith in you.
Make me a channel of your peace.
Where there's despair in life, let me bring
    hope.
Where there is darkness, only light
And where there's sadness, ever joy.
O divine master, grant that I may never seek
So much to be consoled as to console
To be understood as to understand
To be loved as to love with all my soul.
Make me a channel of your peace.
It is in pardoning that we are pardoned
In giving to all men that we receive
And in dying that we're born to eternal life.

GOING DEEPER:

Read It! CCC #2012–16 (The Christian
    life well lived, pleases God).

Do It! Today's reading urges us to "care for widows and orphans." Think of one way to do that this week: Bring a small gift or send a card to a widow in your parish, or invite her for dinner!

The Christian Life

James 5:7–11, 13–16, 19–20

Do you remember the story of Job? That man had everything taken away from him, and yet he still trusted God. The idea that we must be patient even in hard times is the theme of today's Scripture passage too. However, in this passage we also find references to some of the sacraments, such as the anointing of the sick and reconciliation. Even in our darkest moments, God provides ways to strengthen and encourage us!

Be patient, therefore, beloved, until the coming of the Lord. The farmer waits for the precious crop from the earth, being patient with it until it receives the early and the late rains. [8]You also must be patient. Strengthen your hearts, for the coming of the Lord is near. [9]Beloved, do not grumble against one another, so that you may not be judged. See, the Judge is standing at the doors! [10]As an example of suffering and patience, beloved, take the prophets who spoke in the name of the Lord. [11]Indeed we call blessed those who showed endurance. You have heard of the endurance of Job, and you have seen the purpose of the Lord, how the Lord is compassionate and merciful. . . .

13 Are any among you suffering? They should pray. Are any cheerful? They should sing songs of praise. [14]Are any among you sick? They should call for the elders of the church and have them pray over them, anointing them with oil in the name of the Lord. [15]The prayer of faith will save the sick, and the Lord will raise them up; and anyone who has committed sins will be forgiven. [16]Therefore confess your sins to one another, and pray for one another, so that you may be healed. The prayer of the righteous is powerful and effective. . . .

19 My brothers and sisters, if anyone among you wanders from the truth and is brought back by another, [20]you should know that whoever brings back a sinner from wandering will save the sinner's soul from death and will cover a multitude of sins.

LET'S PRAY!

Anima Christi

Soul of Christ, sanctify me,
Body of Christ, save me.
Blood of Christ, inebriate me,
Water from Christ's side, wash me.
Passion of Christ, strengthen me,
O good Jesus, hear me.
Within Thy wounds hide me, suffer me
not to be separated from Thee
From the malicious enemy defend me,
in the hour of my death call me
And bid me come unto Thee that I may
praise Thee
with Thy saints and with Thy angels,
forever and ever, Amen.

GOING DEEPER:

Read It! CCC #1502 (We can pray to God, our healer, for healing for ourselves and for others).

Do It! What can you do today to help someone who is suffering?

Respect Your Spiritual Leaders
1 Peter 5:4—11

*D*o you have a hard time saying yes when someone—a teacher or parent—asks you to do something you don't want to do? Ephesians 6:2 tells us that we must honor our father and mother, that is, that we must respect those in authority. This is true in family life, and it is also true in the Church. God wants us to grow and get strong on the inside, not just the outside! By saying yes to what the Church teaches us through the Magisterium (especially in Scripture and the Catechism) and our priests, we protect ourselves from making spiritually harmful choices.

When the chief shepherd appears, you will win the crown of glory that never fades away. 5In the same way, you who are younger must accept the authority of the elders. And all of you must clothe yourselves with humility in your dealings with one another, for

"God opposes the proud,
but gives grace to the humble."

6 Humble yourselves therefore under the mighty hand of God, so that he may exalt you in due time. 7Cast all your anxiety on him, because he cares for you. 8Discipline yourselves, keep alert. Like a roaring lion your adversary the devil prowls around, looking for someone to devour. 9Resist him, steadfast in your faith, for you know that your brothers and sisters in all the world are undergoing the same kinds of suffering.

10And after you have suffered for a little while, the God of all grace, who has called you to his eternal glory in Christ, will himself restore, support, strengthen, and establish you. 11To him be the power forever and ever. Amen.

Let's Pray!

"Let every one who is godly offer prayer
to thee;
at a time of distress, in the rush of great
waters,
they shall not reach him.
7Thou art a hiding place for me,
thou preservest me from trouble;
thou dost encompass me with
deliverance. *Selah*"
—Psalm 32:6—7 RSV

GOING DEEPER:

Read It! CCC #322 (We can trust in God's providence);
CCC #1546–51 (Ordained ministers act as the presence of Christ to the world).

Do It! Name some ways you can show humility. Share what you can do to seek God's will above your own.

Confess Your Sins

1 John 1:1–10

Bless me, Father, for I have sinned . . ." How long has it been since the last time you received the Sacrament of Reconciliation (went to confession)? Some people say, "Oh, I don't need to tell another human being about my sins. I just tell God about it!" But today's Scripture reading tells us why saying the words aloud and hearing of God's forgiveness through the absolution of the priest is such a powerful source of grace. By bringing our own wrongdoing to light, the sin loses its power, and our resolve to "go and sin no more" is strengthened!

We declare to you what was from the beginning, what we have heard, what we have seen with our eyes, what we have looked at and touched with our hands, concerning the word of life—²this life was revealed, and we have seen it and testify to it, and declare to you the eternal life that was with the Father and was revealed to us—³we declare to you what we have seen and heard so that you also may have fellowship with us; and truly our fellowship is with the Father and with his Son Jesus Christ. ⁴We are writing these things so that our joy may be complete.

5 This is the message we have heard from him and proclaim to you, that God is light and in him there is no darkness at all. ⁶If we say that we have fellowship with him while we are walking in darkness, we lie and do not do what is true; ⁷but if we walk in the light as he himself is in the light, we have fellowship with one another, and the blood of Jesus his Son cleanses us from all sin.

⁸If we say that we have no sin, we deceive ourselves, and the truth is not in us. ⁹If we confess our sins, he who is faithful and just will forgive us our sins and cleanse us from all unrighteousness. ¹⁰If we say that we have not sinned, we make him a liar, and his word is not in us.

LET'S PRAY!
Act of Contrition

O my God, I am heartily sorry for having offended Thee, and I detest all my sins because I dread the loss of Heaven and the pains of Hell; but most of all because they offend Thee, my God, Who art all-good and deserving of all my love. I firmly resolve, with the help of Thy grace, to confess my sins, to do penance, and to amend my life. Amen.

QUOTE OF THE DAY: *"Confess
your sins in church, and do not
go up to your prayer with an evil
conscience. . . . On the Lord's Day
gather together, break bread, and
give thanks, after confessing
your transgressions so that
your sacrifice may be pure"*
*(Didache 4:14, 14:1
[AD 70]).* [61]

GOING DEEPER:

Read It! CCC #1424 (When we confess our sins, God will bring us back to him).

Do It! If you don't have a chance to go to confession this week, sit together as a family and confess some things you may be struggling with in your life. It will help you grow together!

John's Vision
Revelation 1:9—18

The book of Revelation is one of the most mysterious books in the whole Bible, and one that has inspired all kinds of imaginative, and sometimes frightening, interpretations regarding the end of the world. This book was written to the seven churches in Asia, the Roman province in present-day Turkey. Since the number seven stood for completeness, and since the letter is in our Bible, we can be sure it was written for the whole church to read.

I, John, your brother who share with you in Jesus the persecution and the kingdom and the patient endurance, was on the island called Patmos because of the word of God and the testimony of Jesus. ¹⁰I was in the spirit on the Lord's day, and I heard behind me a loud voice like a trumpet ¹¹saying, "Write in a book what you see and send it to the seven churches, to Ephesus, to Smyrna, to Pergamum, to Thyatira, to Sardis, to Philadelphia, and to Laodicea."

12 Then I turned to see whose voice it was that spoke to me, and on turning I saw seven golden lampstands, ¹³and in the midst of the lampstands I saw one like the Son of Man, clothed with a long robe and with a golden sash across his chest. ¹⁴His head and his hair were white as white wool, white as snow; his eyes were like a flame of fire, ¹⁵his feet were like burnished bronze, refined as in a furnace, and his voice was like the sound of many waters. ¹⁶In his right hand he held seven stars, and from his mouth came a sharp, two-edged sword, and his face was like the sun shining with full force.

17 When I saw him, I fell at his feet as though dead. But he placed his right hand on me, saying, "Do not be afraid; I am the first and the last, ¹⁸and the living one. I was dead, and see, I am alive forever and ever; and I have the keys of Death and of Hades."

LET'S PRAY!
The "Our Father," "Hail Mary," and "Glory Be."

Read It! CCC #2853 ("Deliver us from evil" is a hopeful
 anticipation of the glory to come).

Do It! Today's reading is very dramatic! Draw a picture of
 how Jesus looked to John.

Heavenly Treasure

Revelation 3:14–22

*W*e can learn a great deal from the church of Laodicea, which was scolded for being "lukewarm" and spiritually poor. Sometimes, as people are able to provide riches for themselves, they forget their dependency on God. In today's Scripture reading, the Spirit urged the faithful to change and get true riches and white robes (meaning for purity) from Jesus.

"And to the angel of the church in Laodicea write: The words of the Amen, the faithful and true witness, the origin of God's creation:

15 "I know your works; you are neither cold nor hot. I wish that you were either cold or hot. ¹⁶So, because you are lukewarm, and neither cold nor hot, I am about to spit you out of my mouth. ¹⁷For you say, 'I am rich, I have prospered, and I need nothing.' You do not realize that you are wretched, pitiable, poor, blind, and naked. ¹⁸Therefore I counsel you to buy from me gold refined by fire so that you may be rich; and white robes to clothe you and to keep the shame of your nakedness from being seen; and salve to anoint your eyes so that you may see. ¹⁹I reprove and discipline those whom I love. Be earnest, therefore, and repent.

²⁰Listen! I am standing at the door, knocking; if you hear my voice and open the door, I will come in to you and eat with you, and you with me. ²¹To the one who conquers I will give a place with me on my throne, just as I myself conquered and sat down with my Father on his throne. ²²Let anyone who has an ear listen to what the Spirit is saying to the churches."

LET'S PRAY!

Blessed Mother Teresa used to say that the greatest poverty was poverty of spirit. Lord, you have blessed us with so much in the way of material possessions, and we are thankful for your many gifts to us. Help us to rightly order our lives, that we might be pleasing to you. In the name of the Father, and the Son, and the Holy Spirit, Amen!

DID YOU KNOW? The city of
Laodicea was famous for its
medical school as well as its great
wealth from exporting garments
and salves. It was on the Lycus
River, near the hot springs of
Hierapolis (which would have
been lukewarm by the time
they reached the city).[62]

GOING DEEPER:

Read It! The parable of the wedding feast (Matthew
22:2–14); CCC #1065 (Jesus is the "Amen" of God's
revelation to us); CCC #796 (The Church is called the
Bride of Christ).

Do It! Movie Night! Watch *The Miracle Worker*, and talk
about Helen Keller's journey.

The Prayers of the Saints

Revelation 5:1–10

In today's Scripture reading, a mysterious scroll appears, a symbol of the prophecies of God's holy ones. Only Jesus, the Lamb of God, could open it and reveal its secrets. This reminds us that our lives and our futures are safe in the hands of Jesus. We need not fear the future, as long as we entrust ourselves to his care.

Then I saw in the right hand of the one seated on the throne a scroll written on the inside and on the back, sealed with seven seals; ²and I saw a mighty angel proclaiming with a loud voice, "Who is worthy to open the scroll and break its seals?" ³And no one in heaven or on earth or under the earth was able to open the scroll or to look into it. ⁴And I began to weep bitterly because no one was found worthy to open the scroll or to look into it. ⁵Then one of the elders said to me, "Do not weep. See, the Lion of the tribe of Judah, the Root of David, has conquered, so that he can open the scroll and its seven seals."

6 Then I saw between the throne and the four living creatures and among the elders a Lamb standing as if it had been slaughtered, having seven horns and seven eyes, which are the seven spirits of God sent out into all the earth. ⁷He went and took the scroll from the right hand of the one who was seated on the throne. ⁸When he had taken the scroll, the four living creatures and the twenty-four elders fell before the Lamb, each holding a harp and golden bowls full of incense, which are the prayers of the saints. ⁹They sing a new song:

"You are worthy to take the scroll
and to open its seals,
for you were slaughtered and by your
blood you ransomed for God
saints from every tribe and language
and people and nation;
¹⁰ you have made them to be a kingdom
and priests serving our God,
and they will reign on earth."

LET'S PRAY!

Holy, holy, holy Lord, God of power and
might!
Heaven and earth are full of your glory.
Hosanna in the highest!
Blessed is he who comes in the name of
the Lord,
Hosanna in the highest!

SPECIAL WORDS: The "Lion of the Tribe of Judah" and "Root of David" are both references to Christ.

GOING DEEPER:

Read It! CCC #2642 (Faith is pure praise).

Do It! Make a scroll, and write a prayer of praise inside to read at dinner tonight!

A Sea of Martyrs

Revelation 7:9–14

*T*he Church is "catholic" . . . what does that mean? The truth that was passed from Christ to his apostles to spread to the whole world, was entrusted to the Church until the end of time. And though not all Christians are Catholic Christians, everything that Christians believe—the creeds, the sacraments, and the Scriptures themselves—originated and are found in their most complete and fullest form in the Church Jesus promised he would build (Matthew 16:18–19). The word "catholic" means "universal." In today's Scripture reading, we catch a glimpse of just how big that Church really is—and how beautiful it will be when we are all together in heaven!

After this I looked, and there was a great multitude that no one could count, from every nation, from all tribes and peoples and languages, standing before the throne and before the Lamb, robed in white, with palm branches in their hands. ¹⁰They cried out in a loud voice, saying,

"Salvation belongs to our God who is
seated on the throne, and to the
Lamb!"

¹¹And all the angels stood around the throne and around the elders and the four living creatures, and they fell on their faces before the throne and worshiped God, ¹²singing,

"Amen! Blessing and glory and wisdom
and thanksgiving and honor
and power and might
be to our God forever and ever! Amen."

13 Then one of the elders addressed me, saying, "Who are these, robed in white, and where have they come from?" ¹⁴I said to him, "Sir, you are the one that knows." Then he said to me, "These are they who have come out of the great ordeal; they have washed their robes and made them white in the blood of the Lamb."

Let's Pray!

Father, may we sing with all the saints and angels in heaven an unending hymn of praise. Let the church, from shore to shore and from one generation to the next, bless your name! In the name of the Father, and the Son, and the Holy Spirit, Amen!

408

QUOTE OF THE DAY: "Heaven is not divided by the number of those who reign, nor lessened by being shared, nor disturbed by its multitude, nor disordered by its inequality of ranks, nor changed by motion, nor measured by time."

—St. Bonaventure

GOING DEEPER:

Read It! CCC #830–31 (What does it mean that the Church is "catholic"?).

Do It! Discuss: In what two important ways does the Catholic Church live up to its name?

A New Heaven and Earth

Revelation 21:1–4, 10–11; 22:12–13, 20–21

Have you ever talked to a young woman who was getting married, and preparing to make a beautiful home for her future family? She gathers all the things she will need— the linens, the kitchen utensils, the special pieces that will make that home uniquely theirs. However, we find that it is the groom, the Lord Jesus, who has prepared everything for his beloved Bride, the Church, just as he promised (John 14:2–3)! Today's Bible reading is a beautiful image of the Church, the Bride of Christ, finally brought to her heavenly home.

Then I saw a new heaven and a new earth; for the first heaven and the first earth had passed away, and the sea was no more. ²And I saw the holy city, the new Jerusalem, coming down out of heaven from God, prepared as a bride adorned for her husband.

³And I heard a loud voice from the throne saying,

"See, the home of God is among mortals.
He will dwell with them as their God;
they will be his peoples,
and God himself will be with them;
⁴ he will wipe every tear from their eyes.
Death will be no more;
mourning and crying and pain will be no
    more,
for the first things have passed away." . . .

¹⁰And in the spirit he carried me away to a great, high mountain and showed me the holy city Jerusalem coming down out of heaven from God. ¹¹It has the glory of God and a radiance like a very rare jewel, like jasper, clear as crystal. . . .

22 "See, I am coming soon; my reward is with me, to repay according to everyone's work. ¹³I am the Alpha and the Omega, the first and the last, the beginning and the end." . . .

20 The one who testifies to these things says, "Surely I am coming soon."
Amen. Come, Lord Jesus!

21 The grace of the Lord Jesus be with all the saints. Amen.

Let's Pray!

Holy Spirit, help us to live for Jesus. Let the kingdom of God reign in our hearts every day. In the name of the Father, and the Son, and the Holy Spirit, Amen!

Going Deeper:

Read It! CCC #954–959 (The three states of the Church unite us in the communion of saints).

Do It! Which saint are you most looking forward to meeting in heaven, and why? Talk about it at dinner tonight.

Index

Prayers

Verse References

416

417

Notes

1. Michael Buckley, *The Catholic Prayer Book* (Ann Arbor, MI: Charis Books, 1986), 202.
2. *A Prayer Book for Catholic Families* (Chicago, Il.: Loyola Press, 1998), 32.
3. New Advent Catholic Encyclopedia: "Confirmation," "Sponsors," http://www.newadvent.org/cathen/04215b.htm
4. Holy Land Photos: "Camels Drinking," http://www.holylandphotos.org/browse.asp?s=136,297&img=DLANCM02
5. Buckley, *A Prayer Book for Catholic Families*, 193.
6. Halleys Bible Handbook (Grand Rapids, MI: Zondervan, 2000), 137.
7. *Halley's Bible Handbook*, 150.
8. J. I. Packer, *Illustrated Manners and Customs of the Bible* (Nashville, TN: Thomas Nelson, 1980), 721.
9. *Halley's Bible Handbook*, 192.
10. Buckley, *A Prayer Book for Catholic Families*, 68 (adapted).
11. *Halley's Bible Handbook*, 192.
12. *Halley's Bible Handbook*, 199.
13. *Halley's Bible Handbook*, 202.
14. *Halley's Bible Handbook*, 224.
15. *Halley's Bible Handbook*, 236.
16. *Halley's Bible Handbook*, 246.
17. *The International Standard Bible Encyclopedia* (Grand Rapids, Mich: Eerdmans, 1988), 403.
18. 2 Chronicles 32:5. *Halley's Bible Handbook*, 284. See also http://www.holylandphotos.org
19. Packer, *Illustrated Manners and Customs* , 59.
20. *Halley's Bible Handbook*, 413.
21. Buckley, *A Prayer Book for Catholic Families*, 182.
22. *The Catholic Study Bible*: New American Bible, Second Edition (New York: Oxford University Press, 2006) SG 337.
23. *The Catholic Study Bible*, SG 342.
24. *Halley's Bible Handbook*, 446.
25. *The Catholic Study Bible*, 1226.
26. *Halley's Bible Handbook*, 484.
27. Edmisten, Karen. The Rosary: *Keeping Company with Jesus and Mary*, (Cincinnati, OH: Servant Books, 2009) 13.
28. *The Catholic Study Bible*, 1254.
29. Ibid.
30. *The Catholic Study Bible*, 1408.
31. *Halley's Bible Handbook*, 693.
32. Buckley, *The Catholic Prayer Book*, 224.
33. *Halley's Bible Handbook*, 695.
34. Packer, *Illustrated Manners and Customs*, 333.
35. *The Catholic Study Bible*, 1282.
36. *Halley's Bible Handbook*, 700.
37. Packer, *Illustrated Manners and Customs*, 333.
38. Mother Teresa, *In My Own Words* (St. Louis, MO: Liguori, 1996), 4.
39. *The Catholic Study Bible*, 1423
40. *Pedro Sarubbi*, http://www.pedrosarubbi.it. Accessed August 28, 2009.
41. Freese, Brett Leslie. "Medicinal Myrrh." *Archaeology.org*, May/June 1996. http://www.archaeology.org/9605/newsbriefs/myrrh.html (accessed August 31, 2009).
42. "Simon of Cyrene," *Facing the Challenge*, http://www.facingthechallenge.org/cyrene.php (accessed August 31, 2009).
43. "Joseph of Arimathea." *All About Jesus Christ*, http://www.allaboutjesuschrist.org/joseph-of-arimathea-faq.htm (accessed on August 31, 2009).
44. Rhonda Chervin, *Quotable Saints*, (Ann Arbor, MI: Choris 1992), 88.
45. Packer, *Illustrated Manners and Customs*, 507. (Quoting Josephus' Antiquities, 13.10.6).
46. "Synagogue of the Freedmen." *Bible History Online*, http://www.bible-history.com/jerusalem/firstcenturyjerusalem_synagogue_of_the_freedmen.html (accessed on August 31, 2009).
47. *Halley's Bible Handbook*, 731.
48. Buckley, *The Catholic Prayer Book*, 213.
49. Packer, *Illustrated Manners and Customs*, 552.
50. *Halley's Bible Handbook*, 741.
51. Mackall, Dandi. *Kindred Sisters* (Minneapolis, MN: Augsburg Books, 1996), 130.
52. "Areopagus (Mars Hill), Athens." *Sacred Destinations*, http://www.sacred-destinations.com/greece/athens-areopagus-mars-hill.htm (accessed on August 31, 2009).
53. *Halley's Bible Handbook*, 747.
54. *Halley's Bible Handbook*, 751.
55. *The Catholic Study Bible*, 1452.
56. See Acts 23:23-24; see also *Halley's Bible Handbook*, 753.
57. Packer, *Illustrated Manners and Customs*, 635.
58. Paul Thigpen, *A Dictionary of Quotes from the Saints* (Ann Arbor, Mich.:2001), 28.
59. Buckley, *A Prayer Book for Catholic Families*, 68 (adapted).
60. *Halley's Bible Handbook*, 838.
61. "Confession," *Catholic.com*, http://www.catholic.com/ library/Confession.asp (accessed on September 8, 2009).
62. *The Catholic Study Bible*, 1674.

About the Author

Heidi Hess Saxton is the founder of the "Extraordinary Moms Network" (EMN), an on-line, faith-based resource for adoptive and foster moms, and mothers of special needs children. Heidi is a columnist at CatholicMom.com and CatholicExchange.com, and is also the author of several books including *Raising Up Mommy* and *Behold Your Mother*.

Heidi and her husband Craig foster-adopted their two children in 2002. Her family lives in southern Michigan. You may contact Heidi or get information about her books through EMN (http://extraordinarymomsnetwork.wordpress.com), her book website (http://www.christianword.com), or via e-mail: hsaxton@christianword.com.